The
Lost Colony
of the
Templars

Also by Steven Sora

The Lost Treasure of the Knights Templar:
Solving the Oak Island Mystery

Secret Societies of America's Elite:
From the Knights Templar to Skull and Bones

The
Lost Colony
of the
Templars

Verrazano's Secret Mission
to America

STEVEN SORA

Destiny Books
Rochester, Vermont

Destiny Books
One Park Street
Rochester, Vermont 05767
www.InnerTraditions.com

Destiny Books is a division of Inner Traditions International

Library of Congress Cataloging-in-Publication Data
Sora, Steven, 1952–
  The lost colony of the Templars : Verrazano's secret mission to America / Steven
Sora.
       p. cm.
  Includes bibliographical references and index.
  ISBN 1-59477-019-0 (pbk.)
  1. America—Discovery and exploration—Pre-Columbian. 2. Templars—
History, 3. Verrazano, Giovanni da, 1485-1528. 4. Explorer—America—
Biography. 5. Explorer—France—Biography. 6. America—Discovery and
exploration—French. I. Title.
  E103.S67 2004
  970.01'1—dc22
                                    2004018752

Printed and bound in the United States at Lake Book Manufacturing, Inc.

10 9 8 7 6 5 4 3 2 1

Text design by Virginia Scott Bowman and layout by Priscilla Baker
This book was typeset in Sabon, with Bernhard Modern and Delphin as display
typefaces

To my wife and best friend, Terry,
and our sons, Christian and Mike

Contents

Acknowledgments

Thanks first to my family: my wife, Terry, for her support over the years and the miles; and our sons, Christian and Mike, for their interest and assistance.

Thanks to my friends at the New England Antiquities Research Association, especially Suzanne Carlson, Bill Penhallow, and James Egan. NEARA is one of the few organizations I have encountered that is dedicated to truly open-minded research.

Thanks to those who have pioneered the road to a deeper understanding of our hidden history and who have provided me with direction and encouragement, especially Michael Bradley, Gerard Leduc, Warren Getler, Evan Pritchard, Dr. Bob and Zoh Hieronimus, Doug Kenyon, and David Jones.

And most important, thanks to the team at Inner Traditions • Bear and Company. My special thanks to publisher Ehud Sperling, acquisitions editor Jon Graham, marketing director Rob Meadows, my wonderful editors—most notably Jamaica Burns, and art director Peri Champine as well as the many other staff members who assisted with the creation and promotion of this book.

Chronology

325 A.D.   First Church of the Holy Sepulchre built in Jerusalem.

888–911   The sons of Rogenwald, the progenitor of the St. Clair/ Sinclair family, take land in France and northern Scotland.

982   Erik the Red in Greenland.

986   Erik the Red returns to Greenland with twenty-five ships of colonists.

1002   Norsemen arrive in North America.

1066   Battle of Hastings; St. Clairs rewarded with more lands in Scotland.

1095   Pope Urban I calls for First Crusade to recapture Jerusalem.

1099   Jerusalem falls to European armies. Basilica built over the ruin of the First Church of the Holy Sepulchre.

1112   Bernard de Fontaines (later Saint Bernard) and thirty nobles join the Cistercians.

1115–1120   Knights Templar and Bernard's Cistercian order prosper and a secret society, the Order of Sion, connects both from behind the scenes. St. Clair family active in the Templars and the Order of Sion. A wave of Templar-Cistercian building moves across Europe.

1149	Church of Holy Sepulchre rebuilt and consecrated.
1187	Jerusalem falls again to Islam.
1209	Crusade against the Cathars begins.
1291	The last crusader fortress falls; the Holy Land is lost.
1307	Templars in France ordered arrested by the king. The Templar fleet escapes and sails to Sinclair lands in Caithness and the Orkneys.
1314	The Battle of Bannockburn; remnant Templars aid Robert the Bruce in his quest for Scotland's independence.
1317	Knights Templar in Portugal reorganized as the Knights of Christ.
c. 1390	Elizabeth Sinclair (daughter of Henry Sinclair) marries John Drummond.
1390	Henry Sinclair meets Nicolo Zeno, then Antonio Zeno, in Scotland.
1398	Henry Sinclair expedition lands in what will later be Nova Scotia. He explores from Nova Scotia to Newport and declares he will found a colony.
1419	The Genoese Bartolomeo Perestrello, sailing as a Knight of Christ, claims Madeira for his adopted country of Portugal. John Drummond (son of Elizabeth Sinclair and John Drummond) moves to Madeira.
1441	William Sinclair begins employing workers for his Rosslyn Chapel. Complex at Oak Island completed.
1446	Construction starts at Rosslyn.
1478	Spanish Inquisition begins.
1479	Columbus marries Felipa Moniz Perestrello.
1480–1485	Columbus lives in Madeira with Sinclair/ Drummond descendants. Receives the charts of Knights of Christ explorations.
1492	Columbus reaches the Americas.

1502	First Venitian edition of Sannazaro's *Arcadia*.
1515	Francis I crowned king of France; defeats the Swiss.
1517	Martin Luther and others begin Reformation.
1522	Verrazano takes a Spanish treasure fleet. Teutonic Knights lend aid to Martin Luther.
1524	Verrazano reaches the Americas, stays in Newport area, reports on "Norman Villa."
1525	Calvin starts French Reformation.
1526	Esteban Gomez explores the future Hudson River on Saint Anthony's feast day.
1534	Cartier's first voyage.
1535	Cartier in St. Lawrence Seaway.
1572	Saint Bartholomew's Day Massacre of Huguenots.
1598	Huguenots so powerful in La Rochelle that Mass not said in forty years.
1603	A Huguenot given permission to settle Nova Scotia (Acadia). Champlain's first voyage.
1604	Champlain's second voyage; colony established at Port Royal.
1608	Champlain's third voyage; founds Quebec, which grants religious freedom to all.
1609	Champlain discovers the lake that will bear his name. Henry Hudson explores river that will bear his name.
1613	Jesuits take over in Canada and restrict Huguenots.
1618	First time the words *Et in Arcadia Ego* seen on a painting.
1620	*Mayflower* lands.
1630	Compagnie du Saint-Sacrement founded.
1641	Society of Saint-Sulpice founded in Paris.
1654	Large-scale Huguenot immigration to Quebec.

Notable Family Connections

CHILDREN OF
HENRY SINCLAIR (THE DISCOVERER)

Henry   marries Giles (Egida) Douglas
(granddaughter of King Robert III)

John   marries Ingeborg
(daughter of Waldemar, king of Denmark)

Elizabeth   marries Sir John Drummond of Stobhall
and Cargill, the brother of Annabella,
queen of King Robert III

CHILDREN OF ELIZABETH SINCLAIR
AND JOHN DRUMMOND

Walter   remains in possession of lands and titles
in Scotland

John   moves to Madeira; marries Catarina vaz de
Lordelo, widow of Tristao vaz Teixeira, whose
aunt married Bartolomeo Perestrello (brother
of Christopher Columbus's wife, Felipa
Perestrello); upon Catarina's death, John
Drummond marries Branca Afonso da Cunha

CHILDREN OF JOHN DRUMMOND AND BRANCA AFONSO DA CUNHA

John, "John the Scot," born in 1431

Diogo, born in 1432

Catarina, born in 1433

Guimar, born in 1435

Beatriz, born in 1437

Isabel, born in 1438

Joanna, born in 1440

Branca, born in 1442

THE COLUMBUS–SINCLAIR CONNECTION

The wife of Columbus was doña Felipa Perestrello e Moniz. She was a granddaughter (on her mother's side) of Gil Moniz, a Knight of Christ, and daughter of the Genoese explorer Bartolomeo Perestrello, also a Knight of Christ.

Bartolomeo Perestrello also had a son. This son, also called Bartolomeo Perestrello, married Guimar Teixeira, the aunt of Tristao vaz Teixeira, who was the first husband of Catarina vaz de Lordelo. Catarina later married John Drummond, son of Elizabeth Sinclair, a daughter of Henry Sinclair.

Thus, the Perestrello and Teixeira families are connected by marriage. The Lordelo and Drummond families are connected by marriage. And soon the name of Columbus is brought into the Perestrello family. Not so much a family tree as a vine.

The Orders

Cistercian Order. A French order reformed by Saint Bernard. Worked closely with the Knights Templar.

Company of the Sacred Sacrament (Compagnie du Saint-Sacrement). A secretive society operating from the seminary of Saint-Sulpice in Paris. It has been theorized that this order and the Priory of Sion are one and the same.

Knights Hospitaller of St. John. Early order in the Holy Land committed to service. Later became a fighting order and is known today as the Sovereign Knights of Malta.

Knights of Christ. The largest surviving Templar organization, reorganized in Portugal after the Templar order was arrested.

Knights Templar. Originally known as the Order of the Poor Knights of Christ and the Temple of Solomon. Started as a small order in Jerusalem, grew exponentially after returning to France under the sponsorship of Saint Bernard.

Priory of Sion. Also known as the Prieure of Sion. Claimed to have existed for nearly one thousand years. May have provided the impetus for the creation of the Knights Templar.

Society of Notre-Dame of Montreal. Religious group evolving from the Company of the Sacred Sacrament.

Society of St. Sulpice. A priestly society that exists today in France, Canada, and the United States.

Introduction

From La Rochelle to Newport

THE HARBOR OF LA ROCHELLE, FRANCE, faded into darkness as eighteen treasure-laden ships of the Knights Templar abandoned their port. As the ships carrying the knights slipped into the dark Atlantic waters, the army of the king of France prepared to mount a predawn assault against the Templars' Paris headquarters, the Temple. The soldiers expected to find the wealth of the Templars, the largest and richest institution in Europe outside of the Church. Instead, they would find only a handful of knights, whom they placed under arrest.

The fleet sailed past Île de Ré, an island that had long guarded the harbor's tranquillity. La Rochelle had been the first harbor of the Templars, and now it would be their last. Sailing under the skull and crossbones that flew over all Templar warships, the Templar knights aboard the fleet may have been expecting a short sojourn from their own homeland. King Philip IV had other plans, however, and that Friday, the thirteenth of October 1307, marked the demise of their order. The men aboard the ships were outlaws.

The Templar fleet sailed to the one land where neither the tentacles of the Church nor the armies of the French king could reach, Scotland. The leader of that country, Robert the Bruce, had defied England and crowned himself king of Scotland, earning for his efforts the wrath of the pope. Both king and country were excommunicated. In a world

1

where excommunication was still a powerful tool in the hands of the Church, its use here branded Scotland a renegade nation. With the arrival of the remnant Templars, it gained a renegade army whose members, some say, played decisive roles in helping Scotland fight for independence.

The Templars were given refuge in Scotland under the guardianship of the Sinclair clan, an alliance that would have historic consequences. Like the Sinclairs, the Templar knights were Normans who traced their heritage back over five centuries to their ancestors, Norwegian Vikings, who had explored the world from Iceland to Russia and settled in northern France. The arrival of the Templars seems to have reawakened the Sinclairs' seafaring nature. Under Henry Sinclair, the clan mounted an exploratory voyage to the Americas in 1398, reviving a Viking tradition. They left evidence of their successful arrival on Oak Island and New Ross in Nova Scotia, in Westford and Fall River in Massachusetts, at Lake Memphremagog in Vermont, and in the harbor of Newport in Rhode Island. Their impact on the pre-Columbian population in North America spread far and wide.

Compelling evidence also exists that Henry Sinclair even founded a colony, an Arcadia, intended to serve as refuge to those whose beliefs did not conform to rigid Church or dominant state doctrines. The Sinclair fleet, once the Templar fleet, made several voyages to the still "undiscovered" New World, but deprivation and war eventually caused the demise of the colonists' enterprise. Some headed west; others married into the Native population.

The Scottish explorers also brought back evidence of their expeditions. In the Rosslyn Chapel in Scotland, home of the Sinclair family, is stonework that dates to fifty years before Columbus reached the Americas. Carved in stone are the images of American maize and aloe.

Even long after his death, Henry Sinclair exerted an influence on the search for and "discovery" of the New World. His daughter Elizabeth married John Drummond, scion of another of Scotland's wealthiest families. A son, also called John, became an adventurer like his grandfather Henry and soon wound up on the Portuguese islands of Madeira, which had recently been rediscovered by explorers flying the flag of the post-Templar order, the Knights of Christ. Unlike most of the rest of Europe, the Portuguese had allowed the Knights Templar to resurrect their order with only a name change. The grand master of the

Knights of Christ was another Henry, called the Navigator. Their mission was to open the highways of the sea.

When John and Elizabeth Drummond arrived, the Madeira islands were governed by a handful of Italian families who had originated in the same city where Christopher Columbus was born and had joined the Knights of Christ. One such family was the Perestrellos. By 1450 the Perestrello family had intermarried with the Drummond-Sinclair family. In that year Felipa Perestrello was born. It may have been fate or it may have been Columbus's ambition that placed Felipa and him in the same Lisbon church to hear Mass one Sunday. They were soon married, and his new mother-in-law presented him with the maps and charts of her late husband's explorations. As a chart dealer and would-be explorer, Columbus could not have received a better wedding present. Columbus became privy to a body of knowledge unknown to any one person in the world.

The marriage of Christopher Columbus and Felipa Perestrello would create a convergence of knowledge of maritime discovery. The Drummond-Sinclair family, whose heirs married into the Perestrello line, had an unbroken knowledge of Viking exploration in the lands to the west. Sinclair ships carried bishops appointed to Greenland and Vinland even in the fourteenth century, and Henry's ventures in the New World had been privy information within the family. The Perestrello side held the maps and charts of the new Templars, the Knights of Christ, while Columbus brought a lifetime of study of geography and exploration.

Spurred by the charts and other explorers' tales of lands to the west, Columbus made the decision to sail across the Atlantic. He said he was looking for a sea route to the wealthy trading capitals of the East, yet he carried only trinkets and mirrors, not trade goods to impress mandarins and maharajahs.

Thirty-two years after the first voyage of Columbus, however, no such sea route had been discovered, nor the Templar refuge originally founded by Henry Sinclair. Yet Columbus did influence the history of the world by taking a Templar secret public. There was another world over the ocean. Fewer people knew that there was a settlement in that new world, one that had been there for almost a century.

During all this time, the Templar settlement had not been heard from. Like the colonies of Greenland two centuries before, it was nearly forgotten. Only the Church's desire to collect taxes impelled anyone to search for Greenland. The Templar colony would remain secret until the mission was given to another Italian, Giovanni da Verrazano.

Verrazano was a Florentine sea captain, merchant, and navigator nominally in the employ of the French king Francis I. He was also one of those who preserved secrets shared only by a small group of initiates whose goal had been to create a utopian community where church and state did not hinder the intellectual pursuit of man. The earthly paradise was called Arcadia, after the title of a book by Jacopo Sannazaro.

Arcadia and the concept of an "underground stream" of knowledge became a central theme in the sixteenth century. The pages of Sannazaro's work contained a description of a utopia where a beautiful land existed and where freedoms of expression, learning, and religion were allowed. His work was as much a treatise on science, alchemy, and astrology as it was a description of the new Eden. Such science was held in deep distrust by the Church and any claims to a world that differed from the Bible could send a scientist to the stake. Galileo would face the Inquisition for saying the earth moves around the sun.

Under the authority of the Church, knowledge was frozen. Sannazaro's Arcadia was a spark that ignited others to burn with desire for learning. Philip Sidney followed with his own version of Arcadia. Sir Francis Bacon too wrote on the New Atlantis, a colony over the ocean called Bensalem, where scientists and thinkers could learn and experiment without the threat of prison or death.

Verrazano brought Sannazaro's text to Francis I, along with the knowledge that the Arcadia existed, hoping to gain the king's support. He already had the necessary funds. His backers included the Guadagni family of Florence and Bonacorso Rucellai, who had connections to the same Italian banking families that sponsored Columbus. The group believed that Arcadia existed, that it was the colony of the remnant Templars brought to a new world by Henry Sinclair. Verrazano conveyed this to the king, saying that the Sannazaro book was on one level a pastoral tale of shepherds and chaste nymphs in the tradition of the poet Virgil; on another level, it was a real world discovered and settled a hundred years before.

The voyage of Verrazano was rather short as expeditions go. From France, he sailed to the Drummond-Sinclair home in Madeira. He left Madeira on January 17, 1524, for America and returned to Europe in

July of the same year. Rather than spending months exploring the unmapped continent for a route to China (as he had officially proposed doing), he reached North Carolina's coast and headed north. He seems, in fact, to have made no attempt to explore for a route to China and brought no goods suitable for trade or gifts to Asian potentates. Hugging the coastline, he sailed instead past the Chesapeake Bay and on to what is now New York City and the narrow entrance to the harbor that preserves his name. From there he reached the harbor of Newport.

There he met Native Americans whom he described as highly civilized and "inclining to whiteness." His log of the voyage tells of employing a Native to pilot his ship into the harbor of Newport, past the unfamiliar rocks and boulders that might trap even the wariest captain.[1] His letters do not explain just how he was able to converse with the pilot, as commerce and a common language were yet to be established between the Old and New Worlds. Moreover, just how many Native Americans were experienced harbor pilots in 1524 is unknown, given that large vessels were in short supply in Newport Harbor. Verrazano did record the pilot's leader's name, Magnus—betraying at least that a Norse/Norman influence once existed in the region.[2]

The pilot revealed another surprise, too, one that almost certainly pointed toward Arcadia. To reach Newport Harbor from the Atlantic Ocean, one must sail into Rhode Island Sound to the actual Rhode Island. (This island, named by Verrazano for another island, Rhodes in Greece, would later give its name to the small state that surrounds it.) Newport Harbor is found by heading north into what is called the East Passage, between Conanicut Island to the west and Rhode Island to the east. After Verrazano's pilot guided the ship around the southern tip of Rhode Island, they would have come in sight of Newport Harbor on the island's west side. It was here that the structure that stood watch over the harbor—Newport Tower—could be seen. Built to the exact measurements of a Templar baptistery, round or octagonal structures found throughout Europe, the Newport Tower conveyed the message that Sinclair and the Templars had been here. Verrazano stayed two weeks in Newport, his only stay of any length in America. He had found the evidence he needed, as the baptisteries that were built in Europe were the exclusive product of Templar and Cistercian architects since the Crusades. The tower that Verrazano described as a

Norman villa on his map* very closely resembled round and octagonal Templar chapels in the Old World, specifically the Saint-Clare Chapel in France and the round Orphir Church in the Sinclair-owned Orkney Islands.

The round stone tower at Newport is between twenty-four and twenty-five feet in diameter on the outside and eighteen feet in diameter on the inside.[3] Its total height is about twenty-five feet. The tower rises on eight rough-stone columns that are separated by arched entrances. Twelve feet above the ground the tower walls become entire and there are sockets in the masonry for beams, indicating the presence once of a floor that no longer survives. Originally, a second floor existed about seven feet above the first, and a roof that is long gone covered the entire structure. It is estimated that the amount of stone used to complete the structure totaled two hundred tons, 400,000 pounds of rocks gathered and put in place. The man-hours required for such an operation point to a tremendous, probably communal, effort.

On the first floor, twelve and a half feet above the ground, there remains a large recessed fireplace and two flues to vent the smoke on the outside. The fireplace may have served for cooking and heat, but also could have served as a beacon to signal other ships that would have been able to see the flame shining through the slit windows. Before houses were built in the area, the tower's position may have provided a lookout for miles around. Although there is evidence that a staircase connected the first floor to the second, there is none showing a stairway from the ground level. Perhaps a trapdoor served to allow entry or deny entry as needed, a feature employed sometimes in other lookout towers.

There is no other colonial structure that resembles the tower, at least none in North America. Nevertheless, some historians assert it was nothing but an odd windmill. It is true that it would later be called the Old Stone Mill; however, it is unlikely that anyone would have put a fireplace in a grain mill. Because it was mentioned in the December 24, 1677, will of Governor Benedict Arnold as "my Stone-built Wind-Mill," some claim that Governor Arnold had it built. The proponents

---

*There are no Norman villas in architectural terms. Verrazano described it in this way on his map, which generally left little room for longer explanations.

of the stance best summarized in the phrase "no Europeans before Columbus" refer to this fact as evidence of the tower's origin and purpose, although Arnold never claimed to play a role in the construction. Moreover, there actually was a windmill nearby, constructed as they generally are of wood. It was built by Governor Easton in 1663 and destroyed by a hurricane before the end of the century.

In Egypt the pyramids at Giza stand nearly five thousand years after they were built. They convey not only the overt message "We were here" but for those who can understand, they also convey secrets of ancient geometry and astronomy. Similarly, the Newport Tower was meant to tell on a very surface level that the Templars had been to Rhode Island: They built a message in stone that they had survived the purge of an avaricious king and a puppet pope. Like the pyramids, however, the tower has a hidden message, one that can be grasped only by those who can understand the science.

Verrazano was an initiate. His birthplace in Florence and adopted home in Lyon were hotbeds of esoteric thinking and, on occasion, heresy. His social connections were to families known to be adherents of more than one mysterious society and order, and who were versed in the secrets of Templar/Masonic geometry and the understanding of a sacred astronomy that had remained underground for centuries. Verrazano understood the Arcadia as the Refugio, the "refuge," Sinclair had hoped for, and he indicated that on his map by naming the region thus. In fact, he knew he had found the colony the moment he was guided into Newport Harbor. Where, however, were the colonists? He sailed along the coastline of what would become Maine and then headed home. The chart of his voyage recorded the tower as a "Norman Villa," and his report to the king contains no further discussion.

There is no evidence that Verrazano took his ostensible mission seriously. He did not sail into the Chesapeake Bay or even venture into the Hudson. He knew what he was looking for and it was not Asia. His secret mission was to link up with the New World colony of the remnant Templar organization. After his return, France and England would slowly attempt to explore the New World, yet secret societies in both countries would push to create the idyllic land of Sannazaro and the Baconian New Atlantis. Both would allow freedom of religion and of science long held captive by the Church.

Another secret society, the Compagnie du Saint-Sacrement, would lead the way to create the new "refuge." The company was one of several secret societies that would be organized around the Church of Saint-Sulpice in Paris. In time, the Sulpician order also gave rise to the Priory of Sion and the Society of Notre-Dame. Like the Templars, on the surface the Sulpicians were a pious Catholic order while underneath they had an agenda that was often opposite that of the mother church.

Their headquarters itself served as a monument to the sacred geometry, and even today a sun line, called the Rose Line, traces the path of the sun on a sacred day. The same knowledge of the heavens shared by megalithic builders from Scotland to Egypt was alive and well and available in the Church. The knowledge spread from Paris to the Holy Land to the windswept islands in the Baltic and North Seas. So did the power that emanated from Sulpice. It would influence events in Rennes-le-Château, in the European capitals, and eventually in the New World.

The Sulpicians wanted nothing less than to reestablish the Templar legacy in the New World. The apparently unlikely alliance of Catholic Sulpicians and Huguenots would work together first to search for the Templar colony and then to set up Montreal as an Arcadia in the New World.

At Saint-Sulpice in modern Montreal stands the last Templar round church. Upon entrance, there is, for the initiate, a message. It conveys that certain secrets are understood here. The Sulpicians had once held Canada, and their protectors were the Knights of Saint John, known in modern times as the Knights of Malta. They were no match for the Jesuits, however, and as two Catholic orders fought for Quebec, England took away the entire country. The Sulpicians remain, and their influence is strong in both France and North America. This is the story of the ancient wisdom they brought to the New World.

I

Sun Gods and Sea Kings

THE STORY OF ARCADIA and the underground stream appears almost mythical, yet conceals a reality that only a relative handful understood. The idyllic Arcadia on one level was an Eden, a peaceful, fairy-tale land. Yet to the few initiates, Arcadia was a real place. It was a colony in a world barely discovered, and was not subject to the overreaching rule of church and state.

The underground stream existed as a secret society devoted to passing along a secret body of knowledge, known to the ancients but invisible to most, as Europe slowly emerged from a dark age. Every society preserved such secrets through shamans, seers, and small groups of initiates. Though the temptation is always to look east to Egypt and the early Asian civilizations as the basis of science, the western isles, the highway of the Atlantic coast, perhaps had a higher science at a much earlier time. And the Vikings, known more for adventure and plunder, may have served as a conduit for such secrets.

Verrazano served in the role of the Grail knight—an initiate in search of the Holy Grail, the true Arcadia.

NORTHERN ORIGINS OF ANCIENT WISDOM

Centuries before the First Dynasty ruled in Egypt and the early cities of Mesopotamia sprung up in the land known as the Fertile Crescent, man was measuring time by the sun and moon. In the remote Orkney Islands, north of Scotland, and in the Boyne Valley of Ireland, practitioners of the science of astronomy unlocked knowledge of their universe. It is a complicated science, then and now, that measures solar and lunar cycles. The erection of standing stones and chambers, designed to assist the priest or scientist, were put in place by a workforce who most likely did not comprehend the importance of their labors. Myths were created both to serve the unlearned and to pass along secrets to the initiated. Long before Babylonian astronomers and Egyptian pyramid builders measured the heavens, these builders in the remote areas of Western Europe created their own tales of gods and goddesses that told a simple tale on the surface and preserved an encoded body of knowledge beneath. What would later be referred to as an underground stream of knowledge can be found in societies that preserved such secrets to modern times.

The Orkney Islands

North of Scotland across the Pentland Firth are the Orkney Islands. Together, the Orkneys and the Shetlands, still farther north, number more than 150 islands and islets, the largest of which are populated by a hardy people who are used to rough seas and high winds that rage unobstructed across the Atlantic Ocean from Labrador. These turbulent seas pound the western side of the islands, and the combination of wind and water serves to create the world's wildest tidal rips. The firth is regarded as the third most dangerous body of water in the world. When the Merry Men of Mey, a lethal breakwater created by the colliding of two currents, rides through, woe to any sailor caught in the ride. Eerie metal towers rise out of the water to serve as refuge for a capsized sailor, whose death would otherwise be almost a certainty. The towers, however, might just serve to drag out the inevitable, death—not from drowning, but from exposure to the cold.

In good weather, the crossing between Scotland and the main Orkney isle is a regular occurrence with ferries leaving from remote ports like Scrabster and John o' Groat's. Between the two is Thurso,

Thor's River, harkening back to the days when Christianity's reach did not extend this far north.

Orcadian folk are regarded as fiercely independent, a trait they must have in order to survive. The nineteen thousand residents are outnumbered by thirty thousand seals, fifty thousand pairs of puffins, and a quarter of a million guillemots, birds that make their homes in the crags of the sandstone cliffs.

A sturdy Viking heritage still shows itself when a passing cargo ship runs into trouble and is salvaged a bit too quickly. Goods end up in places like Stroma Island, where the sea has pounded holes into sandstone cliffs, and in some places, crafty navigators can enter hundred-foot-long caves from the sea and pull up on dry land at the other end. Such acts no longer require a dragon-prowed ship; a rubber Zodiac with a fast motor attached works just fine.

Incredibly, the islands have been inhabited since at least 4000 B.C., when a prehistoric people built stone houses and solar- and lunar-oriented megalithic monuments well before Egypt was united in the First Dynasty. Separating the monuments are stretches of rough sea, which means the sea was not a barrier to hinder communication; six thousand years ago it was a highway that expanded such communication. Visitors to Skara Brae, the ruins of a community that thrived perhaps five thousand years ago on the largest isle, register awe at this very early knowledge of mathematics and astronomy, as well as indoor sanitation and even hinged stone doors. These people were no hunter-gatherers. Each family had separate living quarters, yet was connected to the others in the village by stone passageways.

The Neolithic (or early Bronze Age) civilization of the Orkneys grew, expanded, and ultimately faded out thousands of years ago. When later residents came across the ruins of the earlier, they attributed the stone villages to pixies. Skara Brae itself would have remained unknown except for the weather. When the unchecked force of the Atlantic beats against the shore for days on end, even underwater rocks are lifted from the seabed. The roar of the surge is heard for miles. The winds build up to speeds that keep all indoors. It was just such a monstrous storm in the nineteenth century that peeled back the soil of Mainland to reveal Skara Brae, waking it from its millenia-long sleep under cover of earth.

Near Skara Brae are the Standing Stones of Stenness and the Ring of Brodgar. Brodgar is one of the most impressive stone circles in the world, in terms of both size and setting. The thirty-six stones, some as high as fifteen feet, sit between two pristine blue bodies of water. In terms of grandeur, it is not massive like the pyramids in Egypt or New Grange in Ireland. The serenity of the setting, however, speaks volumes and tells of a sacredness that existed well before recorded history.

It is unlikely that the handful of Skara Brae residents could have built the ring by themselves. The entire circle is on a plateau surrounded by a ditch cut out of rock. It required a massive amount of labor, as well as a now forgotten technology. As it is more than five thousand years old, the Skara Brae people did live nearby when the construction took place. Most likely, they were only one of many family-community settlements on the island, all of which provided labor for collective projects.

Within a very short distance are the Standing Stones of Stenness. This monument, despite the lonely beauty of its setting, takes a bit of imagination to impress, as it was mostly torn down by a farmer who regarded it as being in the way. Before that, however, it was very similar to the Callanish Standing Stones in the western isles of Scotland, which have not been damaged by modern man. Better preserved, these monoliths, some fifteen feet high, were dragged or carried to their position circa 3000 B.C.

What is remarkable about these monuments is that they are the oldest pieces of evidence we have that the ancients possessed complex understanding of the heavens—a sacred wisdom that would be preserved in one form or another throughout the ages. Significantly, Brodgar and Stenness have been referred to, respectively, as the Temple of the Sun and the Temple of the Moon.

Close to Stenness is another ring temple, Maes Howe, built with massive sandstone slabs. At least one of these slabs weighs more than thirty tons. On the winter solstice the sun rises through the stones of Stenness to enter a doorway at Maes Howe. In the realm of the sun and the moon, symbolically, this was very significant because the sun was often considered to be the male principle; the earth was the female. The standing stones were placed precisely so that on certain days the shaft of the sun's light would pierce the "womb" of the monument's circular center. The sexual connotation was intended. And often the day of the sun's penetration was the winter solstice.

The winter solstice saw the shortest day of the year; in other words, it was the time of the dying sun. On December 21 or 22, the sun shines for the shortest amount of time during the solar year. Even more ominously from the point of view of Neolithic/Bronze Age people, it seems to freeze in a pattern of short appearances for the next three days. Then lo and behold, the days grow longer again. The sun travels farther in the sky. It is, in effect, born again on either December 24 or December 25. The significance of these dates in various myths is no coincidence and points to humankind's endless attempt to make sense of its world through story. The rebirth of the Invincible Sun that the Orcadians tracked is the same rebirth of Sol Invictus that the Romans told of—and is the same resurrection of the Son that Christians celebrate today. In all cases, myths convey the essential truths of our reality.

At least, they convey as much of the truth as the listener is able to comprehend. In other words, a myth is not a simple tale as much as it is a tale told simply. In the Gospel of Mark, Jesus says, "He that hath ears to hear, let him hear" (Mark 4:9). When asked to explain, he answers that not everyone will know the mystery of the Kingdom of God. That is the purpose of parables. Let those who understand, understand.

The birth of the sun at the winter solstice has been told in a mythical fashion wherever there was a priesthood that wanted to preserve such astronomical knowledge. In Egypt, for example, we find Isis and her consort, Osiris. Osiris is killed, but resurrected in his son, Horus, the hawk-headed sun god. This myth differs from the Christian resurrection primarily in that it is the Egyptian mother who effects the resurrection. Christianity simply took out the female principal and made the birth and resurrection two separate events.

We can only guess at the purpose of the massive projects of the ancients. It is true that they served as both a calendar of days and a guide to the changing seasons. Simpler methods, such as sticks in the ground and sundials, would have served the same purpose without years of construction. The more complicated features of the more imposing structures, however, allowed the initiate to predict events such as eclipses. To the ancients, such knowledge was power. The ability to predict the future held the ancients in awe then and continues to fascinate those millions today who require their horoscope before starting out for work. The priestess, shaman, medicine man, and magus were the initiates, and they understood well the effect "predictive" ability could have on the masses.

But parlor tricks do not require pyramids—or megalithic temples. The monuments of the ancients held more than the power of prediction that could be exploited by religious functionaries: They held scientific knowledge. Sir Isaac Newton was among the first to understand just how complex the Great Pyramid actually is. Sacred stone structures were built to exact standards to carry scientific knowledge through the ages. Long after Maes Howe and the Great Pyramid were built, that knowledge was still alive, evidence that it had been preserved, at least for an initiate.

The structure at Maes Howe begs comparison with temples in Egypt, but the passage of time has left us with nothing that will tell a story. It is considered the pinnacle of Neolithic building in the North, with stones weighing as much as thirty tons having been carried and lifted into place. Egyptologists assume that similar stones were either rolled or dragged on sleds to pyramid sites; they were moved on a flat landscape, however. In the Orkney Islands, north of Scotland, there is no such flat terrain for any distance. The job required that much more expertise.

In total it is estimated that there are ten thousand prehistoric sites on the Orkneys,[1] this small remote chain of islands.* The Vikings were the first among modern peoples to wonder about the purpose of the ring stones, particularly Maes Howe. Apparently, they regarded the structure as a vault to guard a treasure hoard or the burial site of a wealthy king. They performed their own "excavation" and presumably left empty-handed, as only bones were left at such sites. They did leave their own graffiti on the hallowed stones, carving depictions that included a dragon and runes. Modern archaeologists have recently continued the inquiry into the nature and function of these stone monu-

---

*Close to a small ferry port in the south of the chain is another site well worth mentioning: the Tomb of the Eagles. Dating between 3530 and 3100 B.C.,[2] the Ibister Tomb of the Eagles was named for the bones of sea eagles found there. Now the sea eagle of Scotland is a remarkable creature that could easily inspire tales of children being stolen by birds. The reality is that these eagles with a six-foot wingspan and a forty-year life expectancy do actually carry off sheep of the full-grown variety. At a wildlife preserve south of Inverness where the birds still nest, naturalists explain that one of the eagles once attempted to carry off a teenage volunteer. This led to a rapid rule change requiring that only adults, two at a time, enter his domain.

ments. The tentative conclusion is that the built-in solar and lunar calculations here are older than calendars found elsewhere.

Ancient Ireland

Another of the great monuments of the North is in Ireland, an hour's drive north of Dublin. Here is New Grange, a solar calculator constructed in an incredibly accurate form five thousand years ago. It is shaped like a large mound with a massive doorway and a so-called light box—a description given by one of the early excavators—over it. As an astronomical clock, it established the time of year called midwinter. As the midwinter sun rose, a shaft of light would enter the box and shine through a long passageway. There it reflected on the farthest interior wall. Once again, the sexual connotation is the heart of the meaning. The dying sun does his part to fertilize the womb of the mother, and the new sun will be born of the shared responsibility of the sun god and Earth mother.

New Grange is a mound three hundred feet across and thirty-five feet high. The outside walls were for thirty meters covered in quartz. Every morning when the sun rose, New Grange would gleam in supernatural splendor and could be seen from miles away. People visiting by land or sea would be in awe well before arriving.

Long after New Grange was built, its architectural device of accommodating the entry of the light on certain days was repeated elsewhere. Two thousand years later, for example, the Temple of Solomon was constructed with three chambers; the deepest interior chamber was the inner sanctum. It is believed also to be astronomically oriented, admitting light in the innermost chamber once a year. It was destroyed in 587 B.C., so there is no way to verify this. Admittance was only to a select few. The rest could visit to view the marvel, but they could not enter the Holy of Holies.

At New Grange, only a handful could fit into the deepest sanctuary, where the initiate could view the effect of the light box admitting the solstice sun. The uniniated could view the display of brilliantly shining quartz and the thirty-six huge stones displaying some form of astronomical significance. They could also view the spirals and zigzag lines carved into stone, possibly hinting at the nature of the monument's significance. But to the deepest mysteries of New Grange and Solomon's Temple, the unlearned were not privy.

Clearly New Grange was not merely a building; it was architecture in its most sacred expression. It is a wonder of the world that does not come up short when compared to Egyptian or Babylonian marvels. In fact, the understanding of architectural effect and degree of astronomical knowledge apparent at New Grange ultimately found their way to Egypt, where pyramids were faced in a white tura limestone to create the same result as the quartz. New Grange, however, was first.

Such knowledge was both encoded and preserved within myth. In Irish mythology, Ogma was the sun god. He hung at the center of all worlds, which revolved around him. He brought the gift of letters—Ogham writing, as we know it today. Although precise knowledge of Ogma has long been obscured, clues of his historic significance remain in the landscape and language. On the island of Skye, a ninety-foot-high pillar of stone, called Uig, once stood. Near Stonehenge is Ogbourne, meaning "born of Og," as Osborn meant "born of Os" in ancient Scandinavia. In County Mayo in Ireland are the Ox Mountains, once Og's Mountains. Moreover, in America, one might call on God's name when surprised, as in "Oh, God!" To avoid being accused of saying God's name in vain, an "Ugh!" might be substituted, especially in print. In Scotland, "Och!" is a similar expression of surprise. In Ireland, "Oc!" will suffice. Noncanonically, Hebrew mythology has the giant Og clinging to the Ark to be saved from the Flood. Canonically, Deuteronomy 3:11 says, "For only King Og of Basan remained of the race of giants."

And Og did actually survive. Og Night is celebrated at Christmas in England, Ireland, Wales, and Scotland. As Eug, he was celebrated along with the Maypole in an ancient fertility celebration that still remains. The second Monday, sometimes Tuesday, after Easter is still known as Ocktide.

As both Ogma and the megalithic monuments of the North suggest, we would do well to question the official chronology of civilization. The far northern isles understood the geometry of the earth and the astronomy of the sky before Egypt and Babylonia, and northerners may have introduced the first alphabet as well. Intriguingly, while Irish mythology has Ogma "bringing" the letters, the first letter of our own alphabet is the symbol of the Ox (although it has been turned upside down since it was introduced by Phoenician sea traders).

We will never know with certainty what became of the cultures that erected such advanced astronomical monuments. History is written by the victors, and if Ogma did indeed bring the letters, he and his people left no records in writing. When the new gods were introduced, *ugly* would not be interpreted as "god-like." Ogma's brother Lugh would become an oafish creature, a "big lug." The rest of the gods were demoted to "ogres" or goblins. Historians and archaeologists further discount the northern peoples' ancient greatness by assigning them names like the Beaker Folk after the simple items that they produced. In the end, historians and archaeologists have failed to accord these master builders the respect they merit. Even worse, they suggest that such people could not have understood the complexities of the very concepts they invented.

Mass migrations occurred around 3200 B.C., when civilizations in Egypt and Sumeria suddenly arose. The emigrations from the northern lands may have been preceded by a rising Atlantic as higher temperatures and the melting of ancient ice swamped coastal lands. A second mass migration occurred between 1550 and 1400 B.C., after the weather deteriorated and the temperature of the isles perhaps dropped far enough to hinder farming. A Golden Age might have ended as the population of the islands headed to warmer climates. In Asia, too, mass migrations led hordes of barbarians into the Fertile Crescent and into Europe. Whatever calamity caused the cross-continental movements, it altered science and religion. The knowledge of astronomy, geometry, and the wonders of the earth and sky would be preserved. In fact, the ancient wisdom of the moon and the sun were brought to other parts of the world.

The Northern Apollo

In the first century B.C., the historian Diodorus Siculus recorded a simple biography of the sun god Apollo. He himself apparently had no understanding of the message it conveyed to the initiated, yet as we have seen, this is how myths are supposed to work. Those with "ears" hear. Diodorus told his readers that Apollo was from Hyperborea, meaning the far north, most likely what is now Britain. He claimed that the god no longer made his home there. He did, however, visit every nineteen years. On the surface, this span of time has little meaning, but the learned would know that it corresponds to the Metonic cycle, a nineteen-year cycle of the sun and moon.

The Metonic cycle was named for Meton of Athens, who lived in the fifth century B.C. He noticed that 235 lunar months made up almost nineteen solar years. Knowledge of this convergence of the cycles of the sun and moon were known much earlier and were preserved in myth.

If the axis of the earth were exactly perpendicular to the earth's orbit, the sun would always rise in the same place in the east and set in the same place in the west. Every day would have the same amount of sunlight as every other day. There would be no seasons. The axis of the earth, however, is tilted at 23.5 degrees, which is why we have seasons and longer and shorter days. From March 20 onward, the sun rises just a little farther north of due east; it sets a little farther north of due west. On June 21 it reaches its limit. For a few days it seems to stand still, the sunrise being at its northernmost point from due east, the sunset being at its northernmost point from due west. This is the summer solstice, and it marks the beginning of summer. The winter solstice occurs one half of a solar year later on December 21 or 22, marking the beginning of winter. The equinoxes are days in late March and late September. When the sun crosses the celestial equator, day and night are of equal duration.

The moon also rises and falls at slightly different angles. These, too, are measurable—including the lunar standstill when the course reverses. Using a lunar-based calendar alone creates problems, as it will slip out of step with the seasons. The ancients attempted to correct this in various ways. The Egyptians added an extra month when needed to keep the summer solstice in the same lunar month. The Babylonians, well before Meton, recognized that the wanderings of the sun and moon, the places on the horizon where they rose and set on various days, were reconciled every nineteen years. Those who understand this relationship, star watchers and shamans, have a very powerful tool: They can predict eclipses. Again, such knowledge was understood before the Babylonian calendar used the cycle in 1000 B.C. The science was carried in the myth of Apollo's nineteen-year journey.

Although the ancient sun watchers from Babylon to the American plains would have clearly understood the science of the sun's path hidden in Diodorus Siculus's tale, by Roman times such concepts remained hidden to all but the most learned astronomers, mathematicians, and architects—and those who could interpret the symbolism of the myth.

Pioneers like Alexander Thom and Aubrey Burl recognized that megalithic stone circles and "wheels" were a measurement system. Phase I of Stonehenge, the so-called Aubrey Holes, can still measure the nineteen-year solar and lunar cycles. In 1963 Gerald Hawkins recognized that combined with Phase II of the building of Stonehenge, the summer solstice sunrise and sunset, the winter solstice sunrise and sunset, and the major and minor standstills could be calculated. Yet this understanding receded at some point from common knowledge, persisting mainly thereafter in silent stone and elusive myth. It is interesting to note that the Greek poet Homer kept Ulysses, too, away from his home for nineteen years.

Might the many stories of Apollo recorded in Greek and Roman myth convey other hidden messages? For most of us who glaze over at such astronomical terms as "declination of the moon," these are just stories. To the initiated, however, they may not be.

Diodorus's tale suggests that Apollo himself originated with a Hyperborean cult. We know that deteriorating weather, a mini–ice age, sent the northerners to other lands. In Egypt, moreover, the meaning of Apollo is "the way opener." Apollo may have left his homeland in 3200 B.C., or much later in 1500 B.C., as cold weather forced migrations everywhere during these two periods. In this harsh domain, where no records were kept, traditions held true until Rome destroyed the groves and schools of the Druids. Like Mayan pyramids covered by jungle, the ancient knowledge was hidden. A dark age descended over the northern isles.

NORTHERN EXPLORERS

In the Orkney Islands, recorded history starts with the Vikings. There is a gap of thousands of years between the civilizations of the megalithic builders and the literate Norse settlers who left their own story in writings called the sagas. Between the second millennium B.C. and the arrival of the Norse, the islands were populated by a people whose history was not preserved. Fishermen plied the seas around the Orkneys, herders raised sheep in the Faeroes and Shetlands, and traders shipped their goods among the islands. A higher knowledge and science is not generally credited to the inhabitants of the islands, as the Viking culture was known more for barbarity. The Norse, however, from their home base to the islands that they settled, did carry and build on a foundation of understanding of astronomy that existed much earlier than their conquests.

The Norse seafarers were as capable as any others in crossing expanses of water. It is to the Norse that we owe the word *skipper*. In the language of the sea kings, a *skip* was a boat. They had been sailing for more than two thousand years before they began expanding their adventures beyond their own lands. From 1500 B.C. onward, Scandinavian ships had rudders and double hulls and were powered by oars. The animal head on the prow was a feature from prehistoric times.[3] A Norse ship dating to A.D. 300 was eighty feet long, twelve feet wide, and three feet deep. In comparison, the *Santa María,* flagship of Columbus's expedition, built one thousand years later, was one hundred feet long.

In the late seventh century, the Norse sea traders had, for several reasons, become the raiders and pirates now known as Vikings. Originally much like any other sea traders, they now began to take what they wanted when the opportunity arose. Finding trade less profitable than plunder, they did not stop at simply stealing from their victims; they also pillaged and burned their villages, stole livestock, and killed or enslaved the people. As early as 681, they attacked Dunbeath and Dunnottar on the northern coast of Scotland and were turned away. It may be that they then made peaceful settlements in the islands that are to the north and west of Scotland. Trade and marriages may have taken place before the dragon ships would "go a-Viking" in the next century. The Shetland chain is only 108 miles from Norway, after all, a two-day sail when the winds were favorable.

In any case, one hundred years after their first attack on the isles north of Britain, the Vikings discovered religion, or at least the easy and rich pickings the churches of the religious offered. The raids began in earnest.

In rapid succession they attacked Christian churches and monasteries. The first raid came on June 8, 793, at the holy island of Lindisfarne, which was founded in 635 by Celtic monks. The attack sent a shock wave of fear into Christian Europe, a Dark Age nightmare against which the Christian isle could mount no retaliation. The West had no means of responding to such a threat. The next year the Vikings raided the monastery at Jarrow. The year after, 795, they attacked Glamorganshire and were actually defeated. They settled in the western isles of Scotland and used the islands as bases for raids on the British Isles and the coast of France.

The Vikings came not from a single country, but rather from a widespread culture we now regard as Norse. The basis of their culture was a middle class of free farmers who became sea traders and sea raiders, often in search of lands and goods. Above were kings and earls *(jarls)*, which the middle class accepted but to which it did not give undue loyalty. Unlike feudal cultures, the Norse placed family units at the center of their structures of obligations. Supporting the middle class from below were slaves, property often captured in raids and bought from other Norsemen.

The Roots of the Sinclairs

The family that was called St. Clair in France and later Sinclair in Scotland was rooted in this Norse culture. The Sinclair family traces its ancestry back to Rogenwald, the earl of Møre and Romsdal, in Norway. He was a favorite of the Norse king Harald, a fact that may have contributed to his common designation of Rogenwald the Rich. It is not known how Rogenwald acquired his fortune, but his family remained wealthy and powerful for a thousand years. Service to his king certainly did him no harm.

By the time Rogenwald was rising to power, the Orkneys, the Hebrides, and the Shetland Islands had been home to Viking sea raiders for a century. Some of the early residents had the audacity not only to attack Ireland and the Isle of Man, but also to raid their homeland in Norway. Rogenwald joined Harald in defeating the isles, and in 888 he received a grant from Harald that entitled him to the Orkney Islands. His people often called themselves after their leader, and the surname Morrison was initially Møre's Sons.

The ambitious Rogenwald had two sons, and they made a pincerlike grab for Scotland. Eynar established the family claim in Scotland's north. Rollo's progeny, traveling by way of France and the Battle of Hastings, moved in from the southwest. The two branches of the family would finally meet outside of Edinburgh at Roslin. Along the way they came to own Caithness, the islands north and west of Scotland, and much of

Scotland north of Edinburgh. The northern end of the pincer struck first when Rogenwald passed his grant to his son Eynar, who became a resident of the Orkneys and whose heirs ruled for centuries afterward. First, Eynar had to deal with the renegades who did not accept his authority, which was easy. Next, he was threatened by the son of King Harald, but he proved only a small threat. Eynar, never known to be political or correct, simply left the prince dead and offered him to Odin. For his offering, he composed a poem:

> *While sturdy spade-beards*
> *Were stalking sheep,*
> *In Orkney I was, busy*
> *Butchering a king's boy;*

He knew the act would create a stir:

> *. . . but hard to hide*
> *What a howling I've caused:*
> *The corbie croaks*
> *Over carrion in Orkney.*

News of the killing was carried by more than croaking crows, and soon King Harald demanded settlement. For the death of his son, a sum of sixty gold marks was paid, Eynar taking it out of his own pocket.[4]

Rogenwald's other son, Rollo, was every bit as ambitious and possibly stronger, although his entry into Scotland was rather delayed. It was said he was so big that no horse could carry him. This accounted for his nickname, Rollo the Walker.[5] From Norway, he loaded his Vikings aboard dragon-headed ships, and his navy set out to conquer lands in the south. These Vikings raided the coast of what is now France and soon settled peacefully where the "Northmen" came to be known as Normans. Rollo made a peace treaty with the French king, Charles the Simple, but it did not start off too peacefully. Asked to kneel to the king, Rollo did, but then grabbed the king by the legs and flipped him on his back. Insulted or not, Charles gave the Viking his daughter, Grielle, in marriage.

In what would become known as the Treaty of St.-Clair-sur-Epte,

Rollo promised to convert to Christianity and was in turn given Normandy in 911. The extent of the territory settled by the Norse is still evident in many place-names. Norse endings in France include –*gard, -land, –tofte,* and –*torp.* Norse prefixes such as Ulf- exist in names such as Ulveville.

Rollo and his Normans were just part of a Norse wave that seemingly was on its way to conquer the world. Swedish Vikings headed east to Russia and south along Russian trade routes. Having sworn an oath *(varar)* to each other, they became a Brotherhood of the Pledge *(vaeringi).* In the Slavic territories, they became known as Varangians. The Swedish Vikings were also called the Rus, and as such gave their name to the land that became Russia. They traded and raided all the way to Constantinople, then known as Byzantium, and brought home enormous amounts of coinage from Arab mints in Baghdad, Samarkand, and Tashkent.[6]

In England, Danish Vikings raided and then settled East Anglia and Northumbria beginning in the middle of the ninth century. They were beaten back for a time by Athelstan, but in 1016 they not only returned but also gained rule of England until 1042. Twenty-four years later, in 1066, descendants of the Norwegian Vikings took power at the Battle of Hastings. Led by William the Conqueror, the Normans (as the descendants of the Norse in France were called) changed the British Isles forever. Not only did they leave their mark upon the English landscape in the same way the Norsemen had left theirs upon that of the French, but they also completed the quest of Rogenwald's sons to grip Scotland from either side: With the Normans came the descendants of Rogenwald and Rollo, now with the surname St. Clair. They chose their name from the holy well of a martyred saint whose pure waters imparted a healing power for the eyes. The nearby town was renamed for the saint and the sacred well, although it was spelled St. Clere.

The Battle of Hastings was a turning point in the history of England. William the Conqueror brought many French nobles with him across the Channel. To ensure that his conquest was not short-lived, he granted land to many of those who fought alongside him in battle, including representatives of the St. Clair family. These St. Clairs who settled in Scotland eventually came to use Sinclair as their family name.

The Norse clearly had the ability and the desire for long-distance travel. They traveled south to Africa and the Mediterranean Sea. They traveled east to Slavic Russia. They penetrated the heart of landmasses as diverse as Britain, continental Europe, and Asia, often following navigable rivers into the interior of Europe and Asia. They also headed west into the unknown. By the time they conquered the English at Hastings, their knowledge of Iceland was already two hundred years old. The first Norse sighting of Iceland was in 860. Even the Norse, however, were latecomers to Iceland.

Across Open Waters

To deny the ability of seafarers to cross the great oceans before Columbus is no longer a tenable position. In the Pacific, ancient Polynesian peoples could sail two thousand miles without seeing land by "reading" the waters. The continent of Australia was settled some forty thousand years ago by a race of sea travelers from Ceylon and southern India who could have only come by crossing immense distances. Evidence that Japanese fishermen reached Ecuador in the third millennium B.C. has been the subject recently of much research by Estrada and Meggers.[7] The Norse, too, had a certain amount of seagoing ability and a great deal of experience.

The voyage from Scandinavia west to North America was really nothing more than a series of short hops, mostly two and three days between sightings of land. From Norway, it usually took two or three days to reach the Shetland Isles. Another two days west brought the longboats to the Faeroes. Three or four days more and the peaks of Iceland rose from the Atlantic. Greenland and then Newfoundland lay beyond only slightly wider stretches of water. A Norse sea trader could make it direct from Norway to Greenland in six days. Nevertheless, the Norse were not the first to reach the fabled land of Thule.

ANCIENT ICELAND

Since the time of Pytheas, an intrepid Phocaean explorer who sailed to the far northern islands in 330 B.C., Iceland had been called Thule or Tilli. The Phocaeans were a Mediterranean people who get credit also for settling Massilia, modern Marseille, six centuries before Christ. Sailing on various ships, including the seventy-foot *holkas,* the Greek trading ship of the day, Pytheas was on a mission to discover new trade for his city-state, which was in competition with the Phoenicians. He describes a journey outside the Straits of Gibraltar, north along the French Bay of Biscay to the Scilly Islands and Alba (England), where he encountered merchant ships covered in hide. The Greeks, and the Phoenicians before them, actively traded with Cornwall and the islands to England's west. At Penmarch, stelae decorated with Greek keys and running spiral designs common to Cretan traders who came even before the Greeks give evidence of the Mediterranean contact. From the tin trade capital of the ancient world, Pytheas headed north to the Ebud Islands, the modern Hebrides, and the Orcadies, the modern Orkneys. These last, loosely meaning "sea pig," may have been named by the Greeks as means of designating that monsters of the deep existed there, possibly the Greek idea of a whale. (Another monster, the walrus, was favored for its ivory tusks and attracted hunters from prehistoric times.)

Somewhere, Pytheas was told of Iceland, just six days west, and he sailed to the island and beyond until he reached the congealed sea where neither man nor ship could travel. The congealed sea of Pytheas was the icy Arctic Ocean.

The people Pytheas had met in the Orkneys, Shetlands, and Faeroe Islands made their living by the sea, as well as by raising sheep. They were some of the earliest travelers among the islands and may have enjoyed the great fishing west of Iceland, but they left no records of their own, and any journey of discovery or settlement was forgotten.

Yet Pytheas was not the only one to make written note of the northwest Atlantic islands before the Vikings. The first-century Roman historian Pliny counted forty Orcades, seven Haemodes (Shetlands), and thirty Hebudes (Hebrides?), as well as the "Sacred Isle" of Ireland. In the early eighth century, the English theologian the Venerable Bede described the frequent voyages that Christian monks from Britain made to the Orkneys, the Faeroes, and Iceland in search of solitude or converts. If Bede is correct, the *Irish* monks had been voyaging to Iceland since the sixth century; this was almost three centuries before the Vikings.

One of the earliest visitors to Iceland from Ireland was Saint Brendan. His account seems fanciful to many, and as a result the authenticity of Brendan's work is hotly debated. When one considers that Europeans, who did little exploring at the time, may well have been strangers to whales, volcanoes, and icebergs, Brendan's account is not so unbelievable. Another pre-Viking writer from Ireland was Dicuil, who recorded the voyage of three priests. Island-hopping from Ireland to the Scottish isles to the Faeroes and finally to Iceland was not beyond their capability, as risky as the voyage was. Dicuil's narrative describes the monks living on the various isles along the way, which would have provided the necessary provisions to keep going.

Clearly, the monks of Ireland were no strangers to sea travel, and they pioneered the stepping-stone method of travel to Iceland. Though the trip from Scotland to the Faeroes could be accomplished in two or three days in a Norse ship, in the open skin boats of the monks it could take much longer. The Irish certainly exhibited courage equal to that of the later Vikings.

Church records are often considered more historically reliable than individual narratives, and such records show subsequent visiting clerics to Greenland and Iceland reporting to Archbishop Angsar of Hamburg as far back as the year 834. This was fifty years before the brother of Rollo took control of the Orkneys, and not that long after the Viking raid on Lindisfarne.[8]

When the earliest Vikings began to settle Iceland in 870, the Irish monks mounted no defense. The monks retreated in the wake of the Norse invasion. Their place-names remain. Names like Patricksfjord indicate that it may well have been an Irish monk who first sighted the fjord. Papey Island and Papafjord are also named for the Gallic word for *priest*.

The introduction to one of the most important Norse sagas, called the *Landnamabok,* describes a trip from Stad in Norway to Horn in east Iceland as generally taking seven days. In the first sixty years of settlement, as many as twenty thousand Norse made the Atlantic crossing.

In Iceland, the Norse settlers returned to farming, fishing, and occasionally trading. On that island, too, they created an early democracy, at least for the minority who were free men. Eighty percent of the population were slaves, either captured in raids or bought from Norse slave owners elsewhere. The body politic had the ability to make law and vote on issues; however, it failed at enforcement. Most issues were settled by murder, always called manslaughter. The stronger neighbor generally beat the weaker neighbor. The murder rate among a free population of 4,500 averaged ten murders each year. Compared to

America's murder capital, Detroit, Iceland was ten times worse. These numbers exclude violence committed on the slave population.[9]

GREENLAND

Circa 920, the navigator Gunnbjorn Ulfsson was blown off course and sighted to the west of Iceland a group of islands that would briefly bear his name, as the Gunnbjorn Skerries. There may have been at that time nine islands in the group, the largest being sixty-five miles long. The ever-changing North Atlantic has seen new islands emerge and old ones submerge even in the last century. Over a longer period, it has seen huge climatic changes as well. Greenland, for example, once may have presented a much more hospitable landscape that it does today. In any case, it was Gunnbjorn's description of the island group that led others to land on and settle in Greenland.

Nearly fifty years after Gunnbjorn's discovery, the Norse spirit of adventure, as well as a tradition of fleeing prosecution for murder, led Snaebjorn Galti to look for the Skerries. He put together a group of companions, and despite an ominous dream of "death in a dread place," they headed for Greenland's east coast. They landed at an icy fjord near Ammassalik, which was opposite the shore where the Skerries were supposed to be. They built shelter from the winter weather, but Snaebjorn and his companions took to quarreling and murder. Only a few survived and made it home to Iceland.

Others may have had better luck. The remarkable tale of Ari Marson is told in the *Saga of the Landnamabok,* the foundation of Norse history in Iceland.[10] While historians regard the sagas in the same way they regard myths, it is an unfair assessment. If a myth is a tale told simply, a saga is an adventure disguised as an often tedious record. The *Landnamabok,* for example, is an extensive listing of three thousand people and fourteen hundred place-names. It was not meant to be sensational by any means.

Marson was a trader who reached North American circa 960, even before Leif Eriksson, and the *Landnamabok* describes his travels in punctuated fashion. It describes a country that lay westward in the sea near "Vinland the Good" and which was alternately called Hvitramannaland (White Man's Land) and Albania (usually translated as "Greater Ireland"). There, Marson encountered Irish emigrants who may have fled before the Norse horde a century earlier, and he was recognized in this new land by Irish traders and baptized by their priest. His story was also recorded in the *Annals of Greenland,* compiled in the eleventh century. Yet despite the evidence of two pre-Columbian texts, Marson's travels to America are basically ignored. Ironically, the Norse, committed to their own explorers, have little regard for records of a pre-Norse, Irish discovery of North America.

As noted earlier, there is evidence that Christian Irish were in Greenland as early as the eighth and ninth centuries. Church documents point to communication between Europe and Greenland in 834, well before the Norse arrived.[11] Such documentation is sparse but does indicate the knowledge of at least one monastic community on Iceland. Moreover, the Viking Gudleif Gudlaugsson reported in 1029 that he, too, had sailed to "Greater Ireland" and met hundreds of Irish. He should have known, as he traded out of the Viking city of Dublin and spoke the language.[12]

Erik the Red

Although we may never know the extent of the pre-Viking Irish presence in Greenland, we can at least say with some certainty that Greenland became a popular Norse destination thanks to a persuasive Norseman named Erik the Red. Erik's father, Thorvald, had come to live in Iceland after being exiled for a murder, and the family tradition of brawling and murder would send Erik himself into exile as well. At the age of twenty-two, he was the head of his extended family. Four years later he killed two of his neighbors in a land dispute. As a result, he was banished and for a while lived in western Iceland. There another dispute, over bed furniture, led to several deaths. Called before Iceland's judicial assembly, the Althing (or Thing), Erik was banished for three years by the elders, who decided he clearly did not get along well with others. He headed to Greenland and made landfall at the same spot where Snaebjorn and his party had taken to warring with each other. Believing the place was bad luck, he rounded Cape Farewell and wintered on a small island, which he named Erik's Island (Eriksey) after himself. When summer came, he headed farther north on the western coast of Greenland, where he made settlement at Erik's Fjord, again named after himself. He called his settlement Brattahlid and built a farm.

After three years of exile, he returned to Iceland to tout his settlement. He named the island Greenland to attract settlers. The ploy worked.

Around 982, Erik returned with a much larger expedition of 750 men and women. Soon there were two settlements, the second farther up the western coast at Nuuk. Despite Erik's promises and the fertile implication of "Green Land," the farming was poor. Driftwood provided fuel as the windswept island had few trees. There was, however, money to be made in the rich stock of walrus and seal, and soon Greenlanders were exporting sealskins, oil, furs, and tusks back to Iceland and farther to Norway.

While the religion of Erik was pagan worship of Thor, the influence of Christianity was making its way from Norway to Iceland to Greenland. Erik's wife, a convert, gave him an ultimatum: Discover Christianity or sleep alone. Lucky for Leif, his son, this happened after his birth.

VINLAND

The sea acted as a highway toward the North American continent. Though the occasional ship blown off course served to add to the body of knowledge shared among the captains and pilots, it was the follow-up voyages by others that led to actual colonies and trade. Leif Eriksson was one of those who brought knowledge of the new lands back to Europe.

Leif Eriksson

Leif Eriksson, also known as Leif the Lucky, was always restless. While his brother Thorstein stayed at home in Greenland, Leif began his voyages at sea by going to Norway. He was only seventeen and in full command of his own ship. There he stayed with King Olaf Tryggvason, who had just become a Christian. Given the choice between converting and becoming a hostage, Leif found it easier to embrace the new religion, and he accepted the faith before heading home. He promised to preach the faith as well, but he must have known his father and other Thor-worshipping Greenlanders had no room for the upstart Christianity.

His homeward voyage was interrupted by a storm, and he decided to summer in the Hebrides, on Scotland's west coast. There, the sagas tell us, he met Thorgunna, a woman of noble birth and possibly a sorceress. She became pregnant with Leif's son, but he wasn't ready to settle down and continued home to Greenland.

Upon arrival, Leif heard about the adventures of Bjarni Herjolfsson and was intrigued. Herjolfsson, a shipowner who spent his summers voyaging among the North Atlantic islands and his winters with his father in Iceland, had heard during his travels that his father had sold his farm and moved to Greenland. Surprised, Herjolfsson received the consent of his men and headed west. After three days of sailing, they were blown off course by northerly winds and lost in a fog that lasted for days. Pushed much farther west than they had intended to go, when they finally saw the sun again and got their bearings, they had to sail east. On the way back to Greenland, the ship passed three separate islands, later called Vinland, Markland, and Helluland.

Against the advice of his crew, he refused to land even to take on water. They ended up sailing nine days before reaching Greenland. The adventures at sea left Herjolfsson shaken. Already wealthy, he gave up the sea trading business and settled down in Greenland on a farm.

Leif chided Herjolfsson for not even landing on the unfamiliar islands. He also bought an eighty-foot ship, and in 1002 traveled west with a crew of thirty-five to America. Three separate sagas, written by hand, record this voyage. The first land Leif and his crew saw was the one Herjolfsson's ship had passed last. It was of little value to settlers as there was no grass and, as far as they could see, was covered by glaciers. They called it Helluland, which means "flatland," literally "slabland." This may have been Baffin Island.

The next place they visited was covered with forests. Leif decided it should be named after its natural resources and called it Markland, meaning "forest land." This could have been Labrador.

It should be noted at this point that historians were very slow in accepting the Norse sagas as histories. Once Norse-style farms were found at L'Anse aux Meadows in Newfoundland, however, that attitude rapidly changed. The ability of Norse sailors to travel six or seven days of open sea between Norway and Iceland should serve as an indicator that they could sail from Greenland to America, a voyage that required fewer days at sea between landings. The sagas also suggest that the Greenlanders no longer needed to rely on the East for timber, as they immediately began importing from Markland.

The third land Leif visited, named Vinland, is the most controversial. It was described as being covered with a "sweet-tasting dew" and with a grass that did not wither in winter. The streams and lakes were full of fish. On the shortest day, the sun was up at nine a.m. and did not set until after three p.m., which indicates a location somewhere between New Jersey and the Gulf of St. Lawrence. They also encountered a tidal shift that left their ship stranded in the shallows. The name Vinland suggests grapes being grown. Understandably, historians have struggled with the description and have placed Vinland as far south as Virginia and as far north as Newfoundland.

In fact, Norse artifacts have been found in Newfoundland, Nova Scotia, Maine, Massachusetts, Rhode Island, Connecticut, and arguably farther south and west. Some of the most intriguing of these are the Norse runes. They are quite controversial, and for every expert who will offer a translation, there is another who will call the runes plow marks or forgeries. The runes certainly present a challenge. There were at least three Norse alphabets, and often the runes were used in code.* While the scattered presence of these artifacts does not help pinpoint the route of early voyages, it is in keeping with Norse wanderlust.

---

*Some of these codes can be deciphered by simple transposition of characters; others were meant to be puzzles. Prior to the acceptance of Christianity, a Norse puzzle master may have been regarded as part sorcerer because while the codes required nothing more than a key to be understood, people who lacked the key probably regarded the characters as magical. In the same way, the megalithic monuments of the northern islands required a key—a starting date, the significance of a certain stone—to be deciphered. In both cases an initiate who held the key was required. After the coming of Christianity, he could just as well have been a monk.

The monks of Scandinavia often used a six-pointed star as their device. The six points did not indicate a Star of David, but rather were used to point out the six principle virtues of God: power, wisdom, majesty, love, mercy, and justice. The monks would leave a word that would in turn be an anagram. A puzzle master could convert the original word into its anagram, assign a letter to each point of the star, and from there be able to decipher the rune.

O. G. Landsverk, a modern master at deciphering such runes, used as an example an inscription found at Nidaros Cathedral, modern Trondheim in Norway: the letters *S-A-K-U-M-R*. Landsverk discovered that this "word" was an anagram for *M-A-R-K-U-S*, the Norse spelling of the Gospel writer Mark.[13] Once this translation was made it was applied to the "Star of Solomon" and the rune deciphered. This form of coded reference was in use more in Greenland and the Orkneys than in Sweden. Nidaros itself served as a base for the Church in the western isles and Vinland.

Leif and his followers put up their booths, stone and turf enclosures, and wintered. When spring came, Leif had them build more permanent houses, but then he decided he wanted to explore further. One member of the scouting party was Tyrkir the Southerner, who had been a friend of Leif's father, Erik. (When Erik was first exiled, Leif was left with the German-born Tyrkir to be raised.) In Vinland, Tyrkir played an eventful role. The last to rejoin the reconnaissance party, he had been delayed by his discovery of grapes and vines. The crew loaded their ship with cut timber and grapes and headed back to Greenland.

Thorvald Eriksson

After Leif Eriksson's return to Greenland, his brother Thorvald in 1004 led another expedition with thirty men. He headed west according to his brother's directions and wintered where Leif and crew had built their houses. In summer he took the ship and sailed south along the coast. Thorvald did not, however, share Leif's luck. The sailors were hit with a gale near a headland, and the ship was stranded on shore with a broken keel. They named the place of their disaster Kjalarness, and erected the keel as a landmark. One likely spot is the northern extent of Cape Cod,[14] another is near Woods Hole to the south of the peninsula. There lies the shifting island of sand called Monomoy, which can still spell disaster to a novice boater.

After replacing the keel, they sailed to the mouth of a great fjord and landed on a hill near the mouth. It was an attractive piece of land, but they had company. Encountering a party of three canoes, the Norse attacked, killing eight men and allowing one to escape. Soon afterward, they were swarmed by natives whom they would call Skraelings.* Thorvald was wounded by an arrow and knew he wouldn't survive. He asked that his body be buried on the headland, at the mouth of the fjord. Once he was buried, crosses were placed at his head and feet and

---

*The origin of the word *skraeling* has been debated, but there is agreement that the Norse meaning was "wretched person." Most historians interpret the word to be a designation given to any of the various Native peoples the Vikings encountered. In Greenland these could have been the Inuit or Eskimo peoples; in North America it might have applied to Micmacs, Beothuks, or an Algonquian-speaking people. In Europe it

the place was called Krossaness. His men left and spent another winter in Leif's camp before taking on a cargo of grapes and timber and heading back to Greenland.

The location of Thorvald's encounter with the so-called Skraelings is an intriguing mystery. There are few fjords in North America. One place that might have been viewed as a fjord is Somes Sound in Bar Harbor, Maine. The eight-mile-long fjord could fit the bill, although the sagas say they had sailed eastward before reaching the fjord. Somes Sound divides Mount Desert Island in two, and the promontory of wooded land at the mouth is picturesque. Another possible location is the mouth of the Hudson. Along the Harlem River there are cliffs, and on the New Jersey side of the Hudson are the even higher cliffs of the Palisades, which might have reminded a Norseman of home in Norway. Like the entrance to Somes Sound, there are islands, and both areas have mountains in the distance.

Thorstein and Gudrid

When Thorvald's men returned home, another Eriksson brother, Thorstein, decided he, too, would find the houses that Leif's expedition erected, and also recover Thorvald's body. He set out with the same ship and a crew of twenty-five that included his wife, Gudrid, but they were immediately hit with bad weather. When they reached shore, they were at the western settlement of Greenland. They wintered there but fell victim to a disease that spread through the party. Its rapid rate of infection and quick death may indicate an early, otherwise unrecorded plague. According to the *Greenlanders' Saga*, Thorstein himself fell victim and apparently died. Gudrid sat on a bench opposite the body. Suddenly, Thorstein sat up, crying, "Where is Gudrid?" His wife was so frightened she could not answer, but he recognized her and told her she would marry an Icelander, survive him as well, make a pilgrimage to Rome, and finally return to Iceland.

---

surfaced as a Danish word used to distinguish the Celtic people. The term did not, therefore, imply that those being referred to were barely more evolved than Stone Age hominids.

Interestingly, the Greeks had typically called foreigners Barbars because their language made as much sense to the Greeks as the braying of sheep: *baa-baa*. The term was therefore a joke word that became a slang word that became the root of our word *barbarian*.

The *Saga of Erik the Red* tells a different version of Thorstein's death. The scene was even more frightening, as Gudrid was standing vigil for a roomful of corpses claimed by the plague. The corpse of her husband spoke with tears in his eyes, saying that the Greenlanders have not observed respect for their dead. Instead of burying people on consecrated ground of the churches, they were burying them on farms with a stake driven into the ground above the breast of the deceased. As the saga makes clear, the Norse were caught between their ancient pagan customs and their recent Christian conversion.

Gudrid respected her husband's wishes that she live a Christian life and make a pilgrimage to Rome.

After her ordeal, Gudrid was taken in by Leif at his farm at Brattahlid. Sometime later, a ship arrived in Greenland from Norway. The owner, Thorfinn Karlsefni, spent the winter with Leif and asked him in the spring to bless his intention to marry Gudrid. After the wedding, Gudrid urged Thorfinn to make a journey to Vinland. Obviously, despite her ordeal with the failed expedition of Thorstein, there was much to be gained. They put together a party of sixty men and five women. Thorfinn asked Leif for his houses in Vinland, but Leif agreed only to lend them rather than give them, and there is no evidence that Thorfinn actually used them. One would think that such a party would have been crowded enough during the sea journey, but they somehow made room for cattle, including one bull.

Thorfinn's story is recorded in three accounts: in the *Flateybok*, also known as the *Greenlanders' Saga*; in *Hauk's Book*, where it was recorded by a linear descendant of Karlsefni; and in the *Saga of Erik the Red*. The three versions are consistent in plot, although diverge occasionally in minor details. Despite the skepticism of non-Norse scholars, the story's accurate representation of human nature and loyalty to historical fact differentiate it clearly from Norse myth.

The sagas agree that after the first winter the company encountered a party of Natives who were so panicked by the bull that they tried to force their way into the houses. Neither the Vikings nor the Natives had the ability to communicate in each other's language, so the scene must have been both frightful and comical. Before long, the Norse brought milk outside to calm the group, who left pelts in exchange for full stomachs. Though the exchange had not gone badly,

Karlsefni and company immediately built a huge palisade around their houses as protection.

It was at this time that the colonists recorded the first European child born in the Americas. Gudrid delivered a boy named Snorri, and as the son of Thorfinn Karlsefni, he would take the name Snorri Thorfinnsson. It may be that he was not, in fact, the first Viking born in Vinland. Among the other women, there could have been a birth, but the sagas—like most early histories—generally tell the tale of the leaders alone.

Soon after the birth, a Native man and woman visited the camp, but were not allowed in. While the woman served as a distraction, the man attempted to steal weapons. Karlsefni laid an ambush for the Natives and many of them were killed, but this new and more deliberate battle left the Norse afraid for their safety. After the following winter, they went back to Greenland.

Before returning home, the party made one attempt at exploration. Among the crew were two Irish scouts, prided for their ability to travel quickly. They were a gift from King Olaf to Leif, and had in turn been lent to Karlsefni. The scouts, Haki and Haekia, were put ashore and told to run as far as they could for forty-eight hours. The sagas report they encountered five people who spoke Gaelic—evidence that the Irish monks and others who were chased across the Atlantic by the encroaching Norsemen had also reached the North American coast. There was apparently little surprise, and the five Gaelic speakers were taken back as slaves.

This extraordinary event could have occurred near the mouth of the Hudson River. There is evidence that the party had lived on the south side of Cape Cod, and their brief exploratory journey was described as a day's sailing past unbroken sandy beaches just about the length of Long Island. At the end of the coast, they sailed past an island they recorded as Straumsey, meaning "current island," an accurate description of Governors Island. From there they entered a fjord, a good description of the Hudson as it flows by the Alpine Cliffs of New Jersey.[15] It was customary to sail as far as one could, and if Karlsefni did, he would have seen the future Albany six hundred years before the Dutch.

Freydis

The following summer, a ship from Iceland brought yet another explorer to the Eriksson household on Greenland. The ship was owned by two brothers, Helgi and Finnbogi, whom Erik's daughter, Freydis, talked into making a voyage to Vinland. Despite the dangers, all the returning ships had brought highly prized grapes, pelts, and lumber. In exchange for her understanding of the route to her brother Leif's encampment, and his willingness to lend their use, the brothers provided the ship and agreed that all would share in the proceeds. The agreement, however, fell apart as soon as they settled in Vinland. Freydis would not let the brothers live in the houses, taunted her fellow Greenlanders into attacking the Icelanders among the crew, and herself killed five women. She swore the Greenlanders to secrecy, but rumors of her crime spread nonetheless. When they reached Leif, he decided as a Christian that he had to get to the truth. The Icelandic version of the law, which was observed in Greenland, required two witnesses. Because Freydis was feared, witnesses were not forthcoming, so this was accomplished by torture. As she was his sister, Leif, wanting to be sure without any reasonable doubt, tortured a third witness into providing testimony, for good measure. With enough evidence, Freydis and her husband were outlawed, ensuring that no one would have anything to do with her or her family. They most likely died in poverty.[16]

The Karlsefni story has a happier ending. Thorfinn and family made one last voyage to Vinland, bringing back the most cargo ever to reach Greenland from the New World. After Thorfinn's death, Snorri took over the family farm while his mother, Gudrid, went on a pilgrimage to Rome. She returned to build a church and serve out her life as a nun. According to the sagas, many prominent Icelanders are descended from Snorri and his brother, Bjorn, including two of Iceland's bishops.

The story of the land called Vinland was no secret in Europe. Certainly, other ships made the journey to the Americas, and it is possible that some never made it back. King Swen of Denmark, with no motive for embellishment, recounted the story of the Norse adventure in the western lands for Adam of Bremen, a Hamburg-based scholar who compiled a history in 1070. Since this was done under his auspices as a rector of a Catholic cathedral school, the Church in Rome may have become aware of the New World as early as this date. It is possible too that Gudrid, the wealthy widow of Karlsefni, brought the story of Vinland to Rome on her visit.

A grave marker in Ringerike, Norway, that dates to 1050 was erected in memory of one lost after being driven from Vinland.[17] By that time the brief age of Norse exploration was over, but this by no means indicates that the westward voyages stopped. From that point on, any number of timber-seeking, tusk-hunting, and fishing ships may have made the crossing from Greenland to North America.

By the early twelfth century, there can be little doubt that the Church knew about both Greenland and Vinland. It was not only aware of the existence of the landmasses to the west, but it also appointed a bishop to watch over the churches being established. In 1112, Eric Gnupson was made bishop of Greenland. There he built a cathedral in Gardar and made a voyage to Vinland that is recorded on the Yale Vinland map.

A WORLD FOCUSED EAST

The Vikings are often mentioned as an entity in history disconnected from the European mainstream. This is only partly true. Twelfth-century Europe did indeed seem to face east, and specifically Jerusalem, while the Norse Vikings addressed most of their attention west, but the Norse and Norman influence in continental Europe should not be underestimated. Three generations after Leif and his family discovered new lands, Norse settlers were sailing west and colonizing Greenland at a time when Europe was preparing for the Crusades. Militarily, Europe was no more united, and possibly the extent of Viking raiding in the south was over. Descendants of the southern wave of Norse expansion now controlled much of France. These French, known as Normans, extended their influence to feudal states all over the Continent.

For example, in 1099 the city of Jerusalem was captured by the European crusaders, an event that at first glance seems immensely distant from the Vikings. The leader of the First Crusade, however, was Godfroi de Bouillon, who married into the Merovingian dynasty of France. He was also a Norman and thus united with the other Norman nobles, including the Sinclair family. His father, Eustache, had fought at the Battle of Hastings with six other members of the family when the Norman wave took England from the south.[18]

In Jerusalem, Godfroi formed the Order of the Holy Sepulchre, and a handful of monks and warriors alike occupied that sacred ground. His victory even caused others among the elite nobles to offer him the title of king of Jerusalem, which he turned down. He did take the title of defender.

Shortly afterward, another order formed, called the Knights of the Order of Our Lady of Sion. The founding members of the so-called Priory of Sion included the Sinclairs and other prominent families, as well as André de Montbard. The same group would create the Knights Templar. André's nephew Bernard would not only take over the Cistercian order, but also grow that order and the Knights Templar and keep burning the flame of the Crusades. Godfroi's niece Melusine would marry the Count of Anjou, thus furthering the influence of the Normans in European state and church concerns.[19]

The Norse invaders were now the ruling class of France. The Viking Norse who had gone west for trade and adventure became the governing powers in Greenland, Iceland, and the Orkneys. The Norse who became Normans in France became the central power by intermarriage and wealth. From this new base they went on to play powerful roles in the governance of Italian states and even Jerusalem. Their influence cannot be discounted on either stage.

The one power, however, they could not overcome was the weather. In the West, specifically Greenland, it would lead to a dwindling of trade and ultimately the failure of the settlements.

The Decline of Greenland

A little more than a century after Erik the Red first sighted Greenland, its Norse population numbered in the thousands. Its residents brought goods from the north and west that were imported by Norway, the Church had officially recognized the colonies with their own bishopric, and the people had achieved a tenuous self-rule. Natural and man-made forces, however, were conspiring to stress the fledgling state.

Despite the deteriorating climate, Greenland was still not cut off from North Atlantic commerce. Erik Gnupson, the appointed bishop from Iceland, arrived in the western settlement of Greenland shortly before the Knights Templar were formed. It is recorded in the Icelandic annals that in 1121 he set sail for Vinland, and histories compiled later call Erik the bishop of Greenland and Vinland. He never returned, however. It is possible that just a few years after the fall of Jerusalem, ships suitable for long-distance travel in the more harsh climate were a scarce commodity.[20] The Church gave up hope for Erik's return, and in 1122 the cathedral he started at Gardar was dedicated without him. The next year the church appointed a successor.*

Around 1260, the bishop of Gardar could not meet his tithe to the archbishop of Nidaros in Norway. The weather had taken a turn toward a much colder climate and the hunt for walruses—the main export used to pay the tithe—was hurt. Pope John XXI was apparently more than annoyed and excommunicated the settlement.[22] (The ban of excommunication was lifted later by Pope Nicholas III.)

Greenland also lost its independence at this time, submitting to Norway and becoming a parish in the Norwegian diocese of Nidaros. The Norwegian king, showing a limit to his wisdom, deemed that only two ships could sail to Greenland each year in order to stop the Hanseatic League, with which Norway was fighting a trade war, from visiting. The Baltic league responded by destroying the harbor in Bergen, reducing the number of visiting ships to zero. Greenland was now isolated, and records of fighting with Skraelings, meaning in this instance the aboriginal Inuit population, made things worse. Communications were so poor that it was said that the bishop of Greenland, Arni, had died in 1328. The archbishop then appointed a successor, only to find later that Arni was alive.

Because of the climatic changes, sea travel became more difficult. For Greenlanders there was no returning to Iceland, as suitable land was no longer available. Many of Greenland's Norse settlers headed west. They were not looking for China as European explorers would

---

*Church records are not too unlike the sagas of the Norse: dry for the most part, but still a history of the human condition. One cannot help but laugh at Greenland's Bishop Nicolaus's request in 1237 to use beer instead of wine for the consecration at Mass. By that time, it is likely that fewer grapes were arriving from Vinland and tradings ships were infrequent. The pope, not amused, turned down his request.[21]

claim two centuries later, rather just better hunting grounds. The lands directly west from Greenland include Baffin Island, Ellesmere Island, and the Canadian mainland.

A great deal of evidence exists that Norse settlers penetrated even the Hudson Bay regions. The archaeologist Peter Schledermann has also found artifacts on Ellesmere Island, demonstrating that the Norse traveled much farther north than their Greenland settlements. This area is called the high Arctic, as it is eight hundred miles from the North Pole. For the Vikings, who most likely sailed across Smith Sound from the northwest tip of Greenland to the closest point on Ellesmere, it was a twenty-five-mile crossing. Among the items they left on the island were chain mail, iron boat rivets, and a carving in the Inuit style depicting a Norseman. Schledermann is now involved in what is called the Payne Lake Project, which is focusing on the Ungava Peninsula and an inland area that shows evidence of Norse occupation. On Ungava several Norse longhouses have been found that date to the eleventh and twelfth centuries. As always, the construction method was to use the available material: stone and timber with turf walls, with fireplaces to keep the occupants warm. As no trees grow within fifty miles, the timber was most likely brought by ship.

Nature was working against the Greenlanders, serving to end what had been an unusually warm era. The glaciers extended again, the growing season shortened, herd animals no longer prospered, and it is possible that the seas became more icebound, making voyages both west and east much more dangerous. When the plague spread through Europe, and even to her far-flung trading posts, the populations in Scandinavia and the northern isles (previously a key factor in the westward migration of the Norse) declined, reducing the need for new lands.

The western settlement had been beset by excommunication, loss of sovereignty, shortages, colder winters, and incessant attacks by the Inuit population. Nevertheless, Greenland's fragile colony did not die quickly. As late as 1323, the papal legate for Norway and Sweden received 1,400 pounds of Greenland walrus ivory that was brought to market in Flanders.[23] The good years, however, were outnumbered by the poor years, and finally, in 1342, the colony ceased to exist. What happened to the remnant population appears to have been recorded by a certain bishop Gisle Oddson, who wrote in the seventeenth century, re-recording more ancient texts. In his words: "The inhabitants of Greenland turned voluntarily away from the true faith and the Christian religion, and . . . turned to the people of America."[24] Although the name America is obviously anachronistic in Oddson's narrative, it does not discredit his report. He had simply replaced "Vinland" with the place-name that his audience would understand more easily.

The second part of his statement, however, is astounding. The bishop claimed in effect that the Norse settlers "went native." Had he written that they stayed on in Greenland, his words could be an interpreted to mean the remaining colonists joined the native Inuit population. Such a development would not have been out of character for European settlers. On every continent to which Europeans sailed, intermarriages between the colonists and the indigenous peoples took place, often accounting for newer cultures. The bishop's statement, however, implied instead that the Norse Greenlanders went west to the new continent, meaning that they may have created a new colony in Vinland or Markland—in other words, modern-day North America. Here too there is evidence of Old World–New World intermarriage. The Payne Lake Project and other research may one day provide the answers.

Europe Takes Notice

European history from 1100 to 1400 is the story of the Crusades, the threat of Mongol invasion, and the series of plagues known as the Black Death. Lands to the west were not of much interest until the period known as the Age of Exploration; this does not mean, as we shall see, that no one took interest.

Yet it is true that most of Europe was focused elsewhere. The rise and fall of the Norse colony in Greenland, oddly enough, coincides with the unraveling of the Crusades and the Knights Templar. While Greenland was struggling against nature, the Native inhabitants, and the harsh separation of icy seas, the Templar order saw that its days were numbered. In 1291 the last Templar stronghold fell to the armies of Islam. They had failed in their attempt to preserve Christian access to Jerusalem. Their critics now turned their attention to the power and the wealth of an order that seemingly answered to no one. When the

French king joined the Templars' list of enemies, the end grew closer.

The Templars had upset Church authorities by supporting the Cathars in the south of France who rejected the authority of the Church. Consequently, they no longer enjoyed the papal protection they once had. And the French king's agenda was clear and bold: breaking the Templar power and taking its wealth. On Friday, October 13, 1307, the temple in Paris came under attack. Thousands were arrested, tortured, and killed, although thousands more and the wealth of the order escaped. Like the last of the Greenlanders, some eventually made their way west.

While Greenland and the Viking practice of island-hopping were hurt by the sudden climate changes and the plague in Europe, Basque fishermen were discovering the New World on their own. Distinct in language and blood type from their neighbors, the Basques have long occupied the coastland of northeast Spain near the border with France. Adept fishermen in their own Bay of Biscay, they may have also fished for cod in the Grand Banks well before Columbus. When French explorers were busy "discovering" America in the sixteenth century, they often noted along the coast the presence of fishing ships and shacks where cod was dried and salted. The Vikings had traveled from Norway to Iceland to Greenland and finally to Labrador, following the route of the cod. How long could such a secret have been kept in a world where Vikings also sailed around Europe?

The Basques left no written records of their travels, as a busy fishing bank might soon mean a depleted fishing bank. They were certainly present, however. It is said that a medieval fisherman caught a cod that could speak. This was surprising, of course, but more so was that he spoke Basque.[25]

There is even evidence that some fishermen stayed and intermarried with the locals. There is a mixed Basque-Micmac people called the Jack-a-Tars in Atlantic Canada who have been there for longer than people have kept records. The word "Jack" is from *Jakue,* a medieval Basque word for God, and *tar* simply means "in relation to."[26] They were a people of a Christian God, and much darker than the next Europeans to visit Labrador.

In the middle of the fourteenth century, then, still one hundred and fifty years before Columbus would set sail, a European–North American commerce was still alive, if not as active as it might have been. Basque fishing fleets plied the Atlantic; Norse ivory traders and even men of the Church sailed through the frigid north. The explorations of fishermen are generally not recorded and are never celebrated as the official discoveries of kings and nations. This does not mean evidence does not exist.

The Caspar Vopel map of 1545 places the name Labrador on what would be the northeast of Canada. There are different versions of how it became a geographical place-name, but *labradore* nevertheless is a Portuguese word for farmer. The same map lists Cape Raso. *Raso* or *raz* is a word Breton seafarers give to the confluence of two currents. Generally, the name serves as a warning of the dangers of steering in such an area. History does record a Breton attempt at colonizing nearby Sable Island by a Breton marquis, Troilus de Mesgouez, but this took place in 1598. Cape Raso is off the southeast corner of Labrador, not far from an even stranger name, Cape d'Temp. The meaning of that name isn't clear, but the mapmaker drew a knight with a red cross on a white shield, an unmistakable reference to the Knights Templar.

Knowledge of the great bounty awaiting cod fishermen in the Great Banks area was not a secret for long. As the climate of the North Atlantic again improved, ships of one nationality and then another left Europe's Atlantic port cities. From Bristol in England to Lisbon in Portugal, fishing fleets raced to the North American coast.

The Last of the Island-Hoppers

While the Grand Banks of Newfoundland was on the way to being crowded with Basque, Breton, and Portuguese cod fishermen and even Biscayan whalers, Greenland was left behind. The western settlements disappeared, but an eastern colony at Osterbygd survived a bit longer. In 1365 Bishop Alfus was appointed to the parish there, but either through reluctance to travel or lack of a ship, he waited three years before making the trip. He died in 1377, and no bishop was appointed for several years.

The last royal carrier was in 1369.[27] This does not mean, however, that there was no contact between Europe and far-off Greenland. The career of one Bishop Henricus is a case in point. Church records show that the Avignon pope appointed Henricus to Greenland in the latter part of the fourteenth century. At the time, there was also a pope in

Rome, and he recalled Henricus under pressure from the archbishop of Trondheim. The king of Norway, as well as his jarls in the Orkneys, supported the Roman pope. In 1394 an Orcadian fleet transported Bishop John of the Orkneys to Greenland to be exchanged for Henricus. John had been in Greenland before and had brought back to the Orkneys a map of the Greenland coast.[28] (The Church had long been the custodian of learning, and most likely the world knew only one better source of knowledge of the oceans, and that was the mariners themselves.) Despite the worsening climate, political loyalties—and perhaps an unsinkable desire for adventure—ensured that Norse seafarers would continue to sail given the least excuse, carrying bishops and making maps for churchmen among them.

Shortly after the exchange of bishops, a voyage of exploration to the western lands was planned. Although this voyage came almost one hundred years before Columbus and almost four hundred years after Leif Eriksson overwintered on Vinland, the planners, Antonio Zeno and the earl of the Orkneys, Henry Sinclair, knew where they were going.

The Orkneys, then and now, are a small place with a strong sense of community.* Seven hundred years ago, news such as voyages to Greenland or the exchange of bishops spread throughout the islands. It was of interest not only to the crew who sailed the ships; Orkney sailors, farmers, herders, and fishermen would all be aware of both the politically inspired change of a bishop and the lands to the west.

Between the Battle of Hastings in 1066 and the late fourteenth century, the Sinclair family had grown their base in Scotland. Through marriage and alliance, Henry Sinclair, now the earl of Caithness (in northern Scotland) and the Orkneys now governed a large geographical area.

His family home in Roslin, near Edinburgh, was near the seat of the

---

*That sense of community has changed little. Despite television, newspapers, and regular ferries, happenings on the islands remain of the most interest. Today, a wedding on the main Orkney isle brings out the whole community. The Kirkwall Cathedral may not fit twenty thousand people, but the park outside and the main street beyond will be filled with celebrants. Residents there have always had a sense of fellowship that extended as far as Orkney residents traveled.

Scottish rulers. From Roslin he would play a role in affairs of government in Norway, Denmark, and throughout his own earldom. Being of Norse heritage, as well as the master of the Orkneys, he was no stranger to knowledge of the lands in the West. It was his ships that carried bishops for the Church. It was his ships that mapped the coast of Greenland. And it was his ancestors who had been sailing to western islands for four hundred years. Greenland, Iceland, and lands farther west were no secret. In 1398 Henry Sinclair acted to further his family's role in the Templar organization by creating a safe haven for the order in the New World.

After Sinclair and Zeno's time, Greenland continued to play a smaller and smaller role in the exploration of the Americas. While it may have served as one more place to land along the island-hopping route to North America, it was bypassed by fishermen who sailed directly west to the Grand Banks. Knowledge of Greenland did not disappear, but records were reduced to a handful of anecdotal events in the fifteenth century. There is a record of a marriage at Osterbygd on September 14, 1408.[29] Thorstein Olafsson of Iceland had landed in Greenland, possibly the result of being blown off course, and took advantage of his predicament by marrying a Greenlander, Sigrid Bjornsdattir.

In 1448 Pope Nicholas V corresponded with bishops in Ireland, recounting tales of what brought about the end of the Church's farthest outpost. The pope blamed an attack by heathen barbarians in 1418, though other records blame English pirates. It may very well have been a combination of both, as Greenland was no longer a strong trading post, but rather a shell of a former colony. In 1540 a German ship called on the community and found one dead Norseman.[30] The age of the sea kings had come to a close.

NEW EXPLORERS AND OLD SKEPTICS

The ability of the Norse to cover great distances is evident, given their documented travels as far east as Kiev and as far south as Italy. Yet we somehow struggle to accept their ability to have sailed west. Perhaps we should ask ourselves where they would have found the climate and inhabitants more hospitable: most likely in the Americas, where the technology of the Native Americans was no match for the Vikings, unless the Vikings were outnumbered. In France, Spain, Morocco, and farther still in Russia, the people were better armed and more hostile.

The evidence is mounting that the Norse—who left numerous records—and others like the Portuguese, Breton, and Basque sailors—who left no sagas—had been living in the Americas for centuries, and that from the tenth century to the fourteenth century, Europe was aware.

As noted, members of the scientific community have long had little regard for the legends and sagas of the Norse. They were forced to reconsider, however, after the summer of 1961, when Helge Ingstad and his wife, Anne Stine, discovered a Viking settlement near L'Anse aux Meadows (Bay of the Meadows) in Newfoundland.

Helge had given up a career in law to explore the Arctic. After years of sailing and trapping, he was appointed governor of remote Spitsbergen, where he continued his studies. Using the Norse sagas as literal descriptions of actual sailing routes, he followed their directions from Rhode Island to Newfoundland's northern tip, where a local fisherman told him about ruins near a tiny village. The village consisted of eleven families and was not approached by any road. After years of searching, the Ingstads had finally found the remains of a Norse settlement. The National Geographic Society lent support for a true excavation, and soon afterward they had acres of evidence, from tiny spindle whorls used in spinning wool to remnants of houses, one measuring seventy feet by fifty-five feet.

Arlington Mallery, excavating between 1946 and 1950, was the first to find remains of Norse houses on Sculpin Island near Labrador. On another island off the coast of Newfoundland, he discovered remains of longhouses and an iron ax and a chisel.[31] The more temporary encampments on Sops Island and Sculpin Island may have been more typical of Norse settlements. As they had done in the Shetlands and the Faeroes, the Norse often established bases on smaller islands where they were protected from the indigenous population.

William Taylor, working for the National Museum of Canada, was among the first to explore in the high Arctic. A local resident led him to an area where he found the remains of a stone longhouse measuring eighty feet by twenty feet. His discovery was not further investigated for a decade, as the search for European artifacts in coastal Canada has been problematic, and it is true that a focus on the history of the colonizers easily undermines the achievements of Native peoples. In this case, however, the local Inuits do not claim the site Taylor studied. In 1972 the archaeologist Thomas Lee excavated longhouses at Ungava Bay, and there, too, local Inuit people told him of legends of "white men" who came to the area.

The site at Ungava Bay has numerous cairns, a stone cross, and stone foundations. Early walrus hunters built such foundations and covered them with their boats as shelter. Skulls found in the stone long-houses are of both Inuit and Norse origin, possibly indicating that the Norse may not always have had poor relations with their Native hosts.

On Skraeling Island, on the east coast of Ellesmere Island, more than eighty objects of Norse origin have been found,[32] including the balance arm of a merchant's scale, which was found by the archaeologist Patricia Sutherland.

Peter Schledermann extended the known range of Viking explorers after his research on Ellesmere Island, where European-style knives, spears, and medieval chain mail were unearthed. On Skraeling Island, a piece of woolen cloth revealing an eleventh-century weave pattern of the Greenland Norse was found, along with tiny Norse carvings. He conjectured that at times Smith Sound, separating Greenland and North America, was only twenty-five miles of open sea and at other times possibly even connected. The Norse settlers of Greenland, hardy enough to cross open seas, could have found the distance to North America much shorter than the often traveled distance between Norway and Iceland.

Norse fishermen, as well as fishermen from the Orkneys, traveled long distances in harsh weather to catch fish and hunt walrus. When they did not have time to construct permanent shelter, they put up temporary "boathouses." One member of the crew with masonry skills would plan a rock shelter. Often only a few feet high, they could then overturn their boat and use it as a roof. So far, forty-five boathouses have been found in the Canadian Arctic, the largest number at Ungava Bay. Wherever such boathouse foundations are discovered, so are stone beacons, some eight to ten feet high, one thirteen feet high. Strategically placed, they guided others to the encampment. Other permanent stone longhouses are evidence that some of the fishermen and walrus hunters settled in for longer periods.

The history of Viking exploration and settlement in Canada is far from complete. The scientific community, however, still resists the implications of even the strongest pieces of evidence. In Barcelona, an American book collector came across a map that was later dubbed the Vinland map. It showed an area that was distinguished as being North America and labeled Vinland. According to researchers, including the historian Frederick Pohl, the map showed Norway, Iceland, Greenland, and the final destination, Vinland. In the area called Vinland, it depicts the mouth of the St. Lawrence River. The map dated from the early fifteenth century, thus before the Vopel map of 1545. It was found between two books of certain fifteenth-century provenance, a typical place to save maps, and wormholes in the map matched wormholes in the two books. Yale University bought the map in 1965, and when historians heaped doubt on its authenticity, Walter McCrone, president and founder of Walter McCrone Research Institute, was brought in. Nine years later, he claimed the map was a forgery because it contained titanium dioxide, which had been invented in the twentieth century. In 1987, however, physicists at the University of California analyzed the map and claimed the amount of titanium was one thousand times less than McCrone claimed. This finding indicates at the very least that the map could be a copy of an original Norse map.[33] Despite no other challenge to authenticity, books and articles continue to view the Yale Vinland map a fraud.[34]

Other evidence, such as an ax at Tor Bay in Nova Scotia, a Norse coin found in Maine, and the controversial Kensington rune stone in Minnesota, is constantly the subject of debate.

Rising above all such evidence of pre-Columbian settlers in the New World is the Newport Tower on Rhode Island, that mysterious structure often called the Norse Tower. Dating the stonework is difficult, and estimates range from the fourteenth to the seventeenth century.* It

---

*This debate has been the subject of many books and articles. The cement between the stones dates to colonial times, as do items found in the tower. It was determined that it would have been repaired in colonial times, however, thus distorting these dates. Manuel L. Da Silva, a local doctor and author, puts forth a great theory that it was built by pre-Columbian Portuguese. Holand builds a case for the Norse. Until my first book, only Michael Bradley and Andrew Sinclair gave credence to the Templar theory.

bears a close resemblance to the Orphir Chapel found on the main Orkney isle. It conforms to the St. Clair Chapel at Le Puy-en-Velay in France. It resembles the Templar monuments on the Baltic Sea isle of Bornholm. It resembles also the Cistercian lavabo near New Grange in Ireland. It is clear evidence that others came to America before Columbus and remained for at least a year, the minimum amount of time they would have needed to build it. The precise placement of its windows that frame lunar events even hints that it is one more key to the science and knowledge of the ancients, if only for those who knew where to look.

The Vikings themselves left no such monuments, although the Normans in France did. In between the Norse excursions in the eleventh century and the French voyages of discovery by Cartier and the English voyages of Cabot in the sixteenth came a group that linked the two. Their ships were manned by allied French and Scottish adventurers and mercenaries, under the protection of the Sinclair family. They were manned by hardy Orkneymen whose ancestors had sailed the cold seas hundreds, and even thousands, of years before them.

They brought with them an ability to create monuments in stone and the knowledge of sacred geometry and astronomy that had originated in places like Stenness and Brodgar on the Orkneys. This knowledge had been carried to the East and preserved by other cultures. It had been transmitted through thousands of years by the initiated. Finally, after being rediscovered by Christian knights and visiting merchants, it was brought to the new Arcadia.

2

The Sun, the Moon, and the Knights Templar

What is God? He is length, width, height, and depth.

SAINT BERNARD OF CLAIRVAUX

 IN THE LATE NINETEENTH CENTURY and throughout the twentieth century, we have been rediscovering what ancient builders already knew. Builders who were initiates of the sciences of astromony and mathematics erected structures from Stonehenge to Lixus to Chichén Itzá that impress visitors with their surface features, yet contain secrets much more impressive if anyone knows how to look.

As we have seen, the megalithic temples of the North Atlantic islands were built so precisely that they pinpoint the winter solstice. The Great Pyramid at Giza, for its part, was accurately aligned with the four cardinal directions. Its north–south axis bisects the delta to the north. Its slope angle aligns it with the sun as it appears on the day of the star Regulus, both as the sun rises and as it sets. Lined with white stone, it created a dramatic visual effect. At the precise moment the sun crossed over the east–west axis of the pyramid, one side was illuminated and visible from a great distance. The effect was as great after noon, when the opposite face was illuminated.[1] A less obvious feature was that the pyramid also solved the problem of how to square the circle by incorporating mathematical relationships and the use of pi.[2]

At Chichén Itzá, in Mayan Mexico, ancient builders constructed the Pyramid of Kukulkan. On the spring and autumn equinoxes, a shadow appears on the northwest edge of the pyramid, an image of a snake undulating down the stairway. To create this effect, the builders must have had both astronomical knowledge and a very sophisticated understanding of the subtle angles of the pyramid walls. The nearby *caracol,* or observatory, has been discovered to contain sight lines for various cycles of the moon and Venus. Similarly, the builders of the Parthenon, of the temples at Luxor, and of the Taj Mahal understood the principles of building and the relationship between astronomy and mathematics so well that they could manifest their wisdom in architectural marvels.

Even the Norse, painted by, mostly deserved, bad press as rapacious barbarians, concealed mathematical and astronomical secrets in their tales. One Norse myth tells of 432,000 warriors emerging from Valhalla to fight the wolf Fenrir at the end of the world. This large number is echoed in the Babylonian records of 432,000 years of reign of the kings before the Great Flood. It is again echoed in the Rig Veda, an ancient text consisting of 432,000 syllables.

Sixty as a number was considered perfect, as time began to be measured by the Sumerians in units of sixty, the hour being divided into sixty minutes and the minute into sixty seconds. The day is divided into twelve hours of day and twelve hours of night. The zodiac has twelve houses. The equinoctal sun occupies each house for 2,160 years and to make a complete cycle of the entire zodiac requires 25,920 years. Dividing the era of a complete zodiac by the perfect number 60 yields 432. It is unclear why this number held importance to the Norse warriors, yet this simply reflects our own shortcomings in understanding our world's history.

The extent of the knowledge of the ancients is something most modern people are still unable to calculate. Such understanding eludes even contemporary scientists, possibly because each scientific field of study is treated as unrelated, at least in the West. (A Japanese architect, on the other hand, may not be concerned about ridicule from a peer group for orienting his plans for good feng shui. Not everyone has remained in the dark.) Yet the wisdom of the ancients was not simply lost, nor has it been rediscovered fortuitously; it was passed from generation to generation by building guilds and closed societies. The Knights Templar and the Cistercian Order of Saint Bernard were two of these.

Until the last decade, the majority of research on the Newport Tower has been in determining an origin and a date. Since 1990, however, it has been found that alignments employing the odd placement of the tower's three narrow slit windows involve the sun and moon, and may also be oriented to major stars including Polaris and Sirius. The astronomer William Penhallow scoffs at the idea that the window placement was random and determined that "[t]hese alignments allow you to keep the lunar months in phase with the solar year resulting in a lunisolar calendar."[3]

The Newport Tower was not the original round church, nor was any of the handful of others in remote places dotting the European landscape. The original round church was, in fact, not in Europe or North America, but rather in the most sacred city in the world, Jerusalem.

After the execution of Jesus Christ, the Romans converted the hallowed ground of his burial place to a shrine to the goddess. Christians who made the pilgrimage to the Holy Land were forced to worship at a pagan site. But Christianity was a powerful force by the fourth century, and the Roman Constantine finally decided he could use it to gain the loyalty of the poor but large population. In 312, at the battle of the Milvian Bridge, Constantine used the cross as a symbol of both Christianity and the Roman military tradition of Sol Invictus. After the battle, he had no rivals for ruling Rome.

From the time that the mother of Constantine, Saint Helena, visited the Holy Land and ordered the Holy Sepulchre built over the tomb of Christ in about A.D. 390, it became a fashion among wealthy Europeans to travel to the Holy Land. The pilgrimage was always fraught with dangers, ranging from bad weather on land and sea to highwaymen and pirates. Europe in the tenth century had three shrines that attracted travelers: Rome as the center of the Church, Saint James's shrine at Compostela in Spain, and Saint Michael's shrine at Monte Gargano in Italy. Pilgrims came from far and wide. The Normans particularly venerated Saint Michael, the fearless soldier of God, and traveled to Italy. But an excursion to Jerusalem was the ultimate pilgrimage. The newly converted Norse of Iceland would often take five years of their lives to make the journey.

PRELUDE TO THE CRUSADES

The fall of the Roman Empire in the fifth century permitted, even necessitated, massive change throughout Europe and the Holy Land. In the north, a weak Europe gave way to the Norse and Norman peoples. Jerusalem to the east and Africa in the south fell to the armies of the Prophet. Shortly after the death of Muhammad in 632, Islam went to war to convert the world. Soon even Sicily, Spain, Portugal, and France fell under attack. For eighty years, waves of Islamic forces saw one victory after another, extending their domain from Mesopotamia to Spain.

The Muslim Arabs controlled Jerusalem beginning in the early seventh century, when the caliph Omar rode in triumphant. He rode straight to the ruins of the Temple of Solomon, where Muhammad ascended into Heaven. Next he asked to see the sites of Christendom. He said his Muslim prayers in the Holy Sepulchre. He granted that People of the Book, Christians and Jews, be allowed to keep their holy sites. However, on the site of the original Temple of Solomon and Muhammad's ascension, he built the Dome of the Rock, incorporating an eight-sided structure, and from the year 681 it became one of Islam's holy places.

In the early eighth century, the Muslim expansion was checked. The city of Constantinople was too strong to be conquered. The Franks held the Muslim advance at the battle of Tours in France. Then the different factions, still organized by family and tribe, turned on each other. The period of Muslim conquest had ended, but a new period of rivalry between Islam and Christianity was just beginning.

In Western Europe, just as Islam was spreading, so was the Norse-Norman rule. The face of Europe changed dramatically between the raids at Lindisfarne and the Battle of Hastings. Ireland and Scotland, England, France, Russia to the Black Sea, and various Mediterranean principalities, including the Italian states, were all altered forever. As Vikings, Normans, Rus, Danes, and Varangians, the descendants of the

Norse entered the European mainstream and ruling classes. Through war and marriage, their influence grew unchecked.

In the eleventh century, the Scandinavian Norse were directing their attention to Iceland, Greenland, and Vinland, while their Norman cousins in France, after Hastings, began focusing on the opposite direction. At sea, the wealthy became so as a result of trade. On land, however, they expanded the feudal system, allowing a handful of rulers to grow wealthy by taxation. They rivaled the Church in their greed to the point that two thirds of a tenant farmer's income went to church and state.

From the days of Sinclair's ancestor Rollo, Europe was in the hands of an elite warrior class. The combination of the Norse cravings for conquest and the wealth that their European lands brought them meant that in the midst of the Church's lands was a large population of nobles who had nothing better to do than fight each other. An increase in wealth through agriculture, a more organized and productive venture, led the nobles to idle and occasionally destructive pursuits, including tournaments. Supporting a knight in a tournament came at a great cost. Petty land disputes were worse, and they were constant. As a burnt village produced no taxes, the Church looked on with horror at the "noble" class. The only value of such tournaments and struggles was to provide an outlet for aggression.

Thus matters stood in the latter part of the eleventh century when the Byzantine emperor appealed to Rome for help to halt a new Muslim invasion in Byzantine territory. Rome agreed. The Church awareness that nothing provides a more effective outlet for pointless aggression than a common enemy probably sped its decision. Ironically, in Jerusalem the Moslems had been generally tolerant of their European visitors, all of whom were considered "Franks" by the Muslims. They allowed royalty to be accompanied by their own armed guards. They even allowed the Hospital of Saint John to be set up in Jerusalem by Italian merchants from Amalfi. (Since the early ninth century, Amalfi had commanded one of the largest trading fleets in the Mediterranean Sea. Although a tiny republic, her maritime law was respected by all, and her influence allowed her to prosper in the western Mediterranean trade.) These merchants, motivated by piety or protective of trade, established in Jerusalem first a church in 1020 and a hostel for poor pilgrims in 1070. They purchased property and built two hospitals, one for men and one for women, near the fourth-century Church of the Resurrection. Since being constructed at Saint Helena's command, the Holy Sepulchre had been a victim of fire, earthquake, and the Fatimid caliph al-Hakim. It was rebuilt in 1048 by the Byzantine emperor Constantine Monomachus, with a timber cone and an open top.

The Hospital of Saint John was staffed by citizens of Amalfi who had taken monastic vows and were under the rule of a master who answered to the Benedictine order. They attended the sick, fed the hungry, and clothed the poor. They were soon raised to their own order, answering directly to the pope, and they replaced their patron saint, Saint John the Almsgiver, who had been a patriarch of Alexandria, with Saint John the Evangelist. Although Amalfi lost its powerful position in the twelfth century, the Knights of Saint John grew in influence.

In the early years, they conducted no military activity at all. Their mission began as humanitarian and in cooperation with their Islamic neighbors. It is very possible that they later provided intelligence to crusading armies because they had been in Jerusalem before renewed hostilities began, but it was not until their order was one hundred years old that the Hospitallers became knights and soldiers. Credit for this shift can be granted partly to the conversion of the Turks to Islam around 970.

In the same way that the Normans spread through Europe, often first as a fighting force, then as a ruling power, the Turks had spread through the Arab world. Turks and to a smaller extent Mongols arrived from the steppes of Asia as an attacking horde of barbarians. Although they soon settled in lands controlled by Islam and converted, they never left behind their warrior instincts. Providing Islam with a new military energy, the Turks of central Asia became the leading armies of western Asia.

When the Byzantine armies met the Turks in battle over Armenia in 1071, the Turkish victory was monumental. Not only did it collapse the balance of power that might have preserved the peace between Christian Europe and Muslim Asia, but it also disrupted the relative peace that had prevailed in the Arab world. A Turkish adventurer, Atsiz ibn Abaq, took Jerusalem in 1071 and then all of Palestine.[4] Fatimid Arabs counterattacked, and Jerusalem was recovered after a bloody massacre.

The Arab world was now divided into Turkish Muslims in the East and various caliphates in Africa and the West. Pope Urban understood that this could be used to the Church's advantage. It is noteworthy that the Christian population was spared from the ensuing massacre.

The West, however, did not take note. The Church, already engaged in helping Spanish nobles recover territory in Spain lost to Islam four centuries earlier, decided to take advantage of a rare opportunity to regain Jerusalem for Christians and used Ibn Abaq's attack as an excuse for entering the fray.

THE FIRST CRUSADE

Shortly after the holy city of Jerusalem was turned into a battle-ground, Europe engaged in a holy war against Islam. The First Crusade began when a Burgundian noble, Odo of Lagery, became Pope Urban II. He was already a reformer, part of the anti-Cluniac movement. The Cluniac order had its roots in reform, but had since become lax. This liberal and licentious order had caused backlash against the Church by the faithful, and many considered such lack of piety as that displayed by the order to be at least partially to blame for the loss of the Holy Land. In 1088 Urban called for a council to be held at Piacenza. There he pushed through new rules. He enforced the ban against clerical marriage. He attempted to end simony, the practice of purchasing and selling ecclesiastical offices. And he attempted to curb other abuses that had caused Church officials to be regarded as a bloated and weathy caste living high at the expense of those they taxed. In time, he even used Islam as a tool to achieve his vision of a rededicated and unified Church.

Because Islam was the enemy of both the Roman and the Byzantine churches, Urban realized that a common crusade against the Muslims could consolidate the power of the Church, which had been fractured both by infighting among nobles in the Western Church and by the schism between Rome and Constantinople. He allowed ambassadors of the Byzantine emperor, Alexius, to address the assembled clergymen and to request their assistance to continue the fight against the Seljuk Turks. Privately, they had reported the fight was going well, and pilgrims were allowed to visit Jerusalem. Publicly, the same ambassadors claimed they needed assistance. With his church convinced, Urban needed the approval of the populace.

On Tuesday, November 27, 1095, the public was admitted to the Council at Clermont, where the pope addressed the need to stop the Turks from marching into Christian lands and defacing Christian shrines. The reward would not be the pay, as little could be promised. Instead, the crusaders could take satisfaction in fulfilling their duty to God and receiving absolution and remission of their sins.[5]

The crowd roared with approval. Possibly by cue, the slogan God wills it! met each pause in Urban's speech. Word of the crusade spread far and wide, and from every corner of Europe men enlisted for battle against the enemies of God.

Secondary to a united Christendom, but still very important to the pope, was another goal that the crusade would solve: It would focus the militant European nobles on something other than squabbling among themselves or testing the authority of the Church. Odo would provide a direction to channel violence, or at least he would try.

Before the First Crusade began, Pope Urban's preaching had a great effect on a cleric named Peter the Hermit. His own People's Crusade began in Germany by attacking Jews and marched across Europe killing Christian Hungarians and Slavs, only to be slaughtered when meeting the Seljuk Turks.

Two months after the disastrous People's Crusade, Norman nobles, including Godfroi de Bouillon and his two brothers, took up the banner and led the more disciplined armies envisioned by the pope. Initially a strong force, the army didn't have much going for it by the time it reached Jerusalem, as its numbers had been reduced by half because of the long journey. Moreover, the People's Crusade had waged a campaign of destruction on the route to the East, dissipating hope for resupply. The first wave of crusaders had also alienated the Byzantine emperor, who was actually in talks with the caliph of Egypt. Not that the second wave was significantly more restrained. It saw two Norman competitors, Tancred and Baldwin, competing for booty. They attacked and looted numerous towns, including Tarsus and Edessa. Then they laid siege to the strategically located Antioch. At last they were resupplied by a fleet of Genoese ships that brought siege weapons, including catapults, along with food and other supplies.

In June 1099, the crusaders and the Genoese were ready to attack Jerusalem, and began a siege that lasted six weeks. Although the armies of the Norman nobles had refrained from attacking Christian posts along the way, like the People's Crusade they were bloodthirsty. When the siege finally broke the defenses of the Holy City, the victory ended in the massacre of all the residents of Jerusalem. It is estimated that fifty thousand Saracens were killed, but the crusaders did not discriminate. The blood of Turks, Jews, and even Christians reputedly flowed knee deep. Many Jews were burned to death in their synagogues. Not since the legions of Titus stormed Jerusalem in A.D. 70 had the slaughter been so complete.

WARRIORS AND MONKS

After the efforts of the First Crusade brought the conquest of Jerusalem, the need to establish a governance served both to ensure peace and to satisfy the need for titles and states by the conquering nobles. Crusader states were set up in the conquered lands and within these states smaller fiefdoms were granted to many nobles. Maintaining a system of supply and safeguarding European pilgrims was the next order of business. Pisa, Genoa, and Venice sent fleets with supplies in the hopes of being granted access to ports. Though the sea provided a safer means to reach the east, others came by land, and even between the cities of Edessa and Jerusalem there were still minor potentates to be dealt with. The need for such security was soon filled.

The Knights of the Temple

Five years after Jerusalem was under Christian rule, a handful of knights led by Hugh de Payens came to the Holy Land. Hugh was a knight and minor noble born near Troyes, and related to the count of Champagne.[6] He met with King Baldwin I, head of the Kingdom of Jerusalem, who was the brother of Godfroi de Bouillon, and presented him with their plans to start a separate order of fighting monks. The knights in Hugh's band were all from the same area in France, and they shared a Merovingian heritage that played an integral role in determining France's rule. King Baldwin agreed to their plans, and they took up residence in the royal palace of Jerusalem, which was believed to lie on the site of Solomon's Temple. As monks, they took vows of poverty, chastity, and obedience in a ceremony on Christmas Day in the year 1119.[7]

Hugh and his eight men may have been inspired both in their goals and in the methods they employed to achieve their aims by the Knights of Saint John, who had long provided charitable service to pilgrims and who had been granted status as an autonomous order in 1113. The new monks also chose a Saint John as their patron, but theirs was Saint John the Baptist, and they boldly claimed that their mission was to make safe the road of the pilgrims who would now want to visit the Holy City. The fact that nine men could hardly accomplish such a daunting task apparently was never questioned, and upon their return to France, the Poor Knights of Christ, also known as the Knights Templar, were accorded disproportionate status and honor.

There are reasons to believe that the Knights Templar had a hidden agenda. Besides the fact that the task of protecting the highways was perilous, if not impossible, they did not actually spend time on the highways. Instead, they spent the first decade of their history excavating the site of Solomon's Temple, specifically under the stables. It is likely they had received some knowledge of either sacred treasure or religious artifacts, and finding them was their primary mission.

One source of information may have been a group of Calabrian monks who had come to the home of the Bouillon family two decades earlier. They were given permission to stay and, finally, a tract of land at Orval in the Ardennes upon which to live. One of this group may have been Godfroi's tutor. At this time, Italy had begun serving as a conduit for the books and charts of the East that had once been moved to Constantinople for protection. Just what new knowledge came to Godfroi via the monks is unknown. When they left, they went to Saint Bernard, who later played a major role in the Crusades.

Or perhaps Baldwin had created the order and sent the new monks home simply to recruit men he could use for his own purposes. We know that Baldwin and his army lived among the Muslim population, whose loyalty was to their own leaders only, and that he had been in secret negotiations with the Assassin sect. Hasan, a leader of the sect, had gone to Aleppo to establish his underground Ismaili movement. Originally under the protection of the local vizier, the Assassins murdered a sheik at Baalbek, whereupon the vizier decided he needed to eliminate the group. The vizier's son ordered the assassination of another leader to make it appear that the sect was responsible. Riots broke out and many Assassins were killed. The head of the sect decided he needed a Frankish ally and met with King Baldwin.[8] With fresh troops that perhaps included new Templars, Baldwin marched on Aleppo. Although the attack failed, it was a starting point for the relationship between the crusaders and the Assassins, and the Templars were center stage.

Recruitment in Europe

The recruitment of new warrior-monks was a much greater success. The recruitment process was certainly helped by the fact that the original members were all of closely linked noble families, and mostly from the French region of Champagne. It also helped that one member was related to the man who would be known as Saint Bernard. Bernard's preaching and fund-raising skills grew both his own Cistercian order, which he resurrected, and the Knights Templar.

The Cistercian order did not begin with Bernard, but rather with Robert, the abbot of Molensme. In 1098 Robert left his monastery with a group of twenty-one monks who were fed up with the impiety and materialism of the Cluniac order. They moved into a swampy, inhospitable area of Burgundy called Cîteaux to set up a new abbey, where they lived following the strict rule of Saint Benedict that had been established in the fifth century. Benedict's rules included work, service to community, prayer, and meditation, but the combination of an austere lifestyle and inhospitable climate left the friars at Cîteaux so weak that an epidemic almost wiped out the earliest members of the order.

Bernard de Fontaines and thirty Burgundian nobles, however, found the Benedictine rule an appealing antidote to the poisonous excesses of the Church. In 1112 they joined the order. Bernard still insisted on strict rules and tight discipline. His rules included not wearing shoes with shoelaces (as they were considered pagan); no hunting, unless for lions; and no shaving of beards, although hair would be cropped short.[9] The order's motto was "Prayer and work," possibly something little seen in the Cluniac order. Instead of the black robes of the Cluniacs, the Cistercians wore white. Bernard insisted on cleanliness, and his monks were required to wash their hands after working.

He founded a chapter at Clairvaux on land given to the order by Hugh, the count of Champagne and a founding member of the Templars. Under Bernard's care, the order made a remarkable recovery, and at the time of his death there were more than three hundred Cistercian houses. His greatest moment came when a student, a Cistercian monk, became Pope Eugenius III.

With the Cistercians well on their way, Bernard turned his attention to the Knights Templar. The two orders started modestly and grew rapidly. The control Bernard was able to exercise with the Templars was due in part to the fact that he was related to at least one of the early members. Sir André de Montbard was a vassal of Hugh of Champagne, and Bernard's uncle. It was his land that provided a home to the early Cistercians under Bernard. Hugh de Payens, another vassal of Hugh of Champagne, was the first leader and a relative by marriage of the St. Clair family. Two members of the ruling house of Flanders and two Cistercian monks were also among Hugh's first eight Templars. Soon noble families throughout Europe rushed to pledge lands and monies to the Templar knights.

Pope Innocent II, who had been a protégé of Saint Bernard, issued a papal bull in 1139 granting the Templars the position of having to answer only to the pope in Rome. At the Council of Troyes, the pope appointed Bernard protector of the order. Bernard helped draw up the Templar Rule of Conduct.

The Knights Templar began providing its forces for various military campaigns in the Holy Land. The order's power grew and members' fearlessness in battle became legendary. Their military code precluded surrender, and at times being outnumbered with horrific odds did not prevent them from charging to their death.

The two military orders, the Templars and the Hospitallers, soon became the standing armies of the Europeans in the Middle East. The various European nobles who administrated the four crusader states were often most concerned about their own power and status, with the result of much infighting. In their midst, a new Muslim leader emerged: Imad al-Din Zengi. One by one, he slew his enemies and then steadily increased his own army with hordes of Kurds and Turkomans from the upper Tigris. In November 1144, they marched on Edessa and prepared for a siege. A surprise Christmas Eve attack allowed them to quickly seize the city and the horde rushed in, killing all the European men and selling the women into slavery. It was a major defeat for the crusader cause. It eliminated Edessa, one of the four crusader states, and with it a geographic wedge between the northeastern and southwestern Turks. It also gave the Arab population renewed hope.

Shock and dismay were the European reactions. In the four decades since the First Crusade, never had the Saracens succeeded in taking back a major city. When Zengi's armies began testing the defenses of another major city, Antioch, the call went out for renewed crusade. The Templar status as a necessary fighting force grew, as Europe's other troops had mostly returned home. Only the Italian merchant cities maintained a regular presence in the region, making sporadic attacks using their own fleets, but often their objectives were their own.

Financial and Military Success

As the need for an even greater military organization grew, so did the status and power of the Knights Templar in Europe. Possibly Bernard's greatest achievement was at Vezelay on March 31, 1146. The need for a new crusade had moved the French king to employ Bernard as the spokesman for his endeavor. Bernard had an unusual fascination with Mary Magdalene and the Black Virgin sanctuary at her pilgrimage site in Vezelay, where the Mary Magdalene relic bones were held. To him, Notre-Dame (Our Lady) was Mary Magdalene, and he wrote the rule of order commanding the Templars to the "obedience of Bethany, the Castle of Mary and Martha."[10] (Bethany refers to the home of Mary Magdalene where she and Martha met with Jesus.)

Kings, queens, and 100,000 knights, monks, and commoners arrived in Vezelay. The cathedral could not hold all the crowd, so Bernard moved the site of his preaching to a field outside town, where he preached his call to arms from a platform. In response, the audience called out for "the crosses," pieces of fabric that Bernard had brought to give to those who enlisted. The hysteria was so great that once his supply of material was exhausted, Bernard took off his own vestments to be cut into crosses. At sunset, his assistants were still cutting and sewing.[11]

The new recruits were not all peasants. Everard of Barre, the grand master of the Templars, signed up a large group of wealthy nobles who were honored to join the Second Crusade with the order. The Templars at this time adopted their Red Cross, the sign of willing martyrs. From Scotland, England, Brittany, and the Lorraine, dukes, earls, and princes donated land to the order as well.[12]

As a consequence of its popularity, the Templars grew to rival the Church itself in ownership of estates. As early as 1128, the order had been given land in the Languedoc, in the Aude Valley near Carcassonne, and as far south as Soure in Portugal. Later in the twelfth century, Eleanor of Aquitaine gave them the right to create a Templar naval port in La Rochelle. As the Templars had their own battle fleet, which alternately acted as a merchant fleet, ports served them well. This one would later play an important role in Templar history. Most of the Templar holdings were in France and England, some in northern Italy.

They also created the first truly international bank. Funds deposited in the London or Paris Temple could be withdrawn in Jerusalem, reducing the need to carry money on the hazardous voyage. As the basis of a bank's ability to earn money for its services is to charge interest or fees for making loans, the Templars soon had many of Europe's nobles in their debt. Although the Templars were sworn to poverty, it was an individual poverty to which they swore. The order itself became wealthy.

The order's success in battle was not always as great as its success in accumulating wealth, but the members' bravery cannot be called into question. Shortly after they lost their patron, Bernard, in 1153, they attempted to besiege the city of Ascalon on their own. With their grand master leading the way, they exploited a breach in the city walls and rushed in. It was most likely a trap. Once inside they found themselves surrounded and hopelessly outnumbered. To a man, every Templar was killed and their bodies hung from the walls.

The next year, led by a new grand master, Bertrand de Blanchefort, the order was drawn into an ambush near Tiberias; hundreds were killed and their grand master captured. Relentlessly, and against all odds, the Templars counterattacked. Thirty knights defeated two hundred Muslims. One telling comment about the victory was that the knights never asked the number of the enemy, only the location.

In 1170, Odo de St. Amand became grand master. The Templars soon met their greatest foe, the legendary Saladin, who rode out of the desert with forty thousand southern Arabians and Bedouins. It may have been the most glorious time for the crusading armies; well-armed

Templars and Hospitallers rode to battle together, as a vanguard leading the larger crusader armies, against Islam's greatest armies. Victories were passed back and forth, with no clear advantage.

As heroic as the Templar knights were in battle and as wealthy as the order became at home, the piety of the warrior-monks was never in doubt. When they camped, the Templar knights always brought with them a portable chapel, a round tent that they placed in the middle of their camp and which contained the trappings of the Catholic Mass. On occasion, pieces of the true cross itself would be taken into battle as inspiration. The chapel was constantly under guard and ready to perform the sacraments for men who would ride into battle.

The Seeds of Craft Masonry

The military exploits of the Knights Templar during the successive periods of military engagement we call the Crusades are well known and documented. Their activities during the numerous lulls between those engagements are less known. In the end, however, these have had the greater consequence.

Ironically, the Crusades served to make a global community of people and cultures separated by seas and long distances. While the wars necessarily spread destruction and death, they also spread learning and knowledge. Returning crusaders filled the libraries of the Italian states with ancient texts of the classical writings on mathematics, cosmography, and geography. These were shared by both Arabic and Jewish scholars and translated into vernacular languages, making available to wide audiences knowledge that until then had been privy to only a few.

First and foremost, the Church stood in the way. Books had long been used to fuel fires rather than minds and were always suspect. The sixth-century bishop Gregory of Tours had said the study of letters had perished, but added that this was good, as the works of the poets led to sin.[13]

By the time of the First Crusade, those who had the good fortune to attend the rare religious schools or receive private instruction came in contact with books; however, the scarcity of schools was not the only barrier to learning. Reading itself was a privilege reserved for those who could afford the luxury of hand-transcribed texts. The community of those devoted to the sciences was necessarily select and small. That community grew as a result of the exposure the Crusades provided to a less insular world.

The community of the learned grew beyond the nobles and their children to include those in their sphere of influence or their employ. Doctors and sea captains, monks and merchants, masons and craftsmen—all benefited from the intellectual treasures the Crusades brought to light and served to advance the sciences themselves.

In particular, building and architecture, based on the science of mathematics and often focused on geometry, grew exponentially. From the birth of the dual orders Templars and Cistercians, building projects spread like wildfire throughout Europe. Fortresses and roads were constructed for practical purposes; cathedrals and churches were built for spiritual ones. The art of construction took on sacred tones, and every bridge, chapel, and cathedral was understood to employ sciences that were the gift of the Great Architect who was the builder of all.

Construction in the modern world may not appear to be part of a divine process, but in the medieval world it was inspired by the divine and not separated from the mystical aspects of religion. The direction an edifice faced, the time when and the place where the sun rose through stained-glass windows, the placement of altars and baptismal fountains: These were of great significance even if that significance was understood only by a select, initiated few.

Most of those who visited cathedrals were amazed by the majesty of the facade, moved by the chanting that perfect acoustics could inspire, and profoundly affected by the altars that perhaps held relics of the Church's most sacred figures. Most supplicants did not, however, understand the even deeper knowledge, or even the symbolism, that was key to the Gothic masterpieces. The builders did understand.

Not only did each cathedral contain mysteries within, but the placement of cathedrals in relation to each other also mirrored the stars. With two exceptions, the cathedrals of northern France represent a map of the constellation Virgo.[14]

A complete brotherhood that guarded these secrets grew out of the building arts. They were learned men, although to various degrees. They were also very loyal to each other. To provide safety for one another as they traveled from city to city to employ their crafts, they formed craft lodges. In each lodge, masons, bricklayers, and architects were bound to each other and would provide a brother with food, clothes, shelter, and camaraderie. The Templars themselves would eventually see the clock run out on their glory days; those bound by oath and secret signs, however, would survive in the lodges of the crafts.

The knowledge that was shared had two purposes. The first was practical, the sharing of the necessary sciences, mutual protection and assistance, and the exclusion of those who could not be trusted as brothers. The second was sacred, the direct connection to the divine. This knowledge was also secret, conveyed only to those initiates who showed the promise of profound understanding. During the Italian Renaissance, it was not an option to challenge the Church, as the Church had no fear in taking on one or one million of those it branded heretics. The way, then, to preserve and spread the sacred and secret knowledge was through other means. Art, music, and architecture were used as the pages of a book that could never be written.

There is no doubt that even the message of Jesus was often encoded and aimed at two distinct audiences. Within the same context, the preaching could inspire the masses, yet give a further message to initiates. The Gospels, which relate the teachings and tales of Jesus, are no different from Norse tales of Valhalla and the Hindu Rig Veda in that they are written on two levels. Jesus frequently used the words "Let those who have ears hear." It was a message that there was more to a parable than the surface story. John used the same line in Revelation, known also as the Apocalypse. Was his story of seven-headed monsters and four horsemen real or did it carry a deeper or even different message? A clue is given at the end of the text (Revelation 22: 18–19), which cautions that adding or taking away any of John's words would be punished severely.

SUN GODS AND CHRISTIAN SYMBOLS

Saint John instituted the sacrament of baptism, the process of cleansing oneself of sin and being reborn to God. This rebirth allows the individual soul to be granted eternal life. John was the "voice crying in the desert" against the state of religion and politics in ancient Judea. He was the precursor. Upon meeting Jesus, he acknowledged the younger man as the true bearer of a new message, yet Jesus insisted that John baptize him. The symbolism of the act was that the faithful would then be born again into God's plan.

John's incessant reproof of the marriage of the tetrarch of Galilee, Herod Antipas, was a danger to his life that he either didn't acknowledge or did not fear. Refusing to compromise his sense of morality, he died at the scheming hand of Herod's wife.

Despite his limited role in bringing actual change to the Judea of his time, Saint John immensely influenced history. It was he who heralded a new world that Jesus would evoke. It was he who instituted baptism and brought eternal life to those who received the cleansing. He even inspired the creation of sects, such as the Mandaeans, that still place him as the central figure in their religion.

During the first few centuries after Christ, John was also central to the new religion. Christianity, however, was an enormously dynamic religion in its early days. Although the act of being baptized in the faith never waned, the role of John the Baptist diminished. Christianity had first appeared as a protest against the all-sacred law of the Hebrews. Jesus's announcement that the law was made for man and not man for the law was a new concept. It was nothing short of an upheaval.

Jesus, however, had a very short ministry, and the faith that grew out of specific cultural conditions changed as conditions changed. Those who became apostles to the new faith knew they had to expand in a Gentile (pagan) world. From the first century onward, the new religion incorporated many of the aspects of the old. For example, Christianity replaced the Mother Goddess, a very important figure in Asia Minor and Europe, with the Blessed Virgin, the mother of Jesus. The old faiths' multitudes of minor gods were replaced by a multitude of saints. Even the Jewish Sabbath, on Saturday, kept holy in early Christianity, was replaced by the Mithraic celebration of the sun god on Sunday.

The sun god has played a paramount role in religions throughout history. In some faiths, it is the sun that grants eternal life to the earth. Its central feast days are December 25 and June 24. In the period just preceding December 25, the sun has its shortest day of the year. It is said to be dying. After three very short days, the length of the day (measured by daylight) increases, so the sun is said to be reborn and resurrected.

June 24 is the longest day of the year. It is regarded as the feast of the birth of Saint John. He is the only Christian saint whose birthday is celebrated. Most saints' feast days are celebrated on the day of their death, as martyrdom was a fast track to becoming canonized. Only the birth dates of John and Jesus are celebrated. The Christian story of John the Baptist making the way for the Lord is not unlike the pagan concept of the old sun dying to make way for the new.

According to the liturgical calendar, John's birthday just happened to fall on June 24, a day that celebrates the sun in cultures from Britain to Syria. For Western peoples, this is midsummer's eve. After the solstice on the twenty-first or twenty-second, the sun tracks its longest path across the sky for three days, then the days start getting shorter. Although the name of the midsummer festival varies from country to country, the feast is celebrated the same way. In the Hyperborean cultures of the north, the sun as a god-man went by the names of Lug and Bel. In Britain, the sacred fires are still lit during the spring and fall celebrations of Beltaine and Lughnasa. Like the knowledge of building structures oriented to the moon and sun, the names of the sun gods may have migrated to the East, becoming Lugal, which in Sumerian means "great man," and Baal, which means "lord."

In Portugal, ancient Hercules, also known as Baal, "the lord," was replaced by the Christian saint John. Each year two major calendar celebrations take place. The summer celebration is from June 13 to June 24. On that last day, midsummer's eve, bonfires that were once lit for Hercules are now lit for John. In Norway, fires lit to Baal, or Balder, have also been replaced by fires lit to Saint Hans, or Saint John.

In Celtic and Druidic calendars, the midsummer month, our June, starts on the modern June 10 and ends July 13. The middle day is celebrated as midsummer's eve and fires to Bel, or Baal, who is regarded as the oak king, are lit on Beltaine.

The Isle of Man retains its own Manx flag depicting a sun symbol. It celebrates the sun god as the principle deity, although under Christianity, the sun god was replaced by Saint John.

It may be impossible to re-create the mystery of Saint John the Baptist and explain why he has taken over the hero-god, sun-god aspects of more ancient religions. One of the few modern John-worshipping religions is the Mandaean sect, a Gnostic faith that believes Yahia Yuhans, its name for John, was the founder of its religion. Members of the sect regard Jesus as a rebellious preacher and heretic. Oddly enough, their Eden, or Arcadia, is an idyllic land to the west that is marked by the star Merika.[15] Their brand of religion may serve as a bridge between the religions of the West, which became monotheistic and focus on the linear birth, then death, then heaven (we hope), and the religions of the East, which are based on the endless cycle of death and rebirth. The cosmic John and Jesus are the representations of the death and resurrection of the sun, an unbroken cosmic cycle.

The belief that Jesus was a heretic may be the result of the sect's geography. Wedged as Mandaeans are among Hebrew, Islam, and Christian religions, they see Jesus portrayed variously as a threat, a prophet (who took on the central role of John for himself), or a savior.

Curiously, this region is also the site of remarkably peaceful religious cohabitation. Near the modern reaches of the Mandaean sects are Syria and the ancient city of Damascus, where resides the temple of the Syrophoenician sun god once known as Hadad. The god of the Aramean people, he held power over the weather—rain, storms, and, most important, fertility. He was also the god of oracles and prophets. His consort goddess was Atargatis. His massive temple existed for at least a thousand years before the city was captured by the Romans, who enlarged the structure to make it a temple to their equivalent deities, Jupiter and Venus. After John was executed by Herod, his head was taken to this temple and a shrine was erected. By the fifth century, it had become a church dedicated to Saint John the Baptist. After the Islamic conquest of 661 and during the reign of the first Umayyad caliph, the place remained a holy shrine for all. The caliph decreed that this was a place of prayer for both Christians and Muslims, and remarkably it was shared by both. The temple was rebuilt over the centuries as a mosque, but the chapel to Saint John remained. A majestic complex evolved, and the Umayyad Mosque in Damascus is considered one of Islam's greatest buildings. It served as a prototype for mosques built in many of the territories where Islam extended its reach.

The mosque itself is basically a simple structure, but with elements that bespeak the same knowledge of architectural symbolism that Gothic builders employed five centuries later. Arcades enclosed on three sides a large open courtyard. In the center of the courtyard is a structure for ablutions that stands between two domed structures. One is the Dome of the Hours, the other is the Dome of the Treasure. This is an octagonal structure held up by eight columns. The ablutions building resembles the Cistercian lavabo in use; the Dome of the Treasure resembles it in form. Octagonal structures were rare in Muslim architecture.

These structures incorporate what Christians recognize as central themes. Baptism and ablutions wash away sins and establish purity in a spiritual sense. The Cistercian lavabo incorporated both cleansing in a spiritual sense and cleansing before meals. The Dome of the Treasure in its octagonal form is incorporated in Christian baptismal fonts. It represents the infinity of life: birth, death, and resurrection. The Umayyad Mosque, despite the differences between Islam and Christianity, demonstrates very similar concepts. Centuries, even thousands of years, separate the building of Templar baptisteries throughout Europe; however, such shared concepts remain.

While the fertilizing aspect of the sun has been pushed out of monotheistic religions, one can only wonder at the secrets in the construction of the Umayyad Mosque. Tellingly, Christian and Muslim women still come to the mosque to pray for help in bearing children. Are they praying to Saint John or to the sun god?

Today the mosque is still open to people of God no matter what faith. Although men and women are advised to dress respectfully, everyone is welcome.

Hidden Messages

In Greco-Roman times, the cult of Apollo still survived. He may have been one of the earliest sun gods and was believed to have been born in the north, in a land called Hyperborea. While classical writers like Diodorus Siculus took this to mean Britain or farther north, the real significance of the tale lay in his return to his home once every nineteen years. On the surface, this information has little meaning, but as we saw earlier, those who had been initiated into the secrets of astronomy knew a nineteen-year pattern of returns made by a sun god refers to the Metonic cycle. The tales of other mythical heroes, too, including Hercules and Jason, incorporate similar knowledge of astronomy that would have gone unnoticed by those who heard the poems being read or recited. The initiate knew there was much more to the tale.

The knowledge held close by the priests in every civilization with superior building techniques goes far beyond what was understood by their audiences. The Mayan calendar that begins in 3113 B.C., for example, was still effective in predicting a major solar eclipse in Mexico in 1991. As startling as that may be, it pales in comparison to the technical ability required to create the illusion of the serpent moving on the steps of the pyramid at Chichén Itzá when the sun sets during the winter and summer solstices. Moreover, the pyramid's four sides each have ninety-one steps, and these added to the platform create 365 steps, representing the solar year. Though the builders and the priests no doubt passed on the deeper significance of their symbols, the tale told to the populace was simply that the shadow snake was their serpent god, Kukulkan.

The incorporation and Christianization of such pagan gods and practices served the Catholic Church well in converting the world. Yet much as the Church as a whole wanted to suppress the beliefs of other religions, individuals and groups within the Church itself have always managed to preserve the ancient wisdom as well as any bard or poet. Zodiacs on church floors, stained-glass windows that shine light on certain days on relevant places, and, as we will find out, the placement of windows even in the Newport Tower demonstrate the eternal return of the sun. As certain stars, importantly Sirius, announced the waking of the sun, John as the Precursor announced Jesus. In Celtic myth, and possibly pre-Celtic myth, one god had to die so another could be born. In this sense, John was the dying god, harvested (killed) every year to make way for the new sun, which would fertilize the next year's crop.

This theme, so common to many early religions, placed great emphasis on cosmic balance. The female principle, Mother Earth, played a role that was at least as important as the male. Pre-Celtic megalith builders may have understood this long before Christianity and Judaism, as is evidenced by their ring temples, which that demonstrate the sun's annual "fertilization" of the womb of the Earth mother. Such themes could be rejected or concealed by new dogma, but they were never truly lost.

Although the Metonic cycle was understood by the Babylonians in 800 B.C., the use of it as a calendar was the invention of the Greek mathematician Meton in the fifth century B.C. It became the basis for the so-called perpetual calendar of the Church, which assisted officials in quickly determining the date of Easter in any given year.

It must be noted that long before Babylonian and Greek mathematicians, such long-term astronomical cycles were understood by cultures living along the shores of the Atlantic from Portugal, to Carnac in France, to Scotland as their monuments, so mysterious until recently, demonstrate.

While Jesus accorded little relevance to the basket of laws found in the Jewish faith and more on the true intentions and values, the architects of Christianity quickly institutionalized new laws. In the new and odd amalgamation of several faiths that became Christianity, the first day of creation was now the first day of the week and of course was Sunday. On this day, Jesus Christ as the Son of God came to earth to redeem man from his sinful ways. It was on a Friday, the sixth day of the week, that he sacrificed himself so that others may live. For three days, a very important span in other religions and later in Christianity, Jesus remained underground. On the third day, his resurrection took place. This was the day after the Sabbath (Saturday), which symbolically was the seventh day. On this "eighth day," the second Sunday, then, was the day of the resurrection. The number eight, turned on its side, remains the symbol for infinity, and so the resurrection taking place on that day has a great deal of meaning.

The sacrament of baptism emphasizes the same theme with different symbols. The child or the adult who accepts the sacrament is reborn to God and therefore resurrected. For this reason, a baptistery could only be round or eight-sided, both shapes that represent the infinite. While these symbols may have been understood from earlier times, Saint Ambrose, who was the archbishop of Milan in the late fourth century, incorporated their explanation as part of his doctrine.

During the birth of the Church and through feudal times, life for many was cheap. The promise of an afterlife was not a casual one, and to Christians, pagans, and adherents of the Islamic faith, it held great significance. Even the Templars, often wealthy nobles, put their faith in their personal rebirth after death.*

Baptism, the Christian expression of the sun god's annual resurrection, became a key tenet of the faith.

---

*It was believed that the skull and the two longest bones were all that was required for resurrection. The skull and crossbones appeared on tombstones as a sign of hope long before it appeared on poison as a sign of danger.

Christianity's Brightest Secret

The difference between the life of the human Jesus and his life as left to us in the Gospels is most likely greater than we can imagine. When Constantine brought together the bishops of the Christian world, they were there to create a religion in the truest sense. The root of the word *religion* means "to bind," and the new Christianity was bound to a dogma. How many bishops were bound to the words of Jesus and how many were bound to Constantine might provide clues as to how the dogma came to its present form.

The backdrop to the early Church was a Roman world where the state religion privileged the sun god Apollo. This personification of the sun connected an even more ancient pagan past with a Christian future. "[The] sun appears as an infant at the winter solstice,"[16] wrote the Roman emperor Aurelian. From there the sun grows old, to be reborn again at the next winter solstice. This was not a difficult concept for the builders of Stonehenge, the pre-Roman Celts, the Mithra worshippers, or the new Christians.

How different is the pagan concept of sacrificing one king or god to replace another from Christianity? The Gospel of John puts words into the mouth of the Baptist: "He must grow greater, while I diminish" (John 3:30)—just as the killing of John Barleycorn must precede the new crop. Notably, after Constantine's fourth-century Council of Nicaea established the divinity of Jesus, a work entitled *De Solsticia* was written explaining the solstices and the conception of the Baptist and Jesus as well as their births.

After grafting the new Christianity onto beliefs as ancient as the megaliths, the Church attempted to exorcise the old. It became wrong to call the sun and moon "lords," as there was a new Lord. Masked dances on the day of the New Year were banned. So was resting on Jove's Day (presumably Thor's Day, as both were on Thursday). Nuptials on Friday were also banned, probably because the day took its name from the Norse goddess Frigg and was the day of the goddess Venus in Rome.[17] Astrology was condemned by Augustine at the end of the fourth century and punished by extreme measures. Astronomy, however, could not be condemned, as monks stood watch day and night to measure the moon and sun. They needed this science to calculate their hours of prayer and to fix the day of Easter.

Like the stargazers in Babylon and Stonehenge, the Christian priests studied the heavens to discover the most sacred days of their year. The sacred days of both sun and Son were not to be left to chance.

Because the majority of the world's people were poor and the poor were often attracted to Christianity in the early centuries, the emperor Constantine decided that enlisting Christians to his cause would give him numerical advantage in defeating his enemies within the Roman Empire. It may also be that he experienced true conversion on the way to the famous battle of the Milvian Bridge when a sign appeared in the sky, accompanied by the words *in hoc signo vinces,* meaning "by this sign you will conquer." His men painted the Chi-Rho, a Christian monogram formed by the first two Greek letters (chi and rho) of Christ (Christos), on their shields and won the battle. Used as an insignia, it looks very much like the cross.

The fact that the symbol of the cross was similar to the Mithraic sun symbol was, most likely, not missed by his own soldiers. Mithraism, the cult of the Persian god of light also known as Sol Invictus (the Invincible Sun), had appeared in Rome in the first century and rapidly become the religion of the legionnaires. Although only men were admitted, the religion shared many elements with Christianity. For Constantine, who played the most significant role in creating the Roman Catholic Church, the gap between them was not difficult to bridge.

Until Constantine, the Christian Church was an amalgamation of sects, with Christ at the center of most, but with little agreement on many articles of faith. Christ's divinity was debated, the role of Mary was not yet apparent, and celebrations were often simply carryovers from the Jewish faith. Constantine made the new Christian religion catholic—that is to say, universal. At the Council of Nicaea, in 325 A.D., the assembled ecclesiasts determined by a narrow margin that Jesus was divine and that Jesus and God the Father were coeternal and "consubstantial," putting to rest a controversy over the relative divinity of Son and Father. The role of Mary was given prominence, allowing Christianity to recruit among goddess and fertility cults. The council also fixed the date of Easter and decided which of the numerous gospels were authentic.

Pagan religions had Attis, Krishna, and Dionysos being born and dying on such important dates as March 25 and December 25, a religious motif that may have existed since residents of Skara Brae erected the sun and moon temples of Stenness, Brodgar, and Maes Howe. It may have existed since the pre-Celtic Irish built the sun and earth temple of New Grange, literally, "New Sun." These gods, of course, were replaced by the Christian religion, which co-opted the sacred days (and even some of the other details) and gave them to Jesus. Jesus and Mithra, for example, were both born on December 25 in a cave and surrounded by three shepherds. Jesus was attended by three wise men bearing gifts. We call them Magi, the title of the Mithraic priests of Persia. The March 25 date was celebrated as the Annunciation, when the angel told Mary she would bear the Savior. Clearly, the names of the gods could change, but the dates themselves were not to be tampered with.

Constantine most likely did not have an understanding of mystic Christianity, nor did the bishops he picked to attend the council. He did, however, convert Christianity to an amalgamate religion in which those of more than one faith could find common ground. Mithra and Jesus, along with a host of savior gods, could share a central day of worship. The message in each was the same: The sun and the Son were reborn to provide Eternal Life. The emphasis placed on Mary allowed the theme of the mother-son relationship, as depicted by Isis and Horus, to become apparent in Mary and Jesus. Other religious motifs, however, such as the roles of the precursor and the consort, did not fare as well. Saint John and Mary Magdalene were demoted. Their once obvious symbolism was forgotten by mainstream Christianity, yet survived beneath the surface in art and architecture.

The Perfect Symbol: The Chapel of the Holy Sepulchre

Although the authenticity of Constantine's conversion remains doubtful, his mother took to the faith in a real sense. It is Helena, later Saint Helena, who gave Christianity its first architectural symbol, the Holy Sepulchre. She is also one of the most famous discoverers of Christian relics. As a true convert, Helena of course made a pilgrimage to the Holy Land, where she unabashedly went on a quest that appears to have been more like a shopping spree. She is recorded as having found the hay of the manger where the baby Jesus lay, the wood of the True Cross, four nails from the Cross, and the bodies of the three Magi. She also found the exact spot where Jesus was buried and resurrected. According to legend, she had a dream that led her to the site, although modern sources say that Christians living in the city knew about it all the time. The Romans in 135 A.D. had built a temple to Venus there. Helena ordered the pagan temple destroyed, and work started on the Holy Sepulchre. It was consecrated in 326.

A domed, circular structure, presently called the rotunda, was built to cover the tomb of Jesus. The design of the rotunda itself is the circle. Jerusalem, and specifically the tomb of Jesus, was the center of the world for Christians. Like the Templar round churches that followed through the ages, it was founded on octagonal geometry manifesting the concept of infinity. The rotunda over the tomb came to be called the Dome of the Resurrection, and from there the original structure grew with the addition of a courtyard and an atrium. Under the southwest corner of the courtyard was the rock of Calvary, the place of the cross. The completed structure never survived the series of invasions in the holiest of cities, but it is believed to have resembled in its complexity the mosque of Umayyad. For the Templar architects who took to building replicas of the Holy Sepulchre Church, it was the simplicity of the octagon within the circle that preserved the meaning.

The Chapel of the Holy Sepulchre, within the rotunda, consists of two chambers, one within the other. In the outer, the Chapel of the Angel, is laid the stone that once closed the tomb of Jesus. In the inner, the chapel proper, is the actual tomb of Jesus. It is the most holy site of Christendom on the planet.

The concepts of birth and rebirth and the eternity of life survived the destruction of the original Holy Sepulchre Church. When it was destroyed, the Islamic Dome of the Rock was built nearby. It employed a circle surrounded by an octagonal arcade of piers and columns. Looking at the transition between the basic octagon and the spherical cupola is described as the transition to heaven from earth. (At least one writer on the Holy Grail literature has come to the conclusion that the Round Table was actually a misinterpretation, and that the place where Arthur and his knights met was within a rotunda rather than around a circular table.[18])

The rotunda and octagonal structures spread to many places soon afterward. One of the first was the Church of San Giovanni in Laterano,

St. John of the Lateran, in Vatican City. Here, in a design that reflects the symbols incorporated in the Damascus Mosque, is an inner octagon supported by eight shafts. In Italy the warmer weather allowed for the baptistery to be a separate building from the rest of the church. Farther north, the baptistery was incorporated as a chapel within a larger church or cathedral.

Many features of the round and octagonal churches that followed the Holy Sepulchre are unique; the theme they all share, however, is that of death and rebirth. The perfect symbol is the circle containing an octagon. The round and eight-sided churches conveyed to some a visual message as important as Christ on the Cross. As Jesus the Son of God died and rose again, the round churches shared the symbol for infinity and the means of baptism, nothing short of initiation into the eternal life.

THE EIGHT SIDES OF THE INFINITE

The Western world takes for granted the incorporation of meaningful symbols in both ancient and modern architecture. The number eight represented the rebirth necessary for eternal life. Today the actual numerical symbol "8" turned on its side represents infinity. In the early centuries of the Christian Church, the symbolism was significant and always incorporated into important structures.

The Church at Philippi

Possibly the first church to follow the plan of the Holy Sepulchre in Jerusalem was built in the ancient town of Philippi. After the death of Jesus, the early Church was divided between those who would admit only Jews and those who would admit everyone. Paul, who was in favor of admitting all to the new faith, was a thorn in the side of James, who took over as head of the Jerusalem faction. For the benefit of all, Paul was sent west to preach. His first stop in Europe was in Greece, in the small city of Neapolis, where his message may not have been welcome to inhabitants who adhered to various rival gods, including Pan.

His next stop was in the town of Philippi, where he had more success. Originally called Krenides after the springs in the area, Philippi was renamed when Philip II of Macedon took the area in the fourth century B.C. In about A.D. 49, Paul founded the first European Christian community there, and this community built the first European Christian church.

This church was replaced with an octagonal church sometime after the Holy Sepulchre was constructed, perhaps as early as A.D. 400. Near it, three basilicas were built, modeled after Saint Sophia in Constantinople. As Philippi was a key city on the trade route from the Adriatic to Constantinople, its location may have served to spread the use of the rotunda design even further.

The Baptistery of Florence

The history of this beautiful city is often centered on the Renaissance era, when art and architecture flowered. However, one of the first true baptisteries built in the octagonal fashion was built here between the fourth and fifth centuries. It was dedicated to Saint John, or Giovanni, and is now centrally located in the Piazza del Duomo. Florence is laid out in four quarters, each having four wards. These all have sacred symbols of dragons, unicorns, and keys, each possibly serving as a key to a greater understanding. In the center of the layout is the baptistery.

Although the original foundation, which itself was built over a temple to Mars, has been worked and reworked, the baptistery itself has been called "the egg from which Florence's golden age was hatched."[19] On March 21, which was once New Year's Day in the Florentine calendar, every child born in the last twelve months was brought here for a communal baptism. Intriguingly, March was once the first month in the astrologer's calendar and the Ides of March began a New Year's celebration in pre-Christian Italy. In ancient fertility cults, the Ides was a dangerous time for kings, who were either symbolically or actually killed to make way for the new king in rituals that ensured the renewal of the kingdom. Among the Persians, who provided at least inspiration for many Judeo-Christian ideas, the savior god was slain at this time. His name, evocatively, was Immanuel, which means "God with us."[20]

Worth noting here is that Florence, whose patron saint was John the Baptist, would become a sanctuary in a religiously hostile world, a place where religious ideas could be exchanged freely and occasionally incubated. In time its Cathar leanings and religious tolerance would keep on the intellectual lights while the Church's Inquisition blacked out learning elsewhere. This was the city where Giovanni Verrazano was born.

Rival Structures of Ravenna

The city of Ravenna, north of Florence, has two octagonal baptisteries, in close proximity to each other and both built around the same time—when the Arian heresy invaded Italy despite the efforts of the Council of Nicea. The Baptistery of the Orthodox is also called the Neonian Baptistery after the Bishop Neon, who decorated it with Ravenna's oldest mosaics. It was built in the fifth century and much of it has been restored, including the mosaics. Upon seeing the mosaic that depicts Christ reaching out his hand to Peter, Carl Jung once commented that he understood it to be conveying the archetypal idea of death and rebirth.

The Baptistery of the Arians was built in the early sixth century during the reign of Theodoric. Like the Orthodox Baptistery, its ceiling shows Christ being baptized by Saint John with the twelve apostles around him. The Arian heresy had other pagan beliefs amalgamated into itself besides denying the divinity of Jesus. Though the Arian heretics and the Orthodox Christians disagreed on the quality of Christ's divinity, both, perhaps unwittingly, incorporated symbols of earlier religions and perpetuated archetypes.

In the Orthodox Baptistery, there is also a depiction of an empty throne with a cross, symbolizing a people awaiting their king. Greek viewers instantly saw the relationship to the empty throne of Zeus, accompanied by the thunderbolt instead of the cross. In the Grail romances, the empty chair in the rotunda, or at the Round Table, signified the seat of King Arthur.

The Baptistery of Frejus

At the time the Romans defeated the Celts in the south, about 122 B.C., Frejus was situated at the mouth of the Argens River and connected to the sea by a canal. The harbor was artificial, built in a swamp. A turret, called Augustus's Lanter, served as a beacon to help Roman ships find their way. Once the river dried up, the port city was a mile from the beach, and the town of Forum Julii, as it was once known, lost considerable importance.

During Constantine's time, Christianity was introduced to Frejus, and Gaul's first octagonal baptistery was built employing the geometry of the model in Jerusalem. It stood on eight black granite columns and endured the test of time as the Saracens attacked and attacked again, destroying much of the city but sparing the baptistery. Today, Frejus is rich in archaeological treasures, many still waiting to be found. In 1986 portions of the ancient docks were discovered under a parking lot. The Roman arena once able to accommodate ten thousand is also still there, as is a theater and an aqueduct. Near the baptistery stands a cathedral.

The Baptistery of Saint John in Poitiers

Poitiers, in central France, has an early baptistery that vies with Frejus's for being the first built in France. Christians were here as early as the third century. In the fourth century, not long after Helena's construction of the Holy Sepulchre, the Baptistery of Saint John was built. Situated less than two hundred meters from the river, it was constructed over an existing foundation. In France, as elsewhere, many such religious monuments were purposely erected over ancient temples, facilitating the transfer of worship of, say, a sea goddess to Mary, who would take on the title Stella Maris, or of various sun gods to Saint John.

The Aachen Cathedral

It is unknown just how many rotundas and octagonal shrines were constructed immediately after the adoption of Christianity as a state religion in Rome. Those listed above may be only a few examples, as many churches did not survive disrepair or centuries of warfare. There appears to have been a rash of building up to the fifth century, then an almost complete halt until a revival of similar construction in the twelfth century. While we don't know the significance, if any, of this cessation, by this time the crusaders began returning from Jerusalem, and a new zeal for religious monuments knew no bounds. Then, just as suddenly, such building was halted again.

During the lull between the fall of the Roman Empire and the Crusades, there was one church built that shows an awareness of the religious symbolism possessed by the builders of the early octagon structures. In Aachen, one of Germany's most sacred spots, the baptistery-style structures did not serve as they often had in the south because of the weather. Thus the builders brought just some of the elements of the style, making the baptistery the centerpiece for the remarkable cathedral there. It was the end of the eighth century and the shifting of control from Merovingian to the Carolingian dynasty that ruled France and much of Germany. Aachen was a holy center and had been so since pagan times. Charlemagne had chosen the city as his capital and the cathedral as his tomb.

Modeled after the Ravenna structures, Aachen's church had eight pillars inside forming an octagon. The octagon was girdled by an ambulatory with tiers of arches. Smaller basilicas were on either side of the structure, resembling the inner construction of the Mosque of Umayyad in Damascus. A more remarkable observation was made by John Young, author of *Sacred Sites of the Knights Templar:* The two concentric circles of columns correspond exactly with the two circles of Stonehenge. He determined that several astronomical calculations had to have been used to allow sunlight through certain windows at the spring and fall equinoxes.[21]

Charlemagne was not a Templar. He preceded them by more than three hundred years. He probably would not have tolerated construction modeled after pagan structures of either the Stonehenge culture or the Islamic. He was a crusader whose reign was full of massacres against those who would not convert to Christianity. He even destroyed the Saxon shrine of Heresburg, the center of mother goddess worship, and another pagan site, the sacred world tree, called Irminsul by the Saxons and Yggdrasil by the Norse.

What Charlemagne missed while he sat on his throne facing the altar of Jesus was surely understood by his architects. They were, no doubt, members of a guild, initiates into a sacred science. This science was not resurrected until the Templar era, and then stopped again after the Templar dissolution.

Lynn Picknett, researcher of historical and religious mysteries and coauthor of *The Templar Revelation,* believes this second halt was intentional. The rotunda shape symbolized the Earth Mother, or certainly the feminine principle in the world. Bernard and his reverence for Mary Magdalene and the chivalrous knights with their appreciation of women in Grail literature may have reintroduced a balanced yin-yang concept of the world.[22] Suppression of the Templars and their "new" religion would have included their round temples as well.

Knights of the Round Table

The Grail romances may have had roots in more ancient traditions, but in the eleventh and twelfth centuries, they were carefully reconstructed around the then modern medieval world. Heroes were knights and kings, ready to sacrifice all with bravery. To writers like Wolfram von Eschenbach, regarded as the greatest of the medieval German epic poets, the Templars epitomized both the Grail spirit and its substance.

When the Templars came to the Holy Land, they saw for the first time what had been created in the days of Constantine, and were exposed to the remnants of cultures even older. Today, we can only guess what texts and artifacts the Templars found on their journeys. We do know that they visited the Holy Sepulchre: It was the ultimate destination for all who made the pilgrimage, as soldier or as tourist.

The Knights Templar were not the only crusaders, nor were they first, to place a great deal of importance on the Holy Sepulchre. The first knights in Jerusalem were led by fellow Frankish nobles including Godfroi de Bouillon, who took the title Defender of the Holy Sepulchre after the successful conclusion of the First Crusade.[23] He also organized the Order of the Holy Sepulchre, whose members wore white robes adorned with the Cross of Jerusalem and the Constantine motto *in hoc signo vinces*. The Templars adopted part of this early order's garb and its cross.* Were they aware of the Mithraic connotations?

Knights of the various orders that spent the Crusades in the Holy Land were like soldiers everywhere. During lulls between fighting, there was plenty of time to learn about the opposing culture. Frederick II of Prussia was one thirteenth-century crusading king who was astounded at the amount of knowledge in the Arab world. In terms of science and medicine, the Westerners were far behind their enemy. He openly courted teachers and mystics alike, and half of his court was Muslim.

Just how much Middle Eastern knowledge was new to Western Europe and how much was already understood can never be known

---

*Like the Knights Templar, the Order of the Holy Sepulchre occasionally found itself on the outs with Rome. Unlike the Knights Templar, such times generally meant being forced into other orders, rather than being arrested and tortured. In the seventeenth century, knights of the order were an elite. They shared noble birth and responsibilities that included making a pilgrimage to the Holy City.

with certainty. The Templars did not create the eight-sided baptistery, although it inspired them to re-create this structure elsewhere. Did they inherit knowledge of astronomy that had already existed in ancient Scotland from a Western source or did they have to travel east to learn such ancient wisdom?

GOTHIC EXPRESSIONS

It was after Saint Bernard began his work to promote both his Cistercian order and the Templar order that the second wave of building roared through Europe. During his lifetime, the Cistercians constructed more than three hundred monastic houses, requiring both residences and places of worship. They became known as the missionaries of the Gothic, and architecture was so important to both of Bernard's orders that the era called the High Gothic started with him and ended at the same time the Templar order was abolished.

The art of architecture was a sacred one. It required knowledge not available to everyone. As a pragmatic science, it was supported by geometric and algebraic formulas that were known only to masters and their apprentices. By the twelfth century, several factors conspired to spark the explosion of building: There were plenty of trained masons and builders, funds for construction were readily available, the guilds provided lodges that facilitated the movement of workers, and the Church was eager to manifest its spiritual truths in stone.

Both the Knights Templar and the Cistercian monks were involved in the wave of construction. Because workers could not regularly travel to places where structures were built, the orders had to deal with the logistics of housing workers far from their villages. The orders provided huts and lodge houses for this purpose, and these smaller structures were built first. Among the Templars, these lodges were called temples. The head of each was the Master Mason. He may have apprenticed with another master for six years or more. He was knowledgeable about tools, machines, and the ability to raise heavy stones, and could plan the construction from the earliest details and supervise until the work was complete.

Saint Bernard's goal in architecture was not simply the detailing of stained-glass windows and statuary to decorate the cathedrals; he had a much greater vision. He understood, and did everything to promote, the greatest secret knowledge of the Templars and their successors, the early Freemasons. That knowledge was geometry. The emphasis was on proportion and balance. The combination of the two produced a harmony of mathematics that can be heard and even felt in the architectural marvels that many of the cathedrals represent. Bernard asked himself, "What is God?" and answered his own question: "He is length, width, height, and depth."[24] The Old Testament provided an equally Masonic statement: "The skies proclaim God's glory, the vault of heaven betrays his craftsmanship" (Psalms 18:22). As God built in heaven, Bernard would build on earth.

Under Bernard's direct influence, the number of cathedrals multiplied. One of the first and indeed the greatest was the cathedral at Chartres; however, the marvel is that at the same time this was being built, there were twenty other cathedrals under construction in France. While they are called Gothic today, they were not built by the Goths, who had settled Europe much earlier. The Goths did not introduce the flying buttresses and ribbed vaulting that played a role in creating the balance the Master Mason desired. The French called the new building art *la mode française*.[25] In *The Templars' Secret Island,* authors Erling Haagensen and Henry Lincoln point out that the word is more likely to have evolved from the term *Art Goth,* or *argot,* meaning a secret language. The secret was the knowledge that was transmitted only to initiates.[26] One master, Villard de Honnecourt, whose sketchbooks provide a remarkable glance into the art of the cathedral builders, used the word *ogive* in referring to the ribs that the new style was adding to the vaults. Derived from *augere,* meaning "to strengthen," these ribs allowed larger and larger buildings.

In 1139, the pope granted the Templar order the right to build its own churches. The first was the Crusader Church built on the grounds of the Holy Sepulchre, which protects the tomb of Jesus. This church was dedicated in July 1149. They were also adept at military construction and built the Castle Pilgrim in Palestine at Athlit, south of Haifa, soon after.

In addition to the ordinary construction of farm buildings, barns, stables, and workshops, the Templars built entire castles. They proved competent and even extraordinary in some cases, strategically building fortified castles on incredibly difficult terrain. In addition to creating fortresses in inaccessible places, they protected those that were easily accessible. Where they built on rivers and coastal ports, they fortified their castles with water gates and hydraulics not generally seen in Europe.

They also spread the use of circular and octagonal chapels and baptisteries throughout their realm. On the surface, the characteristic Templar rotunda symbolized Jerusalem, the center of the medieval world and the city of God that the Templars sought to bring wherever they went. The possible connection between the rotunda of larger churches and the Round Table of Grail literature is not hard to accept. The Grail literature was a blend of history and fiction. The key to both was the inspiration such symbols created. Beneath their Gothic surface, there was a message.

Round Chapels of France

France was the scene of both the beginning and the end of the Knights Templar. Cistercian monks and Knights of the Temple were responsible for some of the greatest works of building art, as well as some mundane structures. The Templars are well known for their strongholds in the north, like the port city of La Rochelle; however, they also were owners of a great deal of land in the south. Here the crusades against Islam were close at hand, where the Christian aristocracy was attempting to regain territory in Muslim Spain, a pursuit known as the Reconquest.

During this attempt to recover the Iberian Peninsula from the Moors, the pilgrim trail from France to Compostela was considered second only to that of Jerusalem. It passed many churches and monasteries before it came to Saint James. The story is told that somehow the apostle James, who is regarded as the brother of Jesus, reached Spain. Traditions vary, and although some claim he traveled there while alive, this does not reconcile with his death in Jerusalem. Alternate tradition has his body miraculously traveling to Spain after his death.

Historically, pilgrims have been able to travel from one holy monastery to another, often finding food and lodging en route to their destination. In this sense, the abbeys functioned not unlike the Masonic lodge system, in which a secret handshake or sign brought a brother Mason a warm place to sleep and a meal. Even now, the monastery system along the modern pilgrim routes allows admittance to those who bring a letter of introduction from their home diocese.

Le Puy-en-Velay is the home of one of those sacred churches on the trail from France to Compostela, and like others has roots in a somewhat mystical and pre-Celtic foundation. At the top of the ancient mount of Le Puy is the Church of Saint-Michel d'Aiguilhe. Saint Michael was a favorite among those who fought in wars, as he was one of the archangels who drove the rebellious angels from heaven. His church was considered a "gateway to the Celestial Jerusalem," implying that it contained a formula in its construction. It was built over a Roman sanctuary to the god Mercury, who was possibly an outgrowth from the even older god Apollo. Significantly, both gods are personifications of the sun, the sacred light. The chapel was built during the early years of the crusaders, and many came there to pray before embarking on the trip to the Middle East.[27]

At the base of the church is an octagonal chapel dedicated to Sanctus Clarus. This was the name chosen by the sons of the Norse invader Rollo, who led the incursion into France. Before the standardization of spelling, the clan was alternately referred to as the Sancto-de-Claro family in written records and as the more modern St. Clair and Sinclair. They had taken this surname because of a holy well of that name located where they had settled. The name had both pagan and Christian meaning, referring to an individual as well as to the concept of sacred light.

The Sinclair family itself spread far and wide, and in the south of France they maintained lands in the area called the Languedoc, which bordered the Pyrennees mountains, an area known as the heartland of Cathar thought in France. The family built more than one religious monument. On their Scottish estate at Roslin still exists one of the most mystical chapels in the world. If one accepts the Henry Sinclair expedition, a Sinclair was instrumental in building the Newport Tower in Rhode Island depicted on Verrazano's map. The structure of the St. Clair Chapel in Le Puy-en-Velay bears a strong resemblance to the tower "discovered" by Verrazano. The scale and dimensions are the same. Only in the building materials and a few Islamic overtones in the French structure is there much difference.

With the science of archaeastronomy only beginning to gain acceptance among a larger community, very little research has been done to see if the Templar and Cistercian round and octagonal towers were built to a plan. When such a study was pioneered in 1996, the results were remarkable. The Newport Tower, the last Sinclair outpost, served as the basis for a December 25 experiment by Douglas Schwartz and James Egan, who photographed a lunar standstill. The light of the rising full moon came through two of the three windows.[28]

Another twelfth-century Templar chapel can be found in Laon, which was actually the capital city of France until Hugh Capet moved the capital to Paris when he created the Capetian dynasty. It lies in the heart of the domain of the noble families of Guise and Lorraine—between Troyes, where the legends of the Grail were brought to life, and the Ardennes Forest, where the last Merovingian king was murdered.

The city has so many churches it was once called *la montagne couronée,* the "crowned mountain." Its position on a spur of rock prevented it from falling to the early Norse invaders, who sailed up rivers like the Seine. In the early twelfth century, the city burned, which was a great excuse to build the Cathedral of Notre-Dame and a separate Chapel of the Templars on the eastern end of town. The Templar chapel included the small octagonal dome that was beginning to be a trademark of Templar construction. Laon is also home to a mandylion—a Christian artifact that the Church says was not made by human hands—that appears to be the face of Jesus on a piece of wood. It is stored in the Cathedral of Notre-Dame, itself an early example of the Gothic style.

While visitors to Saint-Brieuc in northern France are more likely to take in the imposing Cathedral of Saint-Etienne, nearby is the intriguing Templar round church at Lanleff. Today it is in ruins, but at one time the round tower may have been similar to the Newport Tower. The major difference is that this tower stands on twelve columns. Astronomical orientations may have played a role in the construction, as the unusual placement of the windows suggests. And the builders may have taken their cue from an earlier structure. Significantly, churches were often built over pagan structures to assimilate pagan rituals rather than oppose the practioners directly. In some places, however, the rebuilding may have served more than one purpose. Beneath the chapel at Lanleff may once have stood a Celtic sun temple. If the Templar knights and Cistercian monks of Bernard replicated this temple's purpose in the design of their own chapel, they must have understood in much greater detail what was conveyed to those who were not initiated.

The Lanleff chapel's second story is in ruins, and perhaps there were more windows than currently survive. This makes determining any astronomical significance more difficult. The column bases are carved, a feature not found in Newport, possibly because the builders were in a hurry to complete construction. Other carvings described as grotesque beg a comparison with the pillar and other features of the Rosslyn Chapel in Scotland. Once an important Etruscan city called Felsina, Bologna was an independent city-state during the times of the Crusades. Its importance rose and fell with the successes and failures of its ruling families. Through the history of being ruled by one family after another, Bologna built some of Italy's most impressive religious structures.

Saint Petronius founded the monastery of Saint Stefano and a complex of churches in an area where monks from Egypt had settled in early Christian times. A tablet found there indicates it was already sacred ground; possibly the site of a temple built to Isis existed before Christian times. The site later passed into the hands of the Benedictine order, whose massive building of churches and chapels, often re-creating Jerusalem's most holy sites, threatened to outdo Rome itself. The city was then ordered to divert money to its university. Before the wave of construction stopped, a full-size octagonal replica of the Holy Sepulchre was built containing the tomb of the city's patron saint. Interestingly enough, this area in the church had once been the baptistery.

The Templars did not hold a monopoly on the erection of sacred and mystical towers. France offers some most unusual monuments that were built without Templar or Cistercian influence. One type is known as the *lanternes des morts*. These structures are taller than the round or octagonal baptisteries and serve mortality rather than eternity. At the cemetery of the House of God near Montmorillon is an octagonal funeral chapel built to resemble the Holy Sepulchre. It is fifty feet high and forty-five feet in diameter. Openings in a wall suggest an astronomical significance. This particular lanterne was erected by a returning crusader in 1113.

England's Round Churches

England has four major and ten minor places with the distinctive round or octagonal constructions. The minor structures are usually parish churches, although some have a Templar connection. The Temple Church in London and the Holy Sepulchre in Cambridge are the most famous, and others structures exist at Dover and Northampton. While the dimensions of the structures vary, the scale and proportion, reflecting the circle and the octagon and symbolizing eternity, are shared.

Construction on the Temple Church in London was completed in 1185, and in February, Heraclius, the patriarch of Jerusalem, was present for the consecration to the Blessed Virgin Mary. The Knights Templar had moved their headquarters from Holborn, now called Old Temple, to this area during construction. Heraclius was on a mission along with the grand masters of the two military orders, the Knights Templar and Knights of Saint John (later Malta), to appoint a new king of Jerusalem. Baldwin IV was dying, and Jerusalem was split into warring factions at a time when unity was needed. Heraclius offered the title to the English king, who failed to rise to the responsibility.

The Holy Sepulchre in Cambridge was built in 1125 and is the oldest and smallest of the four round churches in England. The original structure, a round stone building on eight columns, resembles the Newport Tower very closely. The floor plan is exactly the same as La Rotunda in Brescia, San Tomaso in Bergamo, and Saint Olaf's Church in Tunsberg. The external diameter in Cambridge was 318 inches, compared to Newport Tower's 296 inches. The original circular structure, on land known as Saint George's Cemetery, was constructed by the Fraternity of the Holy Sepulchre, which that was made up of Knights Templar. The building and rebuilding would continue to the nineteenth century. The original eight columns are still present.

Ireland

In Ireland, near Drogheda and an hour's drive north of Dublin, is Mellifont, a ruined monastery of the Cistercian order. Once outside of Dublin, the drive is pleasant, and one is surprised that such a monument as Mellifont is found by driving on one-lane roads so narrow that one must yield to oncoming traffic by pulling onto the shoulder.

Mellifont's octagonal lavabo, built much like the Newport Tower, has a first floor where it is believed the monks washed before a meal. The second floor has, like Newport, lost its roof. The windows appear to have once been directly over the archway entrances of the first floor. The top of the building is gone, so they are no longer enclosed in stone. There are a couple of other openings, seemingly placed at random.

Mellifont was founded in 1142 by Saint Malachy, who on a trip to Rome had visited Bernard of Clairvoux and was so impressed that he left some followers to study with the saint. On his return, Malachy brought the Cistercian rule to Ireland. He also brought along a Cistercian architect to construct Mellifont, the first such Cistercian construction in the British Isles. Within ten years, six more Cistercian monasteries had sprung up, and in sixty years there were twenty-five abbeys.

The proximity of the Mellifont baptistery to the ruins of megalithic temples must pose intriguing questions to those who follow the historical trail of sacred architecture. Just three centuries before, the area had been the scene of an early Viking invasion and had become a trading center, taking advantage of its location at the mouth of the Boyne River. Mellifont lies just north of the river and directly north of the prehistoric structure of Dowth. To the west of Dowth are New Grange and Knowth, so clearly the area has for a very long time been considered sacred ground. In all, the Boyne Valley is home to more than sixty known passage tombs. Others may well be underground, and some have been bulldozed to make way for farming and herding.

Numerous legends have been invented to explain the construction and purpose of these five-thousand-year-old monuments. They are at once fairy hills and giant graves, constructed by giants or by levitating magicians. They contain bodies, or at least bones, of the dead and, worse, spirits—although none of these tales has ever been enough to keep away grave robbers. But treasures of that sort were not to be found in these tombs. Few contained more than charred bones, indicating the possibility of a ritual or cremation, but in no way giving away the bright secrets known by the builders.

Malachy was very much like Bernard and understood the value of recruiting nobles to his order's defense. His allies included King Donnchad of Airgialla and King Diarait Mac Murchada of Leinster. Lacking money and power, what spell did saints like Malachy and Bernard employ? One possibility was admission to a brotherhood in which only the members could be privy to a sacred knowledge. From the kivas of the American Southwest, to the Arval Brotherhood of Rome, to the round tables of the Knights Templar, such a bond ought not to be underestimated.

Belgium

The Abbey Saint Bavo at Ghent was built in the twelfth century by the Benedictine order. The dimensions of the abbey tower are so similar to those of the Newport structure that it can be called a prototype. The tower is a two-story octagonal building standing on eight columns with arches separating the columns. The lower story was a lavatory, where the monks washed their hands. The upper story was a chapel and a sanctuary. There was no stairway admitting entrance to the first story, implying that a ladder was required and also that once it was occupied, admittance to newcomers was at the occupants' discretion. This curiosity led to the belief in later ages that such structures were simply fortified, albeit small, churches.

The abbey was dedicated to a sixth-century member of the landed gentry who led a riotous existence until the death of his wife. After hearing a sermon, he changed his wicked ways into a most sacred existence, living first as a monk and later as a hermit. His example led to the devotion of many, and after his death the monastery was named for him. The early construction of the tower may have taken place circa A.D. 600; the modern construction took place during the active building and rebuilding period of the twelfth century.

Denmark's Secret Island of the Templars

The greatest concentration of round churches is found on the Baltic island of Bornholm. On the confines of this small island were once fifteen churches; eleven survive today. They are similar in design to the Templar-built Chateau Perelin at Athlit in Palestine.

Oddly enough, the Templars were quite a presence in Denmark during the period of the Crusades. To help hold Wendish pirates at bay in the Baltic, the Templars formed an alliance with the Danish king and the archbishop Eskil.[29] Eskil was the negotiator between the Danes and the pagan Wends from the Baltic states, and his close relationship with Saint Bernard enabled him to carry out the plan.[30] Located between the warring territories, Bornholm played a strategic role in this venture. The archbishop Eskil would spread the Cistercian order east. From 1171 until the final conquest in Estonia in 1219, a crusade was waged against the pagans of the Baltic ports. After peace settled, the Templars and the Cistercians rapidly began building churches. The four round churches on Bornholm are at Olsker, Osterlars, Nyker, and Nylars.

Osterlarskirke is the most impressive, with massive columns and tiny slit windows aligned to the midsummer and midwinter sunrise. In English, the name of the church is the East (Ost) Saint Lawrence *(lars)* Church *(kirke)*. According to tradition, Saint Lawrence lived in the early third century. It was a time when the church was being viciously persecuted. Although the Christians had little wealth, there were always stories that they possessed a treasure. That treasure was the Holy Grail. The chalice that Jesus had used to dedicate the first Christian Mass was the one possession that the pope, Sixtus II, could not allow to fall into Roman hands. The pope in the century before Constantine held a very difficult position. Christianity was not yet the legal religion in Rome and it was often the subject of persecution. The pope as the head of this occasionally outlaw church would be the target. Sixtus II found himself in this situation. Summoned by the emperor, Sixtus II went to his death. Lawrence took the Grail and, days later, fell under suspicion. Given two days to return to the emperor with the riches of the Church, he turned over the Grail to others who would bring it to Spain. Lawrence himself appeared before the emperor with a handful of sick and poor church members at his side. When asked the whereabouts of the treasure, Saint Lawrence pointed to his companions and declared they were the treasures of the Church.

Chained to a grill and roasted over a flame for his levity, he is said to have remarked at one point that he was done on one side and could be turned over. After his death, he was venerated as one of Rome's most sacred martyrs. His symbol is the gridiron. Like the archangel Michael, his courage and joyfulness in times of greatest danger made him a role model for the military. His role in the Grail legend may have endeared him further to the Templars, who expressed their admiration amply on Bornholm.

The island itself, as remote as it is, had like the Orkneys served as a location for pre-Bronze Age stone calendars. Once, thousands of standing stones (today hundreds) provided answers for an initiates-only group of religious leaders.

Sweden

In nearby Sweden, the seal of the city of Konghelle, which once belonged to Norway,[31] depicts a Newport-like tower that is no longer standing. King Sigurd the Crusader returned from the Holy Land with a piece of the True Cross and built Konghelle. The city was attacked and burned by Wends from the eastern shore of the Baltic, today the site of Lithuania and Estonia. Once it was rebuilt, King Erik Magnusson renewed the privileges of the city and approved its seal, which showed the eight-column sanctuary where the True Cross was housed. This is one of the only examples in which a Church relic was stored in a round church. These chapels were in themselves sacred.

In Sweden and Denmark there may have been as many as thirty round structures that share one very important detail: They are usually built on eight columns. The largest is the Church of Saint Olaf in Tunsberg, of which only the foundation and columns remain.

Portugal

The greatest and best-preserved of the round Templar churches is in Tomar, in Portugal, which has survived into the present. The Church of Saint John the Baptist started with an octagonal chapel covered by a rotunda and was modeled on the Church of the Holy Sepulchre in Jerusalem. The structure has sixteen sides and a central octagon called a *charola,* which contains a very small altar. Eight pillars support a two-story structure topped by a dome.

Portugal has possibly Europe's greatest expertise on matters of the seas. The Algarve area served as a crossroads for any merchant venturer who wanted to trade between the Mediterranean and the tin-rich islands of the north. The Phoenicians guarded the Straits of Gibraltar and may have had a long-term monopoly over such trade. Intriguingly, the Phoenicians may not always have been the eastern Mediterranean culture they are thought to be today. Long before they settled and inter-married into the eastern port cities, they may have been Iberian. The single eye once painted on Egyptian and Phoenician ships still graces even small fishing boats in Portugal, betraying an ancient relationship.

The Templars understood Portugal's strategic importance to the coastal European trade. Templar ships reached Lisbon and traveled upriver to Tomar, which became one of their sacred sites.

Scotland

Perhaps one of the least impressive round churches is in the Sinclair domain on the main Orkney island. Built in the late eleventh or early twelfth century, very little is known about it. It is said to have been constructed by Earl Hakon and inspired by the design of the Holy Sepulchre. Originally, it consisted of a circular nave and an apse, but it is in a state of serious disrepair today. The facade is the result of craftsmen using whatever building material was available, typical of much of Scotland's construction in the north. Unfortunately, some of the damage was done by workers in the eighteenth century. As they were building a newer church in the area, they pulled down part of Orphir for its stones. The ruin lies very close to the main city of the islands, Kirkwall.

After the arrest and dissolution of the Templar order in the early fourteenth century, the round churches stopped being built. The Templars had resurrected a secret and sacred knowledge that apparently had placed a great emphasis on John the Baptist in his role as the Precursor. In this respect, John was the sun (as in sun god) who died in order to make way for the new sun (or Son) who was born after the solstice, on December 25. On the other hand, Mary Magdalene was also held in the greatest esteem by Bernard. He had purposely chosen Vezelay, her cult center, to preach the Second Crusade. Was the secret knowledge of the Templars a relationship between Jesus and Mary Magdalene, as Baigent, Leigh, and Lincoln's *Holy Blood, Holy Grail* opened to discussion? Or was the order's secret wisdom more celestial in nature?

Bernard's fascination with the Black Virgin may betray another secret of Christianity. The phenomenon of the black virgin exists all over Europe. Some believe the black virgin represents Isis even though she is depicted in Christian churches. The Roman Catholic Church offers various explanations, including the effect of centuries of exposure to burning candles. The secret of the Church was that it could not divorce itself from the feminine principle in the universe. The sun needed the moon. The god had always had a goddess. As the sun (God) was day, the moon (Goddess) was night. In pre-dynastic Egypt, her name was Neith and of course she was dark. Her later incarnation, Isis, was depicted as the Black Virgin with child. As Isis was the deity of the night, the sun was the deity of the day. Secular depictions of the sun in medieval times had a bearded man with twelve rays emanating from his face. The moon was a female crowned with a crescent.

Bernard's architects were adept in a sacred geometry that originated in the far north and was carried to Egypt, Sumeria, and Babylonia thousands of years earlier. As they resurrected this knowledge (not necessarily for all to understand, but for all to visually appreciate), other bits of ancient wisdom probably emerged as well. Naturally, the Church went into high gear to suppress any deeper understanding, often hiding such science. The Feast of the Magdalene was July 22. Expressed as the number 22 over the number 7 it reveals the fraction 22/7. This fraction is the mathematical concept known as pi, a most important tool in architecture for determining the measurement of the circle.

The original church of Jesus was now the Church of Rome. Gnosis, or direct knowledge, which seems to have been a theme even in the canonical Gospels, was now heresy. Science was part of the quest for knowledge. It too would be regarded as heresy. Heresy would be punished—as 100,000 Cathars, thousands of Templar knights, and untold numbers of "witches" would be made painfully aware of.

In the fourteenth century, the Templars, fleeing persecution, religious turmoil, and a war-torn Old World, carried their science abroad.

Rhode Island

The round stone church guarding the inner harbor at Newport has been controversial to historians for hundreds of years. If this building stood anywhere in Europe, it would be categorized as medieval with little argument. It would be easily compared to any number of similar round chapels and baptisteries built by the Templar order or the related Cistercians. Standing in Newport, however, it presents a great problem. It is not supposed to be there.

Worse still, for those who want to claim it as a windmill or grain mill, it appears on the map of Verrazano's 1524 visit to the Americas, well before the area was supposed to have been settled by Europeans.

As has been discussed, there is evidence that Europeans had visited. Vikings from Norway, Greenland, Iceland, and the Orkney Islands regularly made Atlantic voyages. The Church in Rome was aware of a Vinland well before Columbus. Fishermen of Bristol, of the Breton peninsula of France, and from the Basque coast of southern France and northern Spain made journeys for cod that can never be dated. The Vikings left earthen houses, and the fishermen left wooden huts where they dried their fish. No group is noted for leaving behind stone buildings such as the tower.

The Templars, however, are known for construction, and often a Newport-like baptistery was the centerpiece either within a church or cathedral, as in Tomar, Portugal, or a separate outdoor structure, as in Mellifont in Ireland. Invariably, they took time to build, most likely more than a year, and we can assume that any place where such a sacred baptistery was erected was meant to be inhabited for a long time.

There is only one other round or octagonal tower in North America that resembles the Newport Tower. It is in the city of Montreal, itself named for a Templar fortress, built by an order of priests who more than once found themselves distrusted by their own church.

Montreal

Montreal is the last stop on the trail of round and octagonal holy places, a trail that leads from the Damascus mosque, where the head of Saint John the Baptist lies, through a mysterious Europe where shrines to sun gods and ancient goddesses were the foundations for Christian sanctuaries, to the Templar and Cistercian chapels that served as fortresses and refuge. The tour ends in terms of both space and time in Montreal—in time because the round tower of Saint-Sulpice there was built much later than all the others, in space because it was the last place that a very secret society would hope to place the new Arcadia.

3
The Knights Templar
Death and Rebirth

SOMEHOW, THE TEMPLARS BECAME the new masters of an ancient body of knowledge. The source of this knowledge is unclear and many theories have been offered. Documents found in the Temple of Solomon by the original nine Templars are one possibility. The exposure of West to East, which brought new products such as sugar and candy to Europe, is another. The texts of the Romans and Greeks had been preserved by Islamic scholars and made their way back to centers of Islamic learning in Sicily and Spain. Ironically, although the purpose of the Crusades was to turn back the Islamic tide, a countereffect was that the West came to understand the East better. A concerted effort to learn from those who pursued their science without fear of condemnation as witches, magicians, and alchemists began again.

Regardless of where they found them, the army of warrior-monks had gained the keys to achieving a greater understanding of their world and the cosmos. Their recovered science unlocked that which had been hidden for centuries, at least in the Dark Ages of the West. Cathedrals were soon being built with perfect acoustics, with windows that admitted light on days sacred to important saints and which lined up in the landscape to mirror constellations in the sky. Not all of the Templars' efforts were for lofty purposes, of course; they also constructed bridges some of which survive today.

At the same time, the Knights of the Temple grew from a grand master and eight men into the largest and wealthiest organization in the world. As a fighting force, the Templar military was almost without rival. Answering to no earthly king, it operated with nearly total impunity on the seas and over land. Its various businesses, including estate management, trade, shipping, and banking, grew unchecked because few could challenge the order. At one point, the pope attempted to quell the complaints of kings who had indebted themselves to the order, but even he was ineffective. In the end, it may not have been one event but instead a series that caused the order to collapse.

CRUMBLING FOUNDATIONS

The first threat to the Templars' stability was an end to the organization's greatest reason to be. At the end of the twelfth century, the crusaders finally met with an enemy as strong as their own armies. The difference may have been that the power of the Islamic armies was not divided among managing estates, conducting trade, and delving into arcane science. The armies of Islam had one singular purpose: to defeat the Christian armies. And they were led by a man born Salah ad-Din Yusef ibn Ayyub—the West knew him as Saladin.

The Loss of Jerusalem

Saladin is one of Islam's greatest heroes. He could be gallant and respectful, yet he was feared more than any other Arab leader. Ironically, his burial place is the Umayyad Mosque, a distance measured in feet from the inspirational saint of the Templars, Saint John the Baptist.

The first great victory of Saladin was taking Aleppo in June 1183, which gave him an empire stretching from the Tigris to the Nile. He then began taking one town after another until the massive battle of Hittim.

On July 4, 1187, one of the Crusades' largest battles saw the Templars and the Hospitallers riding headlong into the army of Saladin, which now numbered eighty thousand. Saladin had his men set fire to the grass, and the smoke blew directly into the Christian army. When it cleared, they were surrounded. The ensuing battle left thousands of Christians dead. Saladin marched thousands of captives up a hill to view the sacred lake Gennesaret. He offered these knights their freedom if they renounced Christ. To a man, they refused. All were beheaded. It is said that for three nights afterward celestial lights played on the bodies of the courageous crusaders.[1]

Soon, one Templar castle and then another fell to Saladin until he recaptured Jerusalem. On October 2, 1187, the anniversary of a visit to heaven by the prophet Muhammad, Saladin entered the city. The Templars' Jerusalem temple was surrendered to him, the order ousted from its headquarters.

Europe mounted a counterattack and the war continued. In the ensuing seven battles that comprise the Third Crusade, it is calculated that 100,000 Christians lost their lives, yet new recruits filled their shoes. The ships of Italy's seaports constantly resupplied troops and necessaries to the crusaders. The leadership role was given to Richard the Lion-Hearted, heir to the dukedom of Normandy and the throne of England. He was the great-grandson of Fulk of Anjou, one of the earliest crusaders, and he took up the cross in Tours, on the same spot where Fulk had set out to rule Jerusalem. He was joined by another heroic figure, Frederick I of Germany, who set out with the largest crusader force to have emerged from Germany. The Third Crusade ended in a five-year peace treaty that kept Jerusalem in Muslim hands but allowed Christians to visit the Holy City.

After years of war, the crusading armies experienced a lull that allowed all the orders to devote more time to business, or at least to infighting. The Knights Templar engaged in the slave trade in Acre. Frederick II, commanding the Teutonic Knights, declared war on the Templars and seized their properties and ships. The Teutonic Knights were a Prussian fighting force that, unlike the Templars, were autonomous. They were their own state, in effect fighting for their own leaders. They would fight in Eastern Europe against pagans and in the Holy Land for the crusader cause. The Italian merchants, too, were at war with the Templars, whose fleets grew stronger and stronger, often at the expense of the merchants.

The so-called Fourth Crusade in 1204 never reached Jerusalem or the Islamic armies. Instead, the Christian forces attacked and pillaged the city of Constantinople, seat of the Eastern Church and the Byzantine Empire, driving a wedge between the two churches that crushed not only any hope of offering a joint challenge to the Muslim empires, but also Pope Urban's original hope of uniting the Church through the Crusades.

Before the Fifth Crusade could begin, the Children's Crusade, led by a French shepherd boy, planned to save Jerusalem. Instead, the young crusaders were sold into slavery. From a cynical point of view, the crusades against Islam had as much to do with the Church's desire to control the military nobles in Europe as it did with regaining the Holy Land for Christians. The pilgrims to Jerusalem were harassed more by common thieves than they were by Muslims, who had been accommodating to the point of allowing churches to be established. It is clear that the Muslims were not the enemy of the Church, because they never actually challenged its power.

In contrast, in the south of France was a group that truly challenged the monopoly that the Church claimed on reverence to God. Compared to the threat posed by Islam, this challenge was infinitely more serious to an organization that thrived on a huge hierarchy and an ability to tax everyone in its realm.

The Crusade against the Cathars

Possibly the worst disaster in two hundred years of killing under the guise of religion was a war directed against France's Christians. The war was also a second strike against the predominance of the Knights Templar as a chivalric order. After the death of Richard the Lion-Hearted in 1199, Pope Innocent III became Europe's strongman. He began a half-century-long purge in the Languedoc area of France of the Christian Cathars, from the Greek *katheri,* meaning "pure." Theirs was a movement that sprang up in northern Italy and moved into southern France.[2]

In Italy, the center of Cathar belief was Milan, from which it reached south into Rome and Calabria. To the north, it spread to Flanders and Germany. To the east were the Bogomils of the Balkans, a heretical sect that had been formed in the mid-tenth century and which shared (and probably influenced) the Cathars' belief in dualism.

Uncomfortably vulnerable to all powers, Bogomils were executed by Byzantine Church authorities, forcibly converted by Western Church authorities, and finally stamped out by the Ottomans.

In Italy, the Cathars were dealt with on a local basis, not by crusade. In some cases death was the ultimate price of not recanting the anti-Church Christianity, but never on the scale of the war that took place in France. In 1208 the pope issued a bull of anathema to the Christian sect, which did not, however, recognize his authority. Then on Saint John's Day in 1209, he sent the army into the Languedoc. He was responsible for wiping out tens of thousands of devout Cathars in a war that saw Templar knights on both sides.

Many history books have somehow managed to cling to the portrayal of the Cathars as heretics. They take their place among the Arians (who questioned Jesus's divinity), and witches (who practiced an older nature-based religion), both of whom were persecuted by the Church. Ironically, had the Cathars come into existence two hundred years later, they would have been called reformers. The Reformation, however, did not yet exist, and protesting against the fixed order was simply heresy.

One of the few documents written by a proponent, rather than an enemy, of the Cathars was composed in 1230 by an Italian, John of Lugio. His *Two Principles* outlines the dualistic faith of good and evil that may have been the link between early religions' concepts of the sun and moon and later Templar-Freemason conventions.

The Cathar movement had no formal doctrine and occasionally inconsistent teachings. In general, however, the separate communities of Cathars shared the philosophical concept of dualism, which had been around for thousands of years. The Persian Mazda religion of the Magi saw the forces of good constantly at war with the forces of evil and held that the good thought good thoughts and did good deeds. As a result, they brought the victory of Mazda closer. (At the highest level, Mazda was wisdom.) The Cathars had commandments, a judgment day, and an afterlife reward for the good. Their theology, in fact, was very close to early Christianity, before it came under the influence of Constantine.

In Florence, Cathar beliefs swept the city. There was no institutionalized religion, however, and the Florentine brand of Cathar

thought was simply called the religion of the Good Men. Cathar doctrine was in finding God on one's own, yet they had services and
sacraments. Although they considered matter and life on earth to be
evil, they lived as families. Reputedly against having sex and produc-
ing children, they did not take such a stance seriously until much later
in life, often when close to death. The irony of such a seemingly
blighted outlook philosophically and a joyful simple life in reality is
complicated by the fact that much of what they did believe was fil-
tered through the writings of those who had considered them
heretics.

The Bonhommes, as they were also called in France, postulated a
similar principle of good, which was the light and the spirit, doing battle with the principle of evil, which was darkness and matter.[3] How per-
vasive Cathar-like beliefs were in the north of Italy is difficult to
calculate, as the insular cities and towns did not arouse the ire of others as the Cathars had in France.

The Cathars in France had grown under the protection of several
nobles who were Cathars themselves or sympathizers. Because they
viewed the Catholic Church as the opposite of early Christian principles, they refused both the clergy and the taxes of the Church. It was
a serious threat to an institution that depended on its authority as well
as revenues.

The dove was adopted as a symbol of the direct enlightenment. The
dove as representing such Gnostic thought found its way into art, even
art in church windows. It signified the spirit of God, the Holy Ghost.
The Spirit would show itself in the Word, and according to John 1:1–2:
"And the word was with God and the Word was God."[4] The dove was
also the symbol of Saint John himself, bringing knowledge.

The Church at this point might have tolerated an abstract discussion on the nature of the universe; but once the Cathars' theology led
them to criticize the Church's mode of operation, they could no
longer be tolerated. The war against the Cathar heresy was motivated
by power and not piety. The pope had the power. In his mind, evil was
embodied by anyone whose aim was to dilute the Church's power.
The Cathars preached not only against the need for intermediaries
between believers and God, but also against the Church's power as
expressed in its wealth. The sect believed that access to God was indi-

vidual and direct, with no need for a bureaucracy of impious clerics and power-hungry bishops. In reality, the Church never questioned the piety of the heretics.

Saint Bernard himself had been asked by his pope to look into the Cathar concept of the world. He found them to be devout and living the Christian ideal. Like Bernard, they were truly pious, abstained from excess, and had rejected the corrupt ways of the Church's institutions. Bernard, however, had the power and connections to make change without incurring the wrath of the Church. For a while, the Cathars counted Bernard as an ally, but after his death they became the victim of Rome's backlash.

By the beginning of the thirteenth century, a growing Cathar movement threatened to topple the Church's power to tax. As we have seen, this right was of paramount importance to the organization, as is evidenced in Greenland; the Church was willing to excommunicate an entire colony or country strictly on its inability to pay into the coffers of Rome. The right to govern was apparently more desirable than the right to be a moral authority. The Church harshly defended its right to rule on any issue related to man and God. With no standing army of its own, its power was maintained with revenues, the armies of willing kings, and the right to excommunicate or make outlaws of its enemies. The Cathars for their part presented a threat to the Church that was much greater than that posed by the Saracens.

The first step taken by the Church was meant to be peaceable. Saint Dominic was sent in with others to debate with the Cathar leaders. At Montreal, they engaged Guilhabert de Castres, considered to be the greatest Cathar preacher of the period. The Roman Catholic legates preached for days to little avail. Then a Cathar, Arnald Hot, declared publicly, "The Church of Rome . . . was neither holy nor the Bride of Christ." Instead, he declared it to be espoused of the devil, and the Babylon of Saint John's Gospel.[5] The Catholic bishop gave up and cursed his Cathar audience. Not long afterward, a military response took the place of preaching and debate.

In 1209 an army of thirty thousand, mostly from the north of France, swept through the Languedoc like a Mongol horde. They burned towns and cities, destroyed crops, and in several towns massacred thousands. As with the Christian attacks on Constantinople and Jerusalem, in many towns no one was spared.

The first city to fall was Beziers. Again, the date was carefully picked. It was the feast day of Mary Magdalene. The Cathars debated the importance of Jesus, but believed the earth-bound Jesus was married to Mary Magdalene. At the same time, the Occitan people of the south of France had a special reverence for both Mary Magdalene and Saint John the Baptist. This was true of the Templars as well. On Mary Magdalene's feast day, the city's inhabitants were given the choice of renouncing their faith or going to their death. Every man, woman, and child held together. And died together.

The papal legate had declared, "Kill them all, God will know his own." Launched from the fortress of Citeaux, which once housed the splinter Cistercian order, the army of Simon de Montfort marched south. One by one, the Cathar cities and villages were destroyed, the faithful burned to death. The genocidal crusaders wore the same tunic and cross that they did while fighting Islam. In return for their murderous acts, they were promised heavenly remission of all their sins and, better, earthly rewards of sharing in the spoils. The Church and the French king spent enormous energy in wiping out thousands of Christians and devastating Languedoc. The war raged for forty years. The area was left blighted for centuries.

Bertrand de Blanchefort, the fourth grand master of the Knights Templar, was from Languedoc, as were many other Templar knights. The Templars are recorded as having served on both sides of the final battle, at Montségur. After a lengthy siege, the Cathars and the knights who fought with them were offered their freedom. The catch was they had to acknowledge the Catholic faith as well as the authority of Rome. To a man, and woman, the Cathars refused. They were then sent to the pyres.

The Cathars, like early Christian martyrs, considered death for one's faith the gateway to the afterlife. Coincidentally, Montségur may be regarded as a solar temple.[6] It was constructed such that on the solstice the sun's first rays would penetrate an area called the keep. It was also a fortress "where [the defenders] could touch the sky"—a fitting place to leave the evil earth for the spiritual reward.[7]

There is no record of how the Templars who defended the

Languedoc region were treated. There is little reason to believe that the Church forgot such a rebellious act, which it surely considered a betrayal by its military order. It is equally likely that the Templars did not forget the acts of the Church, which some members of the order likewise may well have regarded as betrayal. It is possible that the Templars' goals—and doctrine—separated at this time from those of Rome's.

The Templars had witnessed firsthand that between the murderous pope and the murderous Saladin there was little difference. A brutal regime is a brutal regime, whatever its claim to legitimacy. Having been philosophically, and on occasion militarily, the defenders of the Cathars, the Templars had joined forces with those who saw beyond the truth as Rome proclaimed it. Moreover, having been in the Holy Land, they may have picked up Johnnite and dualistic beliefs on their own. And, of course, they had come to suspect that the universe possessed wonders unexplained by the Church-sanctioned Ptolemaic system.

Many books have recounted the stories of the pioneers of European science from Leonardo to Copernicus to Galileo, each of whom ran the risks of the Inquisition. The Templar exposure to unbridled science from astronomy to medicine opened up a door that could not then be closed. The Crusades in themselves exposed the dark mind of the Franks to the teaching and philosophy of Arabs and Jews. The Church was proved to have failed Europeans in its bias against learning, and it would prove itself an obdurant obstacle to learning in the future. The foundation of European belief was irreparably cracked.

The war against the Cathars created two new movements within and outside of the Church. Within the Church, the Inquisition was in place by 1234. It wasn't the first time the Church had used torture, punishment, and execution to further the Christian religion; the Inquistion just organized procedures and, by 1257, made them independent of Rome. The Inquisition could seize goods and property and condemn individuals without any semblance of due process. It did not require an army, as it relied on greed and jealousy to prompt people to turn in neighbors and even family members. In France, a single Cathar in a household meant the house could be seized by the Church. Being pious was no safeguard if one was wealthy, and the fifteenth-century Spanish

Inquisition resembled in its lack of moral substance the purges of accused witches later. Where there was money, there was someone who could be accused and a reward to be shared.

The other movement took place outside the Church and took two centuries to incubate. It would bring about new ways to look at the world in a humanistic sense and a new way to approach the divine. The Dark Ages of Europe gave way to the light of learning imported from the East. Not only were new ideas brought home from the East, but much of the lost learning of the West was returned home as well. The works of Cicero, Ovid, and Livy had been preserved in Constantinople. Scholarship and humanism reached the halls where once only rigid doctrine had been taught. The cruelty of the Inquisition and the excesses of the clergy came to be regarded as evil. The Church, very slow to react, would soon see its power disrupted. Yet before a challenge rose up in the form of the Reformation, the church's most powerful organization had already begun to rebel.

Increasing Enmity

At the same time the Templars were playing a significant role in bringing knowledge back from the East, they were losing their reputation as a focused fighting force. First, successive waves of Asian invasions threatened Europe. The fighting orders were not believed to be a match for this massive threat. Only the death of Genghis Khan would stop the invasions that had reached into Eastern Europe.

Second, a war between the Italian merchant cities emerged, with the Templars and the Teutonic Knights supporting Venice and the Hospitallers supporting Genoa. The pope had already spoken out against the orders some years before, condemning them for being more interested in trade and profits than in defeating Christendom's enemies. Although the trade war did not last, the enmity between the orders did. And the growing split between the papacy and the order that was supposed to answer to Rome grew.

The Church had not forsaken Jerusalem entirely, however, and it realized that it would have to destroy Egypt, the center of Arab power, to regain and hold the Holy City. Several disappointing attempts in the middle of the thirteenth century led to the loss of all their important cities with the exception of Acre. Thereafter, a treaty brought some years' peace until a band of European adventurers attacked and killed Egyptian merchants. The sultan of Egypt marched on the Christian army with 200,000 men. Twelve thousand Templar knights and Hospitallers held back the force for days, but the siege of Acre was soon accomplished by burning the last stronghold of the Templars with everyone inside. In 1291, the tenuous 170-year Christian hold on the Holy Land ended in the smoky ruins at Acre. Despite the bravery of both orders, Pope Nicolas IV blamed them for the loss of the city.

Up to this point, the wealth and power of the Templars had grown unchecked, even as the order also grew away from the goals of Rome. A final attempt by the final grand master to gain a foothold in the Holy Land failed in 1302. They abandoned their last fortress at Ruad, on the Syrian coast, and from there the order's future was in jeopardy. The Templar order at home was faced with new restrictions by the Church and the increasing enmity of the European sovereigns and nobles.

BACKLASH AGAINST THE TEMPLARS

Even before the fall of Acre, Edward I of England had acted, claiming that gifts given to the Templars belonged to the order only while it was defending Christendom. As these services were no longer required, in his estimation, the gifts were to be returned. Edward raided the Templars' temple in London to pay his own soldiers, who were fighting in Wales.

His son, Edward II, engaged in a similar robbery, violently confiscating Templar wealth. The exercise was both a monetary setback and, worse, an end to the respect once accorded the knights. The order itself was split and many Knights Templar involved themselves in government disputes and, occasionally, military action.

Symbolizing the changes that were afoot, the Knights Templar established a headquarters on Cyprus, which they had bought from Richard the Lion-Hearted. The Knights of Saint John moved to Rhodes and expelled the Genoese pirates. The Teutonic order moved to Venice and then to Marienburg.

Yet the Knights Templar had as its greatest enemy its own haughtiness. Assuming that accumulated power and wealth would insulate the group from its enemies, it ignored both public sentiment and the threat of kings and the Roman Catholic pope. Following the fall of Acre, the order failed to see the seriousness of its position. Believing that the series of defeats in the Holy Land were directly caused by the infighting between the Templars and the Hospitallers, Pope Nicholas IV wanted the two orders to combine. The Knights Templar brashly ignored his request.

As the fighting in the Holy Land neared an end, the various orders returned home. Teutonic Knights of Germany and Prussia moved back to their headquarters in Marienburg. The Knights of Saint John moved to Malta and later became known as the Sovereign Knights of Malta. The main force of the Knights Templar moved to the island of Cyprus. There it appears the order was under the illusion that business would continue as usual. The order's fleet continued to compete with nonmilitary traders on the sea. Their estates grew in wealth on the land and, unlike the estates of most nobles, escaped the taxes of the king. Their banking empire grew unchecked as well.

One of those in debt to the order was Philip IV, the king of France. His country had been the launching point of the Crusades, and massive amounts of wealth and valuable lives had been lost in the wars. He had also gone to war in Flanders, another costly disaster. Until 1295, the Templars managed Philip's own finances, but in that year he created the royal treasury in the Louvre to handle his finances thereafter. Philip wanted to join the order, and intended to become the Rex Ballator, the Warrior King. The order, however, rejected the king because they feared he would attempt to take over.

To shore up his finances, Philip expelled the Lombard bankers from France and seized as much of their wealth as he could. He next turned his attention to the Jews, making them scapegoats for the country's fiscal distress as he plotted to seize their wealth. When both maneuvers disappointed the king in terms of restoring his treasury, the wealth of the Templars became his primary target. There was, however, protocol to be respected. Philip's second plan of attack required obtaining the pope's aid because he was the only power the order was supposed to adhere to, even though there is evidence that it flouted even this convention. Nevertheless, the king decided he could direct even the pope.

The pope at the time was Boniface VIII, who was not inclined to ally himself with France. A war between families in Italy had caused

Boniface to declare his own crusade against the powerful Colonna family, and his army had defeated the Colonna troops and then ravaged all of their lands in Italy. The family fled to France, and to Philip IV. Subsequently, Philip declared he had a right to tax papal lands, and Boniface reacted by issuing the papal bull *Unam Sanctum,* declaring that the pope was ruler of the world.

Agents of the king were sent to Anagni to arrest the pope, who was already in an extremely weakened state and humiliated by the combined efforts of French and Italian henchmen. He was freed by his own supporters, who learned the pope was being taken to France for trial. The strain, however, led to his death within days. Another pope was soon elected.

The French king then used the same civil servant to go after the next pope, Benedict XI. This pope excommunicated Philip's agent, Guillaume de Nogaret, for his actions against Boniface VIII. Nogaret, in turn, trumped up charges of witchcraft against the pope and possibly caused his death by poison.

The next pope was Bertrand de Got of Bordeaux, who became Clement V. After taking the papal throne, he disappointed the Italians and established the papacy at Avignon. Clement was related to another Bertrand, the Templar grand master, through his mother. He was also as greedy as the French king, using his position to sell anything from annulments to passports. Because he needed protection, he worked to ease the tensions between the king of France and the Templar order, but in the end, he failed.

First, Philip tried to force Clement's hand by submitting a list of charges against the order that had been compiled by the same excommunicated agent, Nogaret. When even the heresy charge was not enough to get Clement to act, Philip began threatening him with his rabid inquisitor. Clement had ordered the grand master to Paris, believing his presence might aid in achieving some form of agreement. When it did not, Clement finally caved in to the king's demands.

End of the Order

On Friday, October 13, 1307, the forces of the king descended on the Templars. All over France, with notable exceptions, the army of the king arrested the knights, seized their preceptories, and attempted to confiscate their wealth. Yet the massive treasure of the Templars, supposed to be in Paris, was gone. Although there is no evidence as to just who tipped off the order, it obviously was notified. The Templars' friends and allies were often close to the king, and the pope himself not only tipped off his relatives in Blanchefort, but also must have made a deal with the king that Templar property there was to be left alone.

It is possible that Philip intended only to seize Templar wealth. The order, Europe's greatest fighting force, apparently submitted to arrest without resistance. The one act the order seems to have taken on its own behalf was to remove the treasure of the Paris temple, Philip's principal target. The plan to do this had to be under the orders of higher-ups, possibly even grand master Jacques de Molay. The wealth in the headquarters of what was the world's largest bank was loaded on a convoy of wagon trains and carried overland to the Templar port city of La Rochelle. There, according to testimony at a later Templar trial, it was taken aboard eighteen ships of the order's fleet and removed from France and the clutches of an avaricious king.

The logistics of such a move is testament to advance knowledge of Philip's plan. The greatest military organization in the world most likely had an equally powerful intelligence system. Certainly in the former Cathar regions of France, Templars fighting on the side of the heretics had been tipped off to forthcoming engagements. In Paris, their world headquarters, intelligence should have been even greater. Oddly, however, they left behind their grand master. Known as a reformer, Jacques de Molay had done what he could to preserve the order and restore it to its core ideals. Either through miscalculation or perhaps as evidence of a split within the Templar organization, the illiterate warrior who held the Templar's highest post was sacrificed.

It is possible that Philip's realization that he had been duped precipitated the extreme violence to which he subjected the Templars. It is more likely that the violence was part of the plan. Individual members, including the grand master, were charged with suspicion of heresy, one of the few crimes for which torture was a standard consequence. They were tortured and beaten, and many were killed. They were ritually humiliated as well, their hair and beards shorn, their garments taken away. And they were forced in private to renounce their order. Five hundred would confess within weeks to everything with which they had been charged, including homosexuality, devil worship, murder of babies, and abominable treatment of sacred Christian symbols.

Charges in some cases were similar to those leveled seventy years earlier against the Cathars when Pope Gregory IX accused them of worshipping Satan and claiming a giant toad appeared in their ceremonies.[8] The Templars were accused of worshipping cats, goats, and a severed head by the name of Baphomet.

Those who had submitted peacefully to arrest were broken by ministers of the corrupt king. Many died of torture or of the harsh treatment in the prisons of the inquisitors, and some were simply killed. Grand Master Jacques de Molay and the preceptor of Normandy were roasted to death over a slow fire. The order was officially dissolved on March 22, 1312. This was the same day that the war against the Cathars was launched at Beziers. It was the feast day of Mary Magdalene.

Despite the horrors the French king wrought, he was successful only in his own country. Perhaps fearing retaliation by Templars in other countries, he did nothing more than harangue the pope to pressure other kings for arrests. The next spring the pope ordered all world leaders to arrest and bring to trial Templars within their realm.

In Lorraine, not yet a part of France, a few nonhysterical trials were held, and a handful of men were sentenced to spend time in monasteries. In England, too, the Templars fared better. Although the pope's power to excommunicate noncompliant monarchs was enough to ensure that England's king arrest Templars in his kingdom, he was not eager to try them, and the ensuing punishments did not come close to the ferocity of those of the French. In Germany the Templars marched into court armed and were quickly exonerated. In Portugal the order came under the direction of the king but remained intact.

The order itself was broken into numerous pieces. Kings took advantage and lands were doled out to the crown, to the Church, and to rival orders. Philip of France was never successful in getting his money. He was also cursed by the dying Jacques de Molay, who said both Philip and the pope would be dead within a year. Both the king and the pope *would* be dead within a year, possibly by poison.

Refuge

Historians now commonly believe that the Templar fleet and hundreds of French knights narrowly escaped arrest and seizure. Speculation on just where they landed generally centers on Scotland and Portugal. Scotland was in turmoil. It had lost a king and with him the ability to avoid England's puppet mastery. Its new king was an upstart who seized control after stabbing his rival and leaving him to die in the Church of the Greyfriars. His rival had been the favorite of the English king. The combination of such a rebellious act and its sacrilegious setting, as well as his declaration that Scotland was meant to be independent, was enough to earn Robert the Bruce excommunication. His country shared the punishment, which essentially made it an outlaw nation. More than one historic source suggests that the Templar knights found kinship with the excommunicated king and refuge in the excommunicated Scotland.[9]

Scotland, despite the intentions and farsightedness of Robert, was not really a country. Various parts of the region and most definitely the islands were ruled by a Celtic-Norman clan system that had member families pledged to a clan leader or noble. With such a system in place over a landscape of mountains and remote islands, it was easy to keep a secret, hide an army, and protect a fleet.

The family of Sinclair was based in Roslin, ruled in Caithness (which extended from Inverness to the most northern coast), and had control of Scotland's numerous islands. The clan was linked by powerful family connections with the not-too-distant St. Clair branch in France. Both sides of the family had been involved with the Templars, and the Crusades in general, since the earliest days. Sinclairs and St. Clairs had fought in the Holy Land, in Scandinavia, in the Iberian wars of the Reconquest, and even in the wars of the Italian merchant cities.

Portugal, too, was a likely place for the Templars to seek immediate refuge. In the hands of a Catholic king who could be as avaricious as France's Philip, the country was one in which the Templars had already made serious inroads. Their castles and monasteries dotted the countryside, and their port cities protected the coast. A deal was struck whereby the members of the Templars could join new orders. The price was the king's right to appoint the grand master and rule on the ownership of Templar property. The advantage of this bargain was that the

Templars would survive as an order, renamed the Knights of Christ, into modern times.

A third possibility is that the fleeing Templars returned to Cyprus. Although Paris was the center of the Templar world and its banking empire, Cyprus was still a nominal headquarters of the Templar order. The ruler of Cyprus was Amalric, who had taken over the country with the help of the Templars. His loyalty to the Templars was greater than his love of the French king or the France-based pope. He simply ignored the orders of both.

The pope's delegate to Cyprus did not arrive from Avignon until May 1308, seven months after the arrests in France. During this time, Amalric allowed the Templars to go on with business as usual. The order armed itself against the pope and is said to have hidden another great treasure. (Underneath Cyprus is an immense network of caverns and caves. If the treasure was secreted somewhere in the catacombs, it was also removed, as through the centuries the area has been regarded highly by treasure hunters. This is one treasure, though, that has never been discovered.) Finally, on June 1 the Templars agreed to be arrested, and they spent nearly two years in the island fortresses under house arrest. In May 1310 they were brought to trial. Without the hysteria that accompanied the prosecution style of the inquisitors of France, the Templars were acquitted.

The pope was furious and threatened to send in the Dominican inquisitors, an army of experienced torturers. A second trial was held, but the outcome was inconclusive. Some Templars were still being held in 1313, but little is known of their fate or of the Templar treasure they once held. As in other places, most likely they were allowed to serve in other orders, quietly living out their lives in monasteries. Others may have escaped into the mercenary ranks of pirates and soldiers.

THE END OF THE CRUSADES

Despite the fatal wounds suffered at the battle of Acre, the Crusades as an enterprise refused to die quietly. As late as 1365, an expedition was mounted that culminated in an attack on Alexandria that displayed savagery on a level that could be compared only with the crusader capture of Jerusalem and Constantinople. Christians, Jews,

Muslims, and even European merchants were butchered. Mosques, tombs, and churches were indiscriminately sacked. Possibly the world's wealthiest city was looted and destroyed. As many as five thousand who survived the wholesale slaughter, Christians and Muslims alike, were sold into slavery. Lines of horses and mules made their way to ships where stolen goods, gold, and artifacts were loaded aboard. Then even the horses and mules were slaughtered. The city, it was said, "stank of death."[10]

The Crusades, which had tried to free Jerusalem from the Muslims, ended with the whole of Eastern Christendom under Muslim rule. Even after Spain and Portugal broke free of Islamic domination, the Turkish Ottoman Empire grew stronger in the East, and would remain in power until the twentieth century. Islam never went on a territory-grabbing warpath again; however, the Ottoman Turks would take Rhodes in 1523 and Venetian-controlled Cyprus in 1570. The Crusades had been a vast fiasco, a spectacular centuries-long failure. The expense of lives and money is incalculable. The cost of the backlash against the Roman Church is also immeasurable. While millions had borne the cost, the perception of the clergy as a fat, tax-hungry bureaucracy had grown. The stage was set for change.

Although the surviving Cathars and Templars had gone underground, they, and the gnosis they had brought to the world, were not forgotten. The evidence of this is both remembered and concealed in the first tarot decks. These contained four suits slightly different from those of modern decks. The swords (spades) and cups (hearts) served as reminders of the male and female energies, respectively. These two symbols were represented more plainly as two triangles (the sword, or blade, pointed up and the cup, or chalice, pointed down) forming the six-pointed star. Scepters (clubs) and pentacles (diamonds) signified power and wisdom. In heaven the symbol of power was the bright light of the sun and the symbol of wisdom was the sacred light of the moon. On earth, Jesus took the role of the reborn sun and Mary Magdalene personified the wisdom of the moon. With meanings beyond this immediate symbolism, the story was also a device used to recall the story of the Templars and the repression of the order.

The tarot's major arcana, the twenty-two trump cards that round out the deck, may have been a means of passing on the story of the treachery of the emperor (Philip IV) and the pope (Clement V), and their destruction of the tower, a symbol of both Mary Magdalene and the Templar's temple. The fool was the seeker of knowledge. Gnostic belief placed the burden of finding the way to truth on the Grail seeker: "Seek, and ye shall find." The joker was the initiate, the wild card that could overturn the game.[11]

With the stage set, the underground orders and secret societies would serve as the wild card in the history of Europe, overturning the powers that were and igniting the light of renaissance and reform.

4

From Scotland to the New World

The Templar Refuge in America

WHILE SOME TEMPLARS may well have found safety in Portugal and Cyprus, the Sinclair family of Scotland accepted their role as guardians of the Knights Templar. The hundreds, possibly thousands, of knights who fled France became part of the Sinclairs' own mercenary force. The vast Templar fleet sailed to the northern isles and joined the Sinclair fleet. And the treasure of the Paris temple itself, now guarded by the Sinclair clan, might certainly have become a target for either Philip of France or Edward of England. As crisis always also presents opportunity, the close of the Templars' reign in Europe influenced the discovery of the New World.

NAVIGATORS AND KNIGHTS

The importance of the Vikings and their emigration from Scandinavia is worthy of a second mention, as one of the important expeditions to the New World was led by a Norse descendant. It is not too generous to say that the sons of Rogenwald of Møre in Norway changed the course of history.

Clan Sinclair

As we saw earlier, while part of the Møre clan reached west to the Orkneys, Rogenwald's son Rollo invaded the Frankish coast circa 890. He captured the stronghold of Saint-Lô and made the castle his base. After marrying the daughter of the French king, he settled down in the territory that later took the name of the invaders, Normandy.

It was also territory that would influence the name of the invaders. The family of the Norse/Norman Rollo picked an area where one of France's noted martyrs, William, had met his death in 884. Possibly Scottish, but also said to be from Kent in England, he traveled to France, where he took up residence by a healing spring. In one version of the story he spurned the advances of a local Salome. It is also possible that William had not taken a vow of silence. Like Saint John the Baptist, he was assassinated after criticizing the behavior of a certain highborn woman. In any case, William's death seems to have been a reenactment of the grisly tale of Saint John the Baptist's demise: Two thugs on the orders of an unnamed woman murdered the hermit by cutting off his head. The name of a nearby holy well replaced the name of the saint and martyr. Both the person and the well became St. Clair. A statue of the saint holding his head stands there today.

The story leaves a little to be desired, as do many of the tales of the early saints. There is a greater possibility that the miraculous healing powers of the St. Clair well predated the arrival of the saint. Sin (moon) and Clair (light) could be interpreted as the sacred light. Sin was the Asian lunar deity who left his name in the Sinai desert, and Sin as Shinann was the Irish lunar deity who is remembered in the Shannon River. Many pagan traditions were either melded into Christian traditions or preserved in spite of them.*

---

*They were also preserved in the names of our days of the week. The Norse and Germanic Tiw's Day became Tuesday; Wotan gave us our Wednesday; and Thor's Day became Thursday. The Norse goddess Frigg left us Friday. Sunday and M(o)onday are also holdovers from more ancient religions, and even the Hebrew Sabbath was the day of Saturn, the lord of the underworld from Roman times.

When the family of Rollo settled on their lands near the Epte River, they helped establish a Norman innovation: They assumed a surname. Up to this point, they had been part of the large Møre clan, but henceforth they were the family of St. Clair—in English and Scottish, more often Sinclair. From this new center, the clan Sinclair prospered and grew. Soon after their chief, Rollo, signed a peace treaty with the French king, branches of the family were established in Senlis, near Paris; and in Rye, in Normandy. They were a power unto themselves and not necessarily pledged to anyone higher, be they Norse or French.

In the eleventh century, another Norse descendant, William the Conqueror, planned an invasion of the British Isles. Reputedly, the St. Clair family did not rush to join his expedition. Nonetheless, the family soon to become Sinclair featured prominently in the invasion that led to the Norman victory at the Battle of Hastings in 1066.[1]

William, the duke of Normandy, was of course successful in his invasion, and to reward those who fought for him, he gave out huge parcels of land.* Nine separate branches of the St. Clair family now held lands throughout the isles. Descendants of Rollo's brother Eynor were already in the north and controlled the Orkneys. The farthest north was the family of William Sinclair, who was six generations down the line in the family tree from Rollo. He had a falling out with William the Conqueror and later met and defeated him in battle. Subsequently, he allied himself closely with King Malcolm III of Scotland, who was allied with Earl Thorfinn of Orkney. William Sinclair went on to marry Thorfinn's daughter. In an age when most families spent their lives on the property of their family or their earl, the extended Møre/Sinclair family already had international connections that were regularly supported by the custom of intermarriage and the capacity to travel to renew their alliances.

This William also founded the Roslin branch of the family, which became the epicenter of power for the family whose influence would extend far and wide. Members of the clan Sinclair were among the prominent crusaders to Jerusalem. They also intermarried with Norwegian and French nobility, and in Scotland with the Bruce clan, which had left the continent under its Norman name, de Brus.

---

*The names of those who joined him are recorded on the Roll of the Battle Abbey, a document deposited in a church in Battle, England, just north of Hastings.

Guardians of the Templars

The fourteenth century at once threatened the family's power and ensured it for hundreds of years to come. The first event of import was Philip IV's October 1307 attack on the Templars. While many individual knights were caught by surprise and forced to endure torture, many others—obviously privy to a prior warning—fled Paris with the contents of the Templar treasury on wagon trains. From the port of La Rochelle, eighteen Templar ships escaped the king's armies and sought refuge elsewhere.

The most likely choice for refuge from the pope was Scotland, which offered several advantages to the Knights Templar. The first was that Scotland was continually out of favor with the Church in Rome. Robert the Bruce had just emerged as the king of Scotland after murdering his rival in the Chapel of the Greyfriars and dumping his body on the altar. The affront to the Church was as great as the affront to England, which was backing the rival John Comyn. As Robert declared himself king, the pope declared him excommunicated and extended the ban to the entire new nation as well. Technically, the Scottish king and the country were outlaws.

The second advantage was that, through intermarriage and political alliance, the relationship between French and Scottish Sinclairs was very strong. (Their relationship with their Norse counterparts was maintained as well, and in the fourteenth century, a clan leader named Henry Sinclair sought marriage to a woman of the Norwegian royalty to cement those bonds.) Roslin was the power base of the Sinclair family outside of France, and was safe from the French king.

The Templar force of thousands made it to Scotland in late 1307. In the early months of the next year, Templars in Ireland were ordered arrested. A handful were, but there was no torture and they were allowed to remain free on bail. In many cases, lands were seized, but no weapons. England's Edward II then ordered Templars in Scotland to be placed under arrest. Remarkably, only two were, and again they were not subjected to the treatment of their French brothers. One of them was the Templar master of Scotland, Walter de Clifton, one of two witnesses who told of the Templars' escape.[2]

Edward realized he now had a problem: There were Templars in England, Scotland, and Ireland, and he was advised that arms were being shipped from Ireland to Scotland. In England, the Templars were often sent to monasteries, most likely to keep them from returning to the military and at the same time preventing a Templar rebellion.

The size of the surviving order may have posed a threat even to Edward's army.

For some time after the arrival of the Templars in Scotland, two waiting games were being played at the same time: the ultimate fate of the French Templars and the fate of Scotland's independence. Then, in 1312, Clement V officially dissolved the Order of the Knights Templar and in 1314 the grand master of the order was burned to death. In the same year, the English and the Scots met in a historic battle.

The Battle of Bannockburn is legendary. When the English arrived on the field of war, their column was two miles long. The forces put together by Robert the Bruce were composed mostly of Celtic troops, including Gall-Gaels from Galloway, Scoto-Picts from Fife, and spearmen and mountain men from the Highlands. As usual, they were outnumbered. Also as usual, they were not armed or trained in the military tradition.

The Scots, however, had some tricks up their sleeve. The first day was a series of skirmishes in which they held their own. One of their more successful strategies was to lead the English cavalry into a field that had been booby-trapped with potholes before the battle. The second day started with the English taking the advantage, but suddenly a fresh force of armed knights, English and French ex-Templars, rode out to rout the English. The tide turned dramatically—fittingly, too, as this was the feast day of Saint John the Baptist, the patron saint of the Knights Templar. Just two years after being officially abolished, the Templars were alive and victorious, and fighting under a new flag.

In general, however, the ex-Templar knights across Europe made up a huge fighting force that no longer had battles to fight or estates to manage. They did have other skills. In Scotland the Sinclair family took the Templars under its wing and helped them find uses for their skills. The ex-Templars helped Henry Sinclair make his navy one of the strongest in the world. Knights who were adept at the building trades were put to work. To shelter their existence and to give them an advantage in their trades, they were organized in trade guilds along the lines of guilds in Europe.

The guild system was a mutual protection society and had been in existence long before the Templars and Freemasons. The building arts had been organized into collegia, or guilds, during Rome's heyday. They suffered during the barbarian invasions but managed to survive and regroup. Master Masons had full power to make contracts for building works that ensured that partners and workmen alike were provided for. While the guilds were free and independent, they did not seek authority from either Roman kings or popes. In Italy's Lake Como, for example, a group of artisans and architects called the Magistri Comacini banded together to fortify an island. From there they taught initiates the sacred precepts of geometry. In some cases, these initiates were monks of various religious orders.

Another group that may have served as a model for both the chivalric orders and Freemasonry was the Italian Order of Altopascio, often referred to as the Order of Bridge Builders. Founded before 1060, it comprised men from Florence and Venice who served to make safe the way to pilgrimage sites much like both the Templars and the Knights of Saint John of Malta, the Hospitallers. Naturally, the order's expertise and charitable work went beyond simply bridges. The monks took up the tau cross, often associated with Egypt.

Imitating the guilds, the Templars had established lodges (called temples) where they might enjoy a home for a time. As the Templars became tradesmen, they continued to pledge themselves to each other whenever one needed work or shelter. It was in this form that they became the early Freemasons. Later, the Sinclairs were named hereditary guardians of the Freemasons. Since they already were the guardians of the Templar order and possibly its savior, the apparent shift in their role actually signified little practical difference.

In 1320 many of Scotland's prominent leaders petitioned the pope to recognize an independent Scotland. A Henry Sinclair was one of them. The Sinclairs rarely occupied the most prominent political positions; they were always active on political and diplomatic fronts, however, wielding power from behind the throne and maintaining a lower profile without sacrificing their control.

They were not afraid to act as leaders on the battlefield. In 1330 Henry's sons, William and John, led a force of men to assist King Alfonso in fighting the Spanish Moors on the plains of Andalusia. William accompanied Sir James Douglas to the Holy Land, where they both fought bravely. On August 25, 1330, William was killed fighting the Saracens. His body was brought back and his tomb is in Rosslyn. It depicts a knight accompanied by a greyhound. William left behind an infant son, also William, who became the head of the clan.

William the son married Isabella, the daughter of Malise Sparre, the earl of Orkney. Isabella tied the Sinclair clan to the bloodlines of the Scottish king Malcolm II and two Norse kings, Magnus I and Magnus V. The Sinclair family had been under siege because of the incessant border wars, but the marriage increased the clan's territorial holdings, and it remained the most powerful in Scotland. In 1344 Isabella became the owner of the earldom of the Orkneys, as well as of Caithness and Strathearn.

The plague years took their toll on Scotland as it did all of Europe, but the Sinclairs managed to fare better than most. They had estates that may have provided earnings and ships that may have been active in trade. As guardians of the Templar/Masons, they also must have provided work for a large number of men whose greatest talent, as Templar descendants, remained their military skills. We know that William Sinclair basically led an army-for-hire business. Besides bringing a force to Spain in 1330, which most likely still included Templar refugees from France, William brought his own forces to Prussia in 1358 as paid mercenaries. There, the Prussian Teutonic knights had found themselves too deep in war against pagan Lithuanians, so William hired out himself and three hundred knights—a massive force considering that each armed knight was usually accompanied by several assistants and that the force brought foot soldiers as well. Launching such an expedition for pay would indicate that the principal business of the Sinclairs was still warfare. William would not return.

His son Henry took over the clan at a young age and sought to ensure its future. Four years after attaining his earldom, in 1362, he sailed to Copenhagen to achieve confirmation of his title. He had several goals in mind, and representatives in that city had prepared the way. He may have married a Danish princess, as is recorded, but if this is true, she never lived to return to Scotland. He also left empty-handed concerning his rights to the Orkneys. Only the Danish king had the right to confirm the earldom, and he dragged his feet for years. Henry sent agents to the Orkneys to stir up trouble against the king's first choice as earl.

Shortly after, he followed in the family's military tradition and went on crusade. He traveled overland through France, where he rekindled family ties with the St. Clair branch, and then reached Venice. At the time, Venice was a key trading center, and its fleets were used to transport crusaders to the Holy Land.

Back home, Henry married a local woman, Janet Halyburton, who gave birth to at least five children. One was Sir Henry, who continued the direct line and married a Douglas, thereby reinforcing the Sinclair-Bruce family connection. Another son was John, who married the daughter of the Danish king. Daughter Elizabeth married Sir John Drummond of Stobhall (of Cargill in Perthshire). John's sister Annabella was the queen of Scottish king Robert III and the mother of James I. Such marriages cemented relationships between Scotland's ruling families and ensured the status of the Sinclairs.

Clan Drummond

The Drummond connection to the Sinclairs is important for two reasons. The Drummonds, like the Sinclairs, were a most powerful family and very close to the crown in Scotland. They served the house of Robert the Bruce and the kings of the Stewart line. Through the marriage of Annabella Drummond and Robert III, all the succeeding kings of Scotland and England had Drummond blood. For five hundred years they would hold key posts in the military and in the government.

Yet the Drummond line had a murky start, with some family histories claiming their origin in a certain Yorik, the grandson of a Hungarian monarch. Yorik was said to have come to Scotland to deliver Margaret, a future queen. In return, he was given land and married into a clan. With little but legend to verify this start, it is more likely that the Drummonds, like the Sinclairs, were a Norman family that intermarried with Celtic Scots upon moving into Scotland.

Descendants of the earliest family members may have taken their name from a region called Drumanach Mor. A Malcolm Beg is usually claimed as the first Drummond, and it is certain that clan Drummond was well rewarded with land after actively supporting the efforts of Robert the Bruce and Scottish independence. Malcolm Drummond was one of those killed at Bannockburn. In 1345 Sir John Drummond married the Maid of Monfichets, and her dowry included estates of

Stobhall on Scotland's Tay River. The estate would be home to two Scottish queens.

The center of Drummond power soon settled in Hawthornden Castle, one mile east of Roslin. Like Rosslyn Chapel, it is said that Hawthornden is built over a network of caves that gave refuge at one point to Robert the Bruce. Despite the turmoils of Reformation two centuries later, the castle survived in the hands of the family until 1970, when it was given to form a trust and a retreat for writers. In between, Drummonds married into Scotland's first families, including the Stewarts, Douglases, Livingstons, Lindsays, and Keiths. They were the earls of Perth and bore titles of duke, lord, and baron elsewhere. In their long and substantial history, Drummonds made a name for themselves in Scotland from Bannockburn and Killcrankie, both disasters for the English, to Culloden, a disaster for the Scots.

The family also had an esoteric side that survived through the centuries. An eighteenth-century Sir William Drummond took a special interest in the knowledge of the ancients, and he may have been among the first to recognize the importance of the zodiac in the history of Israel. He pointed out that there was a connection between Orion and the secret traditions of the Jews. He also believed the biblical story to be the story of the zodiac: The Tribe of Dan, he said, was in Scorpio, the place where the sun dies and therefore the key to the underworld. The Sabbath he connected to the Greek Saturn, meaning that it was not just a time for rest, but rather a time when work and life ceased. William's was not a subject for those afraid of criticism, and despite holding off publication of his *Oedipus Judaicus,* he was branded an infidel. This, however, was better than the treatment a contemporary, Reverend Robert Taylor, received. He was imprisoned for his book, *The Diegesis; Being a Discovery of the Origins, Evidences, and Early History of Christianity,* which traced the pagan influence on the Church. His fate may have held off future Drummond texts. Such writings reveal an esoteric side to the Drummond clan that perhaps was shared with the Sinclairs.

The two clans united when the daughter of the explorer Henry Sinclair married a Drummond. The union of John Drummond and Elizabeth Sinclair, between 1380 and 1390 served to perpetuate a handful of elite Scottish families that dominated the country from the eleventh century. As we shall see, it also spurred Columbus to seek the lands to the west. In 1396 Henry Sinclair was making plans to sail beyond Greenland. Elizabeth, his daughter, was one who was privy to the information, as was her husband, John.

Elizabeth bore three sons: Walter, John, and Robert. Oldest son Walter remained in possession of the land and title to Cargill and Stobhall. The second son, John, headed off in 1419 to seek his fortune in Madeira. Though not too much is known of him, it is recorded that he married Catarina vaz de Lordelo in April 1422. Doña Lordelo was first married to Tristao vaz Teixeira. Teixeira was among the first of the Portuguese explorers to settle Madeira, and an aunt married Bartolomeo Perestrello, whose father was also one of the first three men who reached Madeira for the king. All three were given land. In 1430 John Drummond married a second time, to Branca Afonso da Cunha. This union produced nine children, including a son John, who, like his father, was called John the Scot. The Scottish Drummond clan was now linked to the Perestrello family of Madeira. Both played a role in Madeira from the earliest days of the settlement. The union of the Sinclair-Drummond family and the Perestrello family played an even greater role when young Columbus married Felipa Perestrello.

Henry the Sea King

In 1379, the efforts of Henry Sinclair paid off, and he was finally granted the earldom he had awaited. There were strings attached, and as was custom, semiannual payments from his lands to the Scandinavian king were the most important of them. The Orkneys and the Shetlands were not an easy kingdom to manage. One hundred and seventy islands, possibly only fifty of which were inhabited, provided great cover for pirates and smugglers. How many of those operated with the consent of the Sinclair family is unknown.

In 1380 Henry was thirty-six and had his hands full. Not only was he responsible for the Orcadian population, which meant trying to control a people who traditionally recognized no rule outside family and clan, but he owed allegiance to two monarchs as well. One monarch was Haakon of Norway, who still held claim to Scotland's Orkney Islands, the Shetlands, and Caithness. The other was Scotland's King Robert III, whose claims overlapped with those of the Scandinavian king. As earl of the Orkneys and Shetlands, Henry was a vassal of the Scandinavian king Haakon, yet he was also allowed by King Robert III to rule in much of Scotland. This he may have accomplished by strategic marriages. In addition, he had conflicting loyalties concerning the pope or, more accurately, the popes.

The late fourteenth century was the period of the dual papacy, with one line operating from Avignon and another from Rome. France and Scotland, Spain and Naples recognized the Avignon pope, which obliged Henry the Scottish earl to recognize Avignon as well. England, Portugal, and Norway, however, recognized the Roman pope, which meant that Henry as a vassal to the Norwegian king had to recognize Rome too. Sinclair's Orkney bishopric became a serious problem.

Bishops in this dark era of the Church were as wealthy as any baron, and commonly taxed the populace to a greater degree. There was little moral leadership, and the Church that had taken sides with the corrupt aims of the monarchy in France found itself under attack.* In the Orkneys, Bishop William was no disappointment as a target. On islands where almost everyone was a cousin to almost everyone else, he had declared that all marriages to second, third, and even fourth cousins were null and void. Consequently, as the Church's representative, he had the right to seize people's lands for himself. Henry solved his problem by turning his back. The people killed their bishop.

Sinclair still had his hands full. In 1385 he was back at Roslin, having contracted for a massive new fleet to replace the older ships in his

---

*The so-called Wat Tyler Rebellion of 1382 can be regarded as a revolt against the corrupt clergy. While the official version of the uprising is that a spontaneous rebellion was somehow incited all over the countryside, some see it as the work of a conspiracy. The historian Barbara Tuchman said there was evidence of planning. Winston Churchill said the rebellion betrayed evidence of having been organized by a secret society that sent agents throughout the countryside to prepare the rebels. Mobs attacked churches and clergy as well as tax collectors and castles. The Church and the Knights Hospitallers, who were England's greatest landowners, suffered the most. Churches that had been previously owned by the Knights Templar were spared. John Robinson, in his book *Born in Blood*, makes the point that there was nothing coincidental about which properties were destroyed and claims it was the revenge of the remnant Templar organizations against the Church that had betrayed the order. The end was near when Wat Tyler, presenting demands to the mayor of London, was attacked by a squire and the mayor himself. He was killed almost instantly.[3]

employ. Ships now were stronger and were able to hold cannons, thanks to Carlo Zeno, a naval hero whose pioneering use of the breach-loading cannon saved Venice from the Genoese fleet during the Battle of Chioggia. He was nicknamed the Lion after his victory, which led not only to the signing of the treaty, on June 24, 1381, that ended the long war between Venice and Genoa, but also to the restoration of Venice's maritime power. Venice rose again to control the trade in the eastern Mediterranean in concert with the Order of Saint John of the Hospital, which was headquartered on the island of Rhodes. Zeno was a powerful man in Venice, a city that had served as the meeting point for all the military orders, and his ships regularly transported crusaders. There is evidence that at least one Sinclair had met with him while on crusade in the Holy Land.[4]

Henry Sinclair's fleet played a significant role in maintaining his power, enabling him to fulfill his obligations throughout his sea-crossed realm. With Richard II invading Scotland, Henry needed to be able to move quickly from the troubled Orkneys to his southern stronghold in Roslin. He was also an elector for the united kingdoms of Norway and Denmark, so after the death of King Olaf, he sailed again to Copenhagen to vote for the new monarch.*

Henry's diplomatic commitments and relationships stretched far and wide, responsibilities that kept him away from home. The distraction of Scotland's second most powerful man occasionally caused his own domain to act rebelliously, and Henry periodically used his fleet to display his power. The fleet's greatest role was not military, however, but rather exploratory. A chance meeting on one of Henry's far-flung islands was the catalyst to turning his attention toward the New World.

---

*Upon Olaf's death, his mother, Margaret of Denmark, ruled Norway and Denmark. Desiring Sweden as well, she played and won a political gambit against King Albert of Sweden and created a union of Denmark, Sweden, and Norway called the Union of the Three Crowns. Against all precedent, she named herself regent of her grandnephew Eric of Pomerania, whom she persuaded the three parliaments to accept as king of the tripartite kingdom. Under Eric's rule, the three countries maintained their own laws and customs, and even their own dignitaries.[5] This union survived into the early 1500s.

Eric married Philippa Plantagenet, the daughter of King Henry IV of England. This Henry was the son of John of Gaunt, whose grandson was Henry the Navigator of Portugal.[6]

THE WAY WEST

The Orkneys had never shaken off their Viking ancestry and were always a threat to any ruler who tried to control them. Many of the Norse in the islands, and farther north in the Shetlands, were descendants, like Henry Sinclair, of Rogenwald of Møre. The family loyalty maintained at the highest levels due to diplomatic marriages, however, did not always obtain among the common people. The islanders of the North even spoke a different language from that of the nobles, called Norn. It has never died out and from Iceland to the Orkneys there are efforts in modern times to preserve this Old Norse–based dialect.

North of the Orkneys is a tiny island called Fer (or Fair) Isle. Like the Faeroes, it may have been designated *fer* to imply that sheep were raised there. As remote then as it is today, it was no place for a ship to run aground. The islanders were quick to take advantage of such ill fortune, and no survivors meant simply that none but the islanders could claim the ship's goods. In cases in which crew did survive, the islanders were quick to remedy the problem.

It was from this predicament that Henry Sinclair dramatically came to rescue Nicolo Zeno. Nicolo, a brother of Carlo Zeno of Venice, was on a voyage to make his own name. It almost ended at the hands of Henry's subjects.

The Brothers Zeno

Nicolo's brother Carlo Zeno was the admiral of the Venetian fleet that had been charged with delivering crusaders to the Holy Land. He is the hero who saved his city at the Battle of Chioggia. The Zeno family was among Europe's wealthiest, and Nicolo was inspired by Marco Polo, a fellow Venetian, to travel around the world. Sinclair and Zeno had much more in common than the chance meeting with Carlo years earlier. Both were nobles, and both used sea power to maintain their wealth and power. Nicolo was an elector of the doge, the ruling magistrate of Venice. Henry was an elector of the Scandinavian council. Both families had a military tradition and played roles in the Crusades.

In 1558, letters from Nicolo to his brother Antonio were discovered, inviting Antonio to join Nicolo as the captain (admiral) of the Sinclair fleet. The poor condition of the original documents and the original translation done by R. H. Major may have left something to be desired. It is possible that the seemingly chance meeting between Nicolo and Henry Sinclair had, in fact, been planned.

The evidence of a Sinclair-Zeno relationship during the Crusades, and of Sinclair emulating Zeno in the early use of shipboard cannon, indicates that they may have made further plans. Upon Nicolo's rescue, he was appointed commander of Henry Sinclair's fleet. Because Nicolo had served on his brother Carlo's fleet, Sinclair may have wanted a battle-competent captain. Upon Nicolo's invitation, Antonio joined him in the northern world.

The brothers Zeno may have accompanied Sinclair on a ship-buying trip to England when he needed to come to the aid of Margaret of Norway, whose own fleet was not strong enough to avert a band of pirates known as the Victual Brothers. Henry had his reasons for helping Margaret, besides being her vassal. By strengthening Norway, he hoped his own islands would not be raided. Margaret, whose new taxes were making her unpopular in Iceland—also under Norway's control—had asked Sinclair to pay a visit. He found the Icelandic ports well fortified, and returned home to continue strengthening his own defense.[7] The alliance with the Zeno family helped.

Charting the Western Islands

In 1395, during the Great Schism, Pope Boniface IX ordered an exchange of bishops. Bishop Henry of the Orkneys was to become bishop of Greenland. He would be taken aboard a Sinclair ship commanded by Nicolo Zeno. Bishop John of Greenland would come to the Orkneys, also aboard a Sinclair ship under Zeno's command. The ships sailed out of Kirkwall, the largest city in those islands. Nicolo Zeno used the opportunity during his voyage to Greenland to describe, in letters, the Eskimos, volcanoes, hot springs, and the commerce conducted there. Antonio drew a map showing both sides of the island and claimed that Henry Sinclair had supplied much of the information for it.

Frederick Pohl's *Prince Henry Sinclair* is almost a year-by-year history of the earl's life, and does not include a trip to Greenland by Sinclair himself. If Sinclair provided the details for the Zeno map, it could be that he had made an unrecorded voyage. It also could be that his position as king of the isles allowed him to maintain a library of charts and maps that had been compiled from the regular Norse commerce that had existed for centuries. From Leif Eriksson's days to Henry's, this unbroken commerce was the subject of record, and as the commander of a fleet of ships, it would be inconceivable for Henry to undertake voyages in the same waters without the charts and sailing directions available to traders in lumber, furs, and walrus tusks.

A voyage to Greenland could easily be accomplished in a month, including time to travel the coast and make both the passage west and the return passage home. It is certain that Henry had others in his employ who had traded with Greenland. The Orkneys were a central point between Norway and Iceland. The sail *could* be made direct, without stopping, but the Norse were the greater population in the Orkneys, so there would be ample reason for Scandinavian crews to make the Orkneys a port of resupply, trade, and family visitation. The Norse were predominant in the Scottish islands for as long as they were in Greenland and Iceland.

In *Erik's Saga* we are given the story of Leif Eriksson planning to sail from Greenland to Norway. Along the way he visits the Hebrides, as usual because of a storm, and falls in love with a noblewoman, Thorgunna. She gives birth to his son, who later comes to Greenland, where he is welcomed and acknowledged by Leif.

The North Atlantic islands of Greenland, Iceland, and the Orkneys, Faeroes, Shetlands, and Hebrides were all known to each other in Henry's day, just as they had been in the Viking era between 900 and 1350. With Henry's realm and responsibility extending from Norway to Greenland, there is little doubt that he knew well this corner of the world. The Church, too, knew about the islands, even as far as Greenland. In 1390 the only piece of geographical information that seemed to be missing was an accurate map.

The Tale That Launched an Expedition

Around the same time, a fisherman in Henry's island kingdom told the earl of his adventures west of Iceland. Twenty-six years before, he and his fellow fishermen had started out in four ships. They were blown off course and landed one thousand miles west of Fris, in a place they learned was called Estotiland. The fisherman's description of Estotiland roughly corresponds with a description of Newfoundland or Labrador. They met with a local chief and lived with his people for a short time, one of whom spoke Latin. Later the chief, described as the king, sent them south as part of a twelve-boat fleet to another land called Drogio.

This new country had more bloodthirsty inhabitants, and several of the crew were killed in ritual. The small group that was spared managed to win over its captors by teaching them how to use nets to fish. (Fishing with nets was developed early in the Orkneys, with nets stretching sixty yards long and fifteen yards wide. Nets were laid out at night, and fish, often hundreds of pounds of them, were harvested in the morning.) The natives marveled at the feat. For this, the lives of the fishermen were spared, and they eventually returned home.

For our purposes, the important detail in the fisherman's story is that Estotiland seems to have been home to either Europeans or descendants of Europeans. A Latin-speaking denizen may have been another Norse trader or settler, or even a member of the abandoned Greenland colony. The fishermen's adventure can be roughly dated to 1360, less than twenty years after Bishop Oddson reported on the Christians heading to the New World and going native.

Henry Sinclair had a new passion.

The Uncharted Islands

Were fishermen in fact working the North American Atlantic as early as the fourteenth century? Systematic exploitation of the waters around the known Atlantic islands is in no doubt. Fishing for cod in North America may have begun as early as the Viking days. The Norwegians as early as the twelfth century were undoubtedly the masters of the cod-fishing industry. Cod is high in protein, low in fat, and can be dried outdoors. It could also be stored over the winter months and traded as stockfish. From the high north in the Arctic Sea to the Bay of Biscay, fishing fleets competed for the best areas to cast their nets. Nations, too, fought over the fishing grounds. In 1408 there is record of complaints against fishermen out of Bristol for fishing the waters off Iceland. Bristol had natural advantages as a harbor, and it was geographically situated halfway between the Bay of Biscay and Iceland. Its ships could export woolens to the Continent and return with wine, or they could carry wine and sherry from Iberia to Iceland and return with stockfish. Or they would just harvest the sea.

But evidence suggests, too, that the waters west of Iceland were known to European cartographers. In 1360 Nicholas of Lynne made a voyage to the North Arctic and possibly as far west as the Hudson Bay in Canada. Gerardus Mercator and John Dee both mentioned him in their discussion of England's rights in the New World. They in turn derived their information from the writings of a Dutch explorer, James Cnoyen. Fragments of the record are in the British Museum. According to Cnoyen, Nicholas was a Franciscan or Minorite cleric who had traveled to the New World with eight Norsemen. The dates of Nicholas's last voyage, 1360–1364, are similar to the dates given for King Haakon of Norway's expedition to Greenland. Despite the decline of the Norse sea kings, it appears that the North Atlantic Sea highway was still being officially crossed.

Notably, neither Nicholas nor Cnoyen made claim to new lands even though Nicholas may well have made several voyages. What he accomplished instead was to put together enough information to produce one of the early maps of North America. Though it was too early to make claims on the land (that was still more than a century away), it was a time of mapmaking. The 1414 DeVirga map, believed to be based on the voyage of Nicholas of Lynne, showed a strange new land, Norveca Europa (Norse or North Europe).[8] Norveca and Norumbega were found on early maps and are believed to be derived from the Norse (as are the names Norman and Normandy). On the DeVirga map appear lands that extend directly west of Norway to Florida and the West Indies. Today we know such lands are reached by first heading west, then south; mapmaking, however, was not the exact science that it is today. As a result, the voyages of Nicholas were said to be to the "Polar Regions," yet they seem to have included much more temperate areas.[9]

The friar Nicholas is said to have spent thirty years mapping his Nor-Europa, in the company of Norsemen. It is very possible that these Norse were of the Orkney variety. They would, of course, have had a different agenda themselves, most likely bringing anything profitable home. Needless to say, there are no records of any sponsored expeditions lasting thirty years. But the maps Nicholas drew could well have been the by-products of more than one commercial venture.

Such early maps are often regarded as fanciful because they include unidentifiable islands. Frisland is one example, yet this legendary isle found its way onto an otherwise credible 1154 map by al-Idrisi as Resland, and onto Zeno's map, meaning it most likely did exist in one way or another. There are two possibilities: The island could have been misidentified (some believe it was Iceland) or it could have been one of the isles in the North Atlantic that have actually sunk.

Another of the odd islands that early maps included was Brasil.* It, too, is claimed to be legendary, although it was believed for centuries to be real.

In 1480 Bristol began an annual search for the island of Brasil, or at least that is what city fathers claimed. It is suggested that the Bristol voyage was not one of exploration, but rather a fishing expedition disguised as an exploration to trick the Hanseatic League into not interfering. The *hansa,* a German word meaning "fellowship," was a powerful trade association that attempted to corner the cod market. The league's ships followed the cod across the ocean, possibly as far as Canada, and refused to let English ships fish the rich waters of Iceland. Whether the ships sailing from Bristol were actually fishing or exploring is a question that may never be answered. They often carried salt, to dry their catch, just in case.

Brasil Island, or Hy-Brasil, often surfaced on fourteenth-century maps of the Atlantic just three hundred miles west of Ireland, and it was considered both fact and legend for a long time. It was probably real. Noted on the 1325 chart of the Genoese Dalorto, it appeared on maps until modern times. While many scoff at the notion that Brasil was anything other than Celtic legend, it is tough to land on legends.

In 1674 Captain John Nisbet, of Donegal, did just that. Coming upon the legendary isle after a fog lifted, he sent a small landing party, which claimed to find a castle and cultivated land. Cattle, sheep, and horses were in evidence but people were not. Finally, a Scottish gentleman came forward. He appeared to be living there with male servants, and if there were women and children, they did not show themselves. The men's clothing and language were from an older time, and the island was obviously out of touch with modern affairs. The Scottish gentleman presented the captain with a gift of silver and gold, possibly in hopes that he would leave.

The next year Nisbet's story was confirmed by Alexander Johnson,

---

*Brasil is alternatively spelled Brazil.

who set forth to verify the tale. He reported that the island did exist and that he was treated hospitably.

Remarkably, a sighting of Brasil was documented as late as 1872, shortly after the British Admiralty finally took the island off its chart, where it had been referred to as Brasil Rock. In this year, T. J. Westropp, explorer and member of the Royal Irish Academy, sailed there three times, bringing on his last voyage several others, including his mother, to confirm the island's existence. They reported that the island appeared and disappeared.

Islands do come and go in the actively volcanic North Atlantic, but the problem in discussing them is that the taboo subject of Atlantis lies, along with some of the islands, just below the surface. Whereas sea captains risk their ships if they fail to pay heed to what is submerged, historians risk their credibility if they do.

Brasil is not the only disputed isle in the sea west of Ireland. Near the spot identified by the British Admiralty as Brasil's location is a scrap of land called Rockall. The last to inhabit the tiny isle claimed it for Greenpeace and dubbed it Waveland, a country free from oil exploration and possible exploitation. It appears as Rockall on a 1606 map, although nearly ninety miles from its true location. In 1810 the HMS *Endymion* made the first recorded landing and measured the small island. It was seventy feet high and eighty feet across. In 1824 the *Helen of Dundee* collided with reefs near the rock and most of the passengers were left to drown. Sixteen passengers died as twelve crew members sailed away, and the reef became known as Helen's Reef. In 1846 a clan MacKay member may have landed and annexed the island for his family, a claim that was announced by J. Abrach MacKay, a minor Highland official, in the 1950s—although its veracity is unknown. Another British ship attempted a landing in 1862 when the HMS *Porcupine* put ashore one person, who was unable to make the summit. A fishing boat skipper may have been the first to climb to the top in the 1880s.

In 1904 the *Norge*, packed with immigrants to America, set sail. It was a bad-luck ship from the day it was launched. It ran aground in a fog, collided with a dredger, and hit and sank a Newfoundland fishing boat. Its history ended tragically when it was surprised by the Rockall isle; six hundred were killed. Some survivors made it in lifeboats to as far away as Scotland; others were picked up by fishing boats.

A number of landings were attempted after both World Wars, as the island was believed to have strategic value; however, most were aborted due to rough seas and the rocky shore. One successful landing took place on September 18, 1955, when the British claimed the island from a two-thousand-ton survey ship, the HMS *Vidal*. The British nailed a plaque to the island, hoisted the Union Jack, and fired a twenty-one-gun salute. They also began taking measurements. The island was seventy-three feet by one hundred feet. They also measured the shallow bathymetric features of the Rockall Plateau and assigned names from Tolkien's Ring Cycle to underwater features. Rohan, Gonor, and Eriador seamounts are thus named, as is the Gandalf Spur.

For a brief time this island was the subject of dispute among Ireland, England, Norway, and Iceland. Rockall sits on the Porcupine Bank, which may be as rich in oil as it is in fish. It is also home to a perplexing series of cold-water coral reefs.

Four years after the *Vidal* docked, the British returned to find the plaque missing. The oil debate continued. Geologists declared that Rockall is part of a shallow bank that extends to Greenland, and that between it and England is a break in the seabed some eight thousand feet deep. Therefore, Rockall docs not, by International convention, belong to the United Kingdom. Despite that logic, England issued petroleum licenses in the 1980s while the furor over fishing and drilling rights raged. The result is that four countries still claim the land, although it is too small to even be regarded as an island.

Back in the fifteenth century, however, the island may have been bigger, and there may have been more than one "legendary" isle. Islands are sometimes very small and difficult to find.

John Jay, of Bristol, ordered Thomas Lyde to sail west with a well-provisioned ship to find the island of Brasil. Nine months later, the crew returned no wiser. The next year two ships were sent. The *Trinity* and the *George* were likewise unsuccessful, but each year more ships were sent nonetheless, all returning with no claim of having found this elusive island. It may be that they were more successful than they let be known, as it was recorded that the *Trinity* and the *George* were provisioned with salt, and salt was used for drying cod.[10] It just may have been that Bristol's annual search for Brasil was really a cover for their annual catch of cod— either on the Porcupine Bank or farther west into the Grand Banks.

Just how early and how far Europe's fishermen were sailing for cod will never be known. Nor will details on how many were blown west to American shores, never to return. There is little reason to doubt that Orkney fishermen, as secretive as any, were reaching the Grand Banks well before 1534 when Jacques Cartier, one of the early explorers of the St. Lawrence Seaway, complained that fishermen of various nationalities were already fishing in a land claimed by France.

Henry may have also been aware of Orkney fishing excursions in the west, but was intrigued by the fisherman's story. Quite possibly it was not the first information Henry had heard about land west of Greenland. Both the Norsemen and the Church understood that there was a Vinland despite a cessation or slowdown of goods flowing from it.

THE SINCLAIR-ZENO EXPEDITION

Antonio Zeno wrote home about the encounter with the fisherman and Sinclair's goal of reaching the lands the man described. The fisherman had claimed to travel far south in this new land, so there appeared to be much more to it than the prospects of timber in Markland. The company embarked from the Faeroes, visited two islands that have given historians no end of trouble, and landed on Novia Scotia. Sinclair realized his dream.

Mysterious Islands

In fact, the problems cited by historians as evidence that the expedition did not take place are not that difficult to resolve. The two contested islands, Fris and Icaria, are among the many places whose original names have changed almost beyond recognition as they were translated from one language to another across time. Note the time difference between fourteenth-century Scotland, when the mapping of Greenland and the expedition to Nova Scotia took place, and sixteenth-century Venice, when and where the narrative was recorded.

The expedition had started either north or south of Fer Island, from the Orkneys or the Shetlands. "Fer Island" can become "Frislandia" easily enough without spacing between the letters. Perhaps Zeno, having originally met Henry Sinclair on Fer Island, applied its name to the entire group of islands and dubbed them all Fris or Frislandia on his map.

Fer Island lies between the Orkneys and the Shetlands. For island-hopping sailors, it is a welcome stop in the open sea. On land, residents make their living raising sheep and growing subsistence crops. Because of the extensive sheep raising, the Faeroes and Fer Isle were both given names meaning "sheep island" in Old Norse. Fris, as depicted on the Zeno map, however, covers a greater area and is farther west, which has confounded historians. In the fifteenth century, the language of both island groups was a derivative of Old Norse called Norn. Even though commerce was regular, most inhabitants of the northern islands were isolated, and language and dialect are often problematic.

In the Shetlands, the opening lines of the Lord's Prayer begin: "Fy vor o er I chimeri, halaght vara nam dit." In the Orkneys, the same lines are: "Fa vor I ir I chimeri, helleut ir I nam thite." These are only subtle differences, but the distance between the two places was never more than one measured by hours (today in minutes by air). With the passage of centuries and a translation into a related language, the line reads: "Our father which art in heaven, hallowed be thy Name."

The difference between easily recognizable place-names and the Shetland and Orkney places-names on Zeno's map—recorded most likely in Zeno's best estimation of the local Norn dialects, then translated to Sinclair's fourteenth-century dialect, and then finally translated to the dialect of a sixteenth-century Venetian—does not deserve the weight it is given by skeptics.

Joel Davis, in *Mother Tongue: How Humans Create Language*, points out the dramatic change from Old English in pre-Norman days to Middle English. In Old English the word *leaf* had one spelling. After the Normans exerted their influence, it had seven. In the eleventh century, the modern sentence "Have mercy on my son" was rendered "Gemiltsa minum suna." By the fourteenth, it was "Haue mercy on my sone."[11] These differences reflect changes within one language. Imagine the changes possible when even a literate Venetian tried to transcribe place-names in a country as dialect-fractured as the North Atlantic islands.*

---

*Modern-day New York City has some interesting names that have been transformed over the years from their Dutch origins. Flatbush, in Brooklyn, comes from the Dutch Vlacke Bos. Flushing, in Queens, takes its name from the town of Vlissingen in Holland.

Others claim that Fris was actually Iceland, drawn or redrawn later in error. While the two islands appear as roughly the same shape, Nicolo Zeno specifically mentioned that Sinclair owned Fris. As lord of the isles north of Scotland, Henry possessed many lands, but Iceland was not one of them. The Zeno map does depict an Islanda to the east of Greenland, so there is no evidence that the mapmaker was unaware of that island. Fris is more likely an island in the Orkneys, either Fer Island north of the Orkneys or the similarly-named Faeroes yet farther north. Of the many place-names depicted on Frislandia is Sorand, and at one point in the Zeno narrative he refers to Henry as the ruler of Sorano.

Icaria presents more of a problem. Lying between Iceland and Greenland on Zeno's map, it is much smaller than the renderings of Iceland or Frislandia. It has no place-names. This may mean the island was too small to be covered by older Norse charts. The language of the natives encountered on the island was strange, and throughout the crew of Sinclair's ships only one man, an Icelander, could understand it. Their message was nonetheless clear: It was not safe to land. Without permission to explore ashore, there was no way to find out if a village or town existed, but the expedition managed to learn that the inhabitants had a king they called Icari, as they had all their kings. On the other hand, it may have been a hermit island named by Irish monks. There is no doubt that these intrepid friars made numerous unrecorded discoveries. As mentioned, the Norse found evidence in Iceland of Catholic monks who may have been there for centuries. They typically chose the smaller islands as refuge from the pirates who plagued religious communities. Monks from Kerry, where the missionary Saint Patrick once lived, may have brought their name with them and dubbed their lonely new home Ker Isle, which could have become Keris. Inevitable transcription errors would be enough to render that as Icaria. If so, the Sinclair expedition may have seen the end result of six centuries of isolation.

Icaria has a second problem, however; there is no easily observable island where Zeno placed it. This mystery was solved by Captain Arlington Mallery, a navigator and cartographer who rediscovered the sixty-mile-long Icaria just where Zeno indicated—but underwater. It has been sinking for the last several centuries as part of the changing undersea around Iceland and Greenland.

There is more than one reason to believe the island described as Icaria may have existed. The annals of Bishop Gisle Oddson, copied from older records of Iceland and Greenland, describe a volcanic eruption on Iceland in 1342: "More than half of the Reykjanes Peninsula disappeared, and the Island Edley, forty miles west of Reykjanes, blew up. The maritime provinces of Selvoge . . . gradually sank into the Atlantic."[12] Islands have reappeared as well, due to the same volcanic activity. And subsequently disappeared again.

In the New World

Once the Zeno expedition managed to pass through several course-altering storms west of Greenland, they determined that the route to Estotiland lay west. From the drawing on Zeno's map, they clearly had Newfoundland in mind. Settled in the past by Norsemen from Iceland, Newfoundland had once supported as many as three hundred early colonists. The isolation must have been worse than that experienced on Greenland, and whatever colonies survived from 1100 to 1350 may have "turned native" at that time. The knowledge of Newfoundland under any name was most likely available to Sinclair.

He, however, was interested in lands farther south. He didn't bother to anchor. Instead he sailed on to Nova Scotia. Finally, they passed Cape Trin and arrived in Trin Harbor, named for the day they landed, Trinity Sunday. The date was June 2, 1398. Pohl places these points at Cape Canso and the harbor of modern Guysborough in Nova Scotia. Today Guysborough honors Henry Sinclair with a statue in that harbor.

While Antonio's damaged letters do not provide some of the most important details, they do describe enough landmarks that Sinclair's travels on Nova Scotia can be followed. Some of these, such as a smoking hole and a spring of pitch, are unmistakable. In fact, outside of the Stellarton area where both are located, the only near-Atlantic deposit of pitch is in Trinidad.

Zeno also recorded that upon landing Sinclair immediately sent one hundred men to survey their area. At the very least this would indicate that two hundred men landed. He ends by saying again that Henry split his fleet, sending Zeno and part of the expedition home while he and the rest stayed to explore, and that Henry's intention was to found a settlement.[13]

How long did Henry stay behind? The period after May 1398 is the only gap in his well-recorded life. There are two famed biographers who wrote about the affairs of the early Sinclairs. Father Hay has Henry returning to the Orkneys in August of 1400, when he fell in battle with the English. Raphael Holinshed has him suffering the same fate, but in 1404. Because Antonio Zeno returned to Venice in that year, it could be taken as evidence that Henry Sinclair lived for six years following his discovery.

A more important question can be posed: Did he make a second journey? His vow to create a colony could have been fulfilled shortly after returning home. He may have left men in place somewhere between Nova Scotia and Newport and sent more to turn his discovery into a true settlement. Unfortunately for Henry, the splitting of his fleet, absence, and distraction from affairs at home might have served to invite the English to strike. He had maintained control in the northern islands through the occasional visits of his fleet. The divided fleet and a long absence gave the English king the opportunity he needed.

As we have seen from the back-to-back explorations of the Norse, Henry and family could have made several voyages. There is evidence that years of man-hours were required to build both the underground complex on Oak Island and the baptistery in Newport—two signs of long-term settlement. There is further evidence that construction on the Oak Island complex was started in 1441. Sometime after that, the voyages may have stopped and the colonies been cut off.

CONSEQUENCES IN EUROPE

We have little more than the letters and partially reconstructed maps of Antonio Zeno for evidence of the first voyage. As pilot and commander of Henry Sinclair's fleet, Zeno did not actually "discover" the New World for Europe, as Norse sailors had made a multitude of voyages there for exploration and trade. For the Norse, though, this land was just an extension of not-so-hospitable North Atlantic lands. Zeno did recognize it as a New World, as it was not on any map known in Venice. Nearly one hundred years before Columbus, it was Zeno's map that referred to these lands as having been discovered. It was Henry Sinclair who would recognize the lands both as a New World and as a refuge from religious intolerance and constant warfare in Europe, long before the Pilgrims and the Huguenots.

Soon after Zeno's voyage, some new places turned up on European maps. The Borgia map of 1450 depicted the old Norse destination as Greater Albania (Great White Man's Land) and showed a Hansa ship anchored there, indicating that at least one more secretive trading guild was aware of the western lands. A Hansa map dated to 1475 and called the *Rudimentium Novitorium* depicts Vinland, evidence that the Norse destination had not been forgotten. It also shows a fortified church at the mouth of the St. Lawrence River. This is four hundred years after early Vikings and still seventeen years before Columbus. While the Newport Tower could be construed as a fortified church, it was nowhere near the St. Lawrence. Gerardus Mercator, who made his most famous maps after Columbus, depicted this same church in 1569.

In the mid-sixteenth century, Mercator and other famed cartographers, such as Abraham Ortelius and Girolamo Ruscelli, used the evidence of the Zeno exploration, obtaining their information from the Zeno family. Their records had gathered mold and dust for 150 years until a descendant remembered playing with them (and destroying a great deal) when he was a child. In 1558, as printing was available, this Zeno descendant published a narrative account of the Sinclair-Zeno voyage and made it available for the public, at least to those able both to buy and to read such a document. Some evidence suggests that it had already been available privately and may have been shared among other scientists of the day. For two hundred years, this early voyage was accepted as factual. It was only much later that any doubt was cast.

Immediately after the narrative's publication in Venice, Richard Hakluyt included it in his work *The Principle Navigations, Voyages, Traffiques, and Discoveries of the English Nation*. It was accepted in its own time, but later rejected because some of the landmasses and names do not correspond with real geography and historically verifiable placenames on modern maps. One explanation is that much Renaissance cartography did not yet include the projections of Mercator, greatly decreasing accuracy. Another explanation is that merchants and adventurers alike often protected routes and wrote and drew maps in a coded language. Potentially, the descendant of Nicolo Zeno failed to understand the code when compiling his ancestor's letters.[14] Nor was he knowledgeable about the science of cartography. Third, he suffered a serious language barrier, as had his mapmaking ancestors, in translating Norse and Norn names into Italian. At least Antonio had the opportunity to ask questions of contemporary speakers had he so chosen.

Several Renaissance cartographers are responsible for making enormous strides in mapping the world. Abraham Ortelius was one of the greatest, and he claimed that though Columbus should get credit for discovering the south, Zeno had been mapping the north part of the same continent a century earlier. Ortelius's map was produced in 1570, and the Estotiland of Zeno is the Labrador of modern Canada.

The year before, in 1569, Mercator, too, based his very influential map on the charts of the Zeno expedition. His maps of 1587 and 1595 still included Frisland, as did the Emery Molyneux globe of 1592 and Hessel Gerritsz's map of Hudson's explorations in 1612.

Venice and Genoa had never enjoyed amicable relations, as they competed in trade and, occasionally, in battle. Yet citizens of both cities made their mark on the world by leading discoveries on several continents, often in the employ of merchants and sailing under the nominal protection, or at least the permission, of foreign kings.

John Cabot, a Genoese, sailed out of Bristol in 1497 to discover Newfoundland for the English. Antonio Zeno sailed out of Scotland's outer islands. It is possible and in many cases likely that Zeno's maps were known to Cabot. It is certainly likely that the crew of Zeno's expedition, and their descendants, passed on knowledge of the voyage to fishermen and traders.

Columbus, also of Genoa, sailed for Queen Isabella of Spain. He was known to have sailed to Bristol, to Ireland, and even to Iceland. As a cartographer and a chart collector himself, it is difficult to believe that he was unaware of what the fishermen and traders among the North Atlantic islands already knew. For Columbus, whose name means "the dove" (the symbol of enlightenment), his own enlightenment would also come from a more direct source.

5

The Templar Trail in America

THE ONLY WRITTEN RECORD we have of Sinclair's voyage to the New World is that of his commander, Antonio Zeno. Zeno's narration tells us that Henry split the force so that Zeno could return to Scotland and Sinclair could explore further. This was sometime in 1398, before winter set in.

It would have been no surprise if the entire voyage turned around. Most of the records of voyages from 1492 to the seventeenth century portray European sailors as ill prepared and often scared to be at sea for any length of time. Moreover, wintering in the North Atlantic continent was usually a disaster for English settlers, who had little inclination to work and never enough food to carry through the season.

Sinclair's company was different. Even though they were not battle-tempered veterans of the Crusades, which at this point were two generations in the past, they had often been called to serve as mercenaries. They were certainly trained in the building arts. And they were teamed up with the men of Sinclair's navy, who came from the Orkneys.

A harsh climate and rough seas in those remote islands have long nurtured unusual stamina among their inhabitants. Two hundred years after Sinclair, the Hudson Bay Company of Canada decided it was best to recruit in the islands for those men who would brave the Canadian wilderness. Subsequently, nearly ninety percent of the fur traders and trappers would be from the Orkneys. Two centuries later, it was Orkneymen who explored the Arctic.

Winter in New England would not be a problem.

Sinclair's exploration of the New World started soon after landing in the place he called Trin. From Nova Scotia, they headed south and west, leaving clues along the way from Atlantic Canada to Newport, Rhode Island.

BIAS AGAINST THE EVIDENCE

If a new pyramid is discovered in Egypt, historians and archaeologists have little trouble assigning a date and a dynasty. If a mummy is found in Peru, there is a ready explanation that can be fit, without much controversy, into what is already known about Peru. When a Templar baptistery, effigies of knights in armor, castle ruins, and a complex treasure vault are found along the northeastern coast of North America, it is somehow hazardous to one's academic career even to mention the possibility of a pre-Columbian visitor or colony.

From Nova Scotia to Rhode Island are numerous unexplained phenomena that the scientific community either ignores or downplays as historical anomalies or accidents of nature. Some of these are ancient, some may be from the Norse era, and more recently other evidence may prove the precolonial visit of Sinclair. Among the ancient there are rock-built structures that calculate summer solstices in Connecticut and Rhode Island and a megalithic complex in southeastern New Hampshire. They all point to a much earlier culture that erected similar monuments in the Orkneys, the Hebrides, and various places in Ireland, Scotland, and England. In Europe these monuments are taken for granted, although they are beginning to be seen as part of a more appreciated heritage. In America, they are an embarrassment.

Thus, solar temples become root cellars, stone houses and monuments become cattle pens, and dolmens and standing stones become geological anomalies. Or even worse: Many simply get plowed over. The structures that manage to survive ignorance are still awaiting a more enlightened appreciation from the experts and scholars. On the lawn of a Westchester County firehouse in North Salem, New York, is a three-legged dolmen. In France when such a pre–Iron Age construction is found in Carnac, it's called a dolmen—that is, a "table" rock set up for some unknown purpose. In New York and New Jersey, such stones are explained as products of the Ice Age, despite legs that are two-thirds above ground, one-third below. So, too, runs the explanation for a twenty-five-foot standing stone along the Susquehanna River at (where else?) Standing Stone, Pennsylvania. Science would have us believe the Ice Age erected it.

The Susquehanna River has been the digging ground for numerous archaeologists, from amateurs to the Harvard professor Barry Fell. Inscriptions on stones found there have been interpreted by Fell as a Celto-Iberian script shared in Spain and North Africa. Skeptics claim that plow marks and weathering created the markings.

There is another North Salem, this one in New England. It is in New Hampshire is a quiet community of well-tended homes. Here lie the Mystery Hill structures, billed as America's Stonehenge. They comprise a series of rock-cut rooms, a sacrificial table rock, and small passageways. The structures are surrounded by standing stones in an alignment that very much resembles Skara Brae and the surrounding area in the Orkney Islands.

Skara Brae and the Ring of Brodgar may date to 2500–3000 B.C. The North Salem complex in New Hampshire dates to 3500 B.C., the time frame when the erection of megaliths ceased in England and France and along the Atlantic coastline. Historians often blame the end of this culture on deteriorating climate, which opens up the possibility of transatlantic sailing during the earlier, warmer phase. It also suggests that such megalith builders tried to establish themselves in a prehistoric America.

Europe has taken great steps to preserve monuments like Skara Brae, even though explanations of just who built them and how are not yet complete; American structures, however, are less fortunate. New England, and the rest of the contiguous forty-eight states, is not supposed to have had a Neolithic culture capable of crafting solar and lunar temples. For too long, the blatantly incorrect stereotype of Amerindian culture has been of nearly naked savages living in the woods, certainly without much in the way of knowledge and always devoid of a systematic spiritual expression. It was a trend that started as early as the Spanish conquest of Mexican peoples, whose cities were greater in size and population than Seville or anywhere else in Europe. The myth of the primitive savage was created to provide an excuse to evict, enslave, and ultimately destroy as much of American civilizations as possible.

Today, the myth still pervades scientific reasoning.

Yet hints of change do exist. The ceremonial cities in Cahokia, Illinois, and Etowah, Georgia, have until recently been in persistent danger of being absorbed into the surrounding trailer parks and golf courses. Sun circles in Miami, Florida, medicine wheels in Wyoming, and monumental effigy mounds from Ohio to Iowa are now beginning to get a new appraisal. It is becoming permissible in academic circles to entertain the idea that the peoples once labeled primitive had astronomical knowledge and used so-called medicine wheels to a purpose not unlike that of the pre-Celtic Europeans' ring stones. It is not, however, acceptable to propose that outside cultures may have braved the oceans.

The iron curtain of academic boundaries that pertains to pre-Columbian ocean crossing to the Americas is enforced by attitudes of political correctness. To declare that a European or Asian culture influenced early North American peoples has been declared racist, as it implies that such indigenous culture was not intelligent enough to have originated these ideas. Ironically, the same closed minds that once allowed conversion by the sword have survived only to enforce closed-mind thinking in the opposite direction. Both stereotypes prevent the expansion of knowledge, and both allow the destruction of anything that does not fit into the curriculum.

The result of such narrow thinking is still evident. The Hill of Cairns, in Bolton, Massachusetts, was paved through by Interstate 495. If you are lucky enough to be caught in the sprawling traffic during a weekday rush hour, one of the cairns can still be seen from the highway. As many as four hundred once existed.[1]

In New York's Putnam County, where it is not uncommon for a home on an acre of property to be valued at one million dollars or more, there exist numerous stone chambers. The entranceways often include a lintel stone placed over the doorway, not a feature in native North

American construction, but a typical feature in European structures. Generally, the chambers are simple and straight, but some have side passages. Some of these form crosses, although similar European chambers in the form of the cross precede Christian crosses by thousands of years. In New York, seventeen known chambers have been destroyed in the last twenty years, some of which were built to the same purpose as the gigantic New Grange mound in Ireland. The equinoctial sunset penetrates the innermost wall on two or three days of the year. If open-minded archaeological investigation were allowed, these chambers might be a historian's dream. Instead, they are nothing but builders' nightmares. If reported, the chambers require evaluation, and even a cursory investigation will hold up a project and raise cost. How many have simply been bulldozed is impossible to determine.[2]

In fairness to American engineers and developers, it is appropriate to note the moving of Abu Simbel in Egypt to accommodate the building of the Aswan Dam. What was cut into one massive rock thousands of years ago was cut apart in the 1960s and moved, costing the temple its most sacred secret. The original temple contained a 260-foot-long hallway that allowed sunlight to pass through each October 17 and illuminate statues of the sun god. The Sphinx, the most enigmatic and possibly the oldest monument in Egypt, presents a similarly disheartening case. It has lost its beard, has had its neck deteriorate to the point that it may soon collapse, and has had its nose blown off by Napoleon's cannons. In comparison, the paving over of an ancient cairn or two might seem insignificant.

The wealth of unexplained structures—from beehive cairns and dolmens, to stone tunnels and walls, to solar and lunar monuments and standing stones—means that there is much to pre-Columbian and pre-Viking American history that has yet to be discovered. More modern evidence—such as anchor stones, medieval armor and carvings, and even precolonial cannon—help us limit the suspect anomalies to evidence of a twelfth-century Viking Norse or fourteenth-century Orkney presence. Perhaps one candidate for the oddest yet most blatant evidence is the complex underground structure at Oak Island.

THE EVIDENCE

When Henry Sinclair and Antonio Zeno parted company, Henry indicated that he was going to spend time investigating his new world in the hopes of someday establishing a colony there. There is no direct proof of the route Henry and his men may have taken, or just what was done on subsequent journeys to the New World. There is, however, some very unusual and unexplained evidence that has been unearthed throughout Nova Scotia and New England.

The Mystery of Oak Island

In 1795, four hundred years after Sinclair's expedition, three young men on Oak Island found a depression in the ground under a tackle block hanging from a tree. Hunting for pirate treasure was the rage, as the coast of New England and maritime Canada had been plagued by pirates for centuries. The nearby port of La Have had a pirate culture that is still evident in the names of eateries, tourist maps, and geographic features. Mahone Bay, for example, was named for the low-lying Turkish pirate ships that would never have made it across the Atlantic, but with which the Templar fleet was well acquainted. Oak Island lies in this bay.

The three young men started digging, first encountering a row of flagstones, then, at ten-foot intervals, oaken platforms. At ninety feet, the excavators found an inscribed and coded stone. When its simple transposition code was broken, the stone revealed that a treasure could be found forty feet farther below. Fast forward two hundred years: The treasure, despite a toll of six human lives and two million dollars, has not been recovered.

Along the way, however, it was discovered that a massive complex of drains and water tunnels booby-traps the Money Pit, foiling digging by flooding the shafts. The clog-proof drains were covered in coconut husks. Years of investigating the island have also turned up numerous inscribed stones that may combine to form a map and a solution to the puzzle of just how to reach whatever is in a secret vault below.

Stranger still is that carbon dating places the structure as early as 1490 or as late as 1660. The problem presented by the date is that Europeans were not supposed to be on Oak Island in 1490, as Columbus, Cabot, Verrazano, and Samuel de Champlain all crossed the

Atlantic later. With the possible exception of Champlain, who arrived in 1604, there is no evidence that any of these explorers would have brought funds to start a colony (or to hide.)

Those whom we can suspect of visiting the Americas well before any organized European expeditions are Irish monks, Vikings, and Basque fishermen. The monks sought solitude, the Norse exploited timber and walrus tusks, and the Basques brought only salt to preserve their cod. None would exhibit wealth that was so great it must be buried, and certainly none is credited with the technology to create such an odd construction. Those who came after, including Acadians, had little motive or means to conduct such an operation in secrecy.

My own conclusion, detailed in *Lost Treasure of the Knights Templar,* is that the Sinclair family, valuing their rescued Templar treasure hoard, built and used the Money Pit as a vault to safeguard the Templar wealth.

The gold and silver, precious jewels, and religious relics that had been rescued from Philip IV's reach and placed on a fleet of ships had been secreted in the caves of the Esk Valley surrounding the Sinclair ancestral home in Roslin. The treasure had been relatively safe until the Sinclair family found themselves on the outs with both the English government and the early stirrings of the Reformation.

Henry had made his initial voyage in 1398, and it is believed he returned to Scotland in 1400. He may have made a subsequent visit between 1400 and 1404, when he was killed. This second voyage may have been conducted without Zeno, which would account for the absence of its record. Henry himself did not make public the story of his further explorations or his goal of establishing a colony, but, then, he and his family were well versed in keeping such secrets. They had preserved the Knights Templar and helped resurrect them as guild craftsmen and Freemasons. His castles and the caves in his domain had served as the vault for a treasure wanted by both the government and the Church. In 1400 Henry may have seen the value of the New World as a place to plant a colony free from the harsh religious climate of Europe and to create a place where thousands in his care could start an Arcadian utopia in peace. He may have also sponsored one or more colonization efforts, the ends of which he did not live to see. He was not alone in understanding the tyranny of a one-religion world. Those who sought to reform the

Roman Church, however, were just as uncompromising in their approach and attitudes. Catholics burned heretics; Protestants burned "witches." Both fought wars against each other for centuries to come.

The years between 1398 and 1404 would not have been when the Money Pit complex was excavated; it was, however, the time when it was placed on a map, one that would not be shared with anyone outside of the close circle of Sinclair family and allies. Even forty years later, there may have been no immediate need to move the treasure from its lair beneath Roslin, but the writing was on the wall. Calvinists in Scotland soon began burning churches and destroying religious artifacts. Such destruction later became official policy under the English king Henry VIII, and we can safely assume that the well-connected and foresightful Sinclairs had learned of danger early and protected their assets.

In 1441 another Sinclair, William, brought in masons and builders to begin construction of one of the most enthralling monuments of religion found on the planet, the chapel of Rosslyn. When complete, the chapel would be a record in stone that could tell as much as the Bayeaux tapestry, yet only to the initiated. To some, the inclusion of Celtic symbols implied a sanctuary where all who believed in a god were welcome. To the initiated, the hanging man, apprentice pillar, and severed heads were clearly Masonic. Yet who among even the Masons and guild craftsmen would have been aware of other clues, such as the presence of aloe and American maize carved into stone? These exist as a permanent record of the Sinclairs's seafaring voyages, made ninety years after the Templar order was "dissolved" and ninety years before Columbus was credited with discovering a continent.

While other clues to the chapel's purpose exist, the greatest enigma is that the actual construction of the chapel began five years later than the workers were brought to Roslin. They could have been put to other tasks, but none is recorded. It is my contention that the builders first were transported to Nova Scotia to erect the colony Sinclair had envisioned and at the same time to construct the complex tunnel and vault that would later be called the Money Pit. They then returned home to Roslin to build the chapel.

The Money Pit's construction period has been estimated at one year. The difficult part of this hypothesis is that for at least a year the contingent of Sinclair workers and soldiers had to live somewhere. Henry, of course, did not survive to see the construction, but his family carried on. If Henry had brought no fewer than two hundred men in his discovery voyage, William may have brought many more for the construction. Where did they live?

The Mystery Walls

A handful of interesting sites around Mahone Bay have defied explanation. In October 1992, the researcher and treasure hunter Jack McNab discovered a rectangular stone structure measuring seven feet by nine feet. William Crooker reported on McNab's discovery in his 1998 book, *Tracking Treasure*.[3] McNab also found three stone formations that he believed to be fireplaces and stones that appear to be grave markers. The structure is in Waverly, Nova Scotia, just outside of Halifax. There is no record of anyone building such structures, and no excavation has been done. Consequently, the area and its unusual structures have come to be known as the Mystery Walls of Bayers Lake. Further exploration has extended the area, which has grown to yield the discovery of a thirty-eight-foot longhouse that is not duplicated, so far, by any known structure in Nova Scotia, in addition to the "walls." A stone wall or fence extends four hundred feet and is built of three-foot-high rock along the top of natural rock cliffs. So far, the area is known to have this massive wall, at least two stone house foundations, and a collapsed subterranean chamber—none of which was known to Halifax residents until 1990. And none of which can be explained by colonial development.

If a Sinclair-led expedition did create a secret vault, it would not have been prudent to have surrounded it with temporary dwellings for hundreds of men. Such development, even if cleared later, would leave clues of human occupation. The evidence could later serve as a beacon to the inquisitive. Instead, a base some hours away that housed the majority of the workforce, and ships that conveyed only those workers desired, would have risked less chance of discovery. Halifax is a fine natural harbor. Its distance from the Money Pit could also have served to keep secrets even within the force, as certainly no one could trust hundreds with such rich information.

The Waverly–Bayers Lake area is now surrounded by industrial and commercial development. The discoverer and others have sought professional opinion to at least prevent further development from destroying future discoveries.

Nova Scotia is replete with roads and wells, dikes and dams, foundations and cellars that are not explained by its known history. Because cod-fishing Basques and fur-trapping French had intended only short visits, they can be eliminated from the list of suspects. Whoever built such structures meant to stay longer. The older anomalies imply that a culture hundreds or even thousands of years before the Vikings might have extended their range from Europe to Canada. Clues are seen in ancient structures in Scotland.

Scotland and the islands to the north are home to some curious ancient architecture that goes unexplained. The Maes Howe prehistoric complex dates to 2500 B.C., when the Pictish peoples inhabited the region, preceding the Scotti, who came later from Ireland. The Picts built their houses into the earth, and their stone and sod dwellings appeared after years of disuse to be very tiny because dirt and dust filled the insides and raised the floors. Soon these empty houses were called Picts' houses and later pixies' houses. They were the wee people who live on in the Celtic imagination.

The type of construction that they started, however, was not abandoned. Later inhabitants of Scotland and the isles used a similar construction, more out of necessity than design. At Jarlshof, in the Shetland Islands, is a Norse-constructed farmhouse. It is unknown if an important figure such as a jarl, or an earl, ever lived there, but its large size, seventy-two feet by sixteen feet, inspired Sir Walter Scott to give it that important name Jarl's Hof (or Jarlshof), as this means "Earl's House." The "house" is constructed on an earthen floor with walls of large rocks piled on top of each other. The rocks are chinked with earth, which insulated the dwelling in the cold Shetland winter. Posts and beams supported a roof that did not survive.

This type of construction is found in Norse Atlantic settlements everywhere on different scales.[4] The Norse settlers who came to the Shetlands in the ninth century were the forebears of the Norsemen descendants who made up Earl Henry Sinclair's fiefdom in the fourteenth and fifteenth. Like farmers everywhere, they relied on available materials, importing only what was necessary. Henry's navy was a combination of two groups of men. Some were nobly born knights who were heir at least to titles, if no longer to property. The others were people pledged to the earl who were probably both skilled craftsmen and unskilled laborers.

Any construction that required time also required housing for laborers and architects. Until proper excavation is accomplished, there is little way to tell if the "mystery walls" of the Halifax area date to a Viking era or to a later Scottish expedition.

The Cross

Even closer to Oak Island is the small community of New Ross. There, in 1979, resident Jean Harris and her husband made a discovery in the backyard of the home where they had been living for seven years: They unearthed walls, some five feet thick, others three feet thick. They also found several huge stones with inscribed letters, although to date none has been deciphered. Jean tried to invite museums and universities to investigate her property, but no one was interested in what she claimed was a castle mound.

No one, that is, until she reached Michael Bradley, who had written on pre-Columbian Atlantic crossings. Although his *Holy Grail Across the Atlantic* was cautious in accepting the owner's claims, he noted that the "castle" ruin had two levels: An older large-stone foundation supported a newer rubble-stone construction of walls. The ruin started in the back of the Harris home and extended over a hill. Notably, this area is close to the Gold River, which was once so full of gold that it simply washed down the riverbed.

The Harris family eventually moved out and a man named Alva Pye bought the property. He was a local and remembered the walls being much higher in his youth. He outlined several landmarks, including an ancient ten-by-twelve rectangular outline of stones and a standing stone that was apparently placed by what was once a well. His goal was to rebuild the "castle," but he also eventually moved on.

Today another owner rents out the home. The town of New Ross, known as The Cross in earlier days, is easy to locate and only a twenty-minute drive from Oak Island north on Route 12. Finding the ruin is also easy, as everyone in town, skeptical or not, knows the story. The former Harris home is across the street from the local Masonic Lodge. In 2001, the occupants were renters and the response I received to my request to look around was a pleasant "Why not?

Everyone else does." The site is unimpressive, as well as home to poison ivy and an ample number of bees. At the same time, it is difficult to imagine a natural explanation for the site.

Most likely, New Ross was home not to a castle, but to a Norse-like stone longhouse. Henry's crew may have included French masons and craftsmen, but his sailors were Orkneymen, all descended from the Norse who had settled the islands and stayed long after the Orkneys were given up by the Norwegian king. Just as they could erect stone longhouses at home, they could quickly build similar structures in the New World to serve as a headquarters for the builders, miners, and explorers who would have made up William Sinclair's enterprise.

The New Ross site may have been selected for another very good reason. It lies halfway between the mouth of the Gold River in the south, where among other islands in Mahone Bay is Oak Island, and another Oak Island directly north of the Cross, where the Gaspereau River reaches the Bay of Fundy. This is an intriguing coincidence, as oaks do not grow where acorns do not fall. Both Oak Islands had to have been seeded by someone. Because Champlain noted the oak trees, the planting must have taken place well before the 1600s. Both the Gaspereau River mouth and the mouth of the Gold River may have been signposted by oaks planted to serve as beacons to the informed, letting them know they had found the right location.*

Champlain noted that along the Bay of Fundy were numerous abandoned mines. He called this region the Bay of Mines; it is now the Minas Basin, part of the larger Bay of Fundy.

The Louisbourg Cannon

When the Sinclair-Zeno expedition first reached Nova Scotia, the site of its first landing is said to have been Chedabucto Bay in the center of that province. Modern-day Guysborough commemorates the landing with a statue of Henry Sinclair. As far as Oak Island is from Guysborough in a southerly direction, the site of the future fort of

---

*A less interesting coincidence is that both Oak Islands are now attached to the mainland. In the north, the infamous tidal changes and the lower waterline have connected the island to the mainland. In Mahone Bay, a causeway connects Oak Island to the shore to bring construction vehicles across. Both islands are private property requiring permission to visit.

Louisbourg is in the opposite direction. Louisbourg had been chosen by the French as the site of their first armed settlement in Nova Scotia. The fort was one of colonial Canada's largest and was built to maintain an army. In fact, the huge enterprise of constructing Louisbourg inspired some to believe a payship for the builders or for soldiers stationed there was diverted for safekeeping. The Oak Island complex may then have been constructed to protect the large payrolls from piracy.

Henry Sinclair would not have done more than pass the future site of the fort on his initial voyage; there is some evidence, however, that one of his boats was in the vicinity. The historian and distant relation Andrew Sinclair notes that a Venetian-style *petriero* cannon was dredged in the Louisbourg harbor in 1849. This is the same cannon that had been introduced as seaboard firepower in Italy by Carlo Zeno, and Andrew Sinclair saw these same weapons in the Museo Storico Navale in Venice.[5]

The Hanseatic League, competing with Norway for the North Atlantic trade, may also have been a source of that cannon, as a Hansa map of the early St. Lawrence River depicts what appears to be a fortified church at the river's mouth. It is possible that the cannon was tossed overboard from a merchant ship, or that it was a casualty of some unrecorded naval skirmish. The cannon had a design flaw that occasionally caused it to explode when used to fire missiles. While Zeno recorded his voyage, no mention of dispatching a cannon was made.

Nor, however, did he mention coasting Newfoundland. In 1501, a hundred years later, the Portuguese explorer Gaspar Corte Real did. He tells of meeting up with the Beothuk natives on the island and capturing nearly sixty, who seemed primitive in comparison to the residents of Nova Scotia and New England. They made a living by hunting, the prey including, according to Corte Real, a large hairy deer—probably moose. Oddly enough, they possessed a broken gilt sword and silver earrings, both of which were determined to be of Italian manufacture.[6] The earrings were specifically found to have been made in Venice.

The Yarmouth Inscribed Stone

Then as now, the fastest route from Halifax to the New England coast is southeast along the coast of Nova Scotia, past Oak Island to Yarmouth, and across the Gulf of Maine to the mainland. There is nothing between Yarmouth and Maine except water, and today ferries such as the *CAT* make the trip in a matter of hours. As a result, Yarmouth has become an important small city on the southeastern tip of Nova Scotia.

It also is part of the mystery of the island. In 1812, a four-hundred-pound stone was found in a protected part of Yarmouth's harbor. Called the Runic Stone, it bears thirteen runic-style characters that have been variously declared Norse, Basque, Egyptian, and Phoenician. Several translations have differed enough to seem almost comical. As discussed earlier, Norse runes were often encoded, serving to withhold their meaning from all but the intitiated. A Norse-style anchor stone was found nearby.

Of course, evidence that Norse ships visited Yarmouth cannot prove that Sinclair, too, visited that harbor. It is possible that Norse maps, which have not survived the centuries, included alternative directions for getting to the mainland and that Sinclair followed these.

Lake Memphremagog

Some three hundred miles west of Yarmouth is Lake Memphremagog, stretching sixty-five miles from Magog in Canada to Newport, Vermont. Sleepy home to permanent and summer residents who own cottages on the lake, it is also the source of irrepressible evidence that pre-Columbian Europeans visited the area. In the 1950s, decorative metal chest armor turned up near the shore of the lake. It was discovered by a farmer who sold it to another local. Although it was stolen from the Magog resident who purchased it, it was photographed. The *Vermont Patriot* also tells of a much earlier find of chain mail in Irasburg, very close to the lake, in 1826. What became of the artifact is unknown.[7] In the mid-1980s, a stone-carved gargoyle head was found four and a half miles away in a stream that empties into the western side of the lake. Art historians compared it to the gargoyles found in France, and particularly to the work done in the Rosslyn Chapel in Scotland. Stone cannot be carbon-dated, although the records of building the Rosslyn Chapel tell us that gargoyles of this sort were being carved at the beginning of the fifteenth century—precisely when the Sinclairs diverted the crews that would build the chapel to Nova Scotia to construct the Money Pit.

Near where this carving was found, an iron spearhead turned up.

Native Americans did not work in iron, and early colonists used firearms, so the spear has joined the other artifacts as part of the lake's mysterious past. Medieval infantry circa 1400–1500 still used spears, however, and medieval weapons makers, of course, worked in iron.

Among the other oddities discovered at or near Lake Memphremagog that point to a precolonial European period are a ruined dam, an iron-reinforced wooden boat, and a plank-built barge. While early colonists in the area perhaps built a dam, this particular dam dates to between 1450 and 1550.[8]

In 1998 one cottage owner found on a boulder what appears to be an outline of a fourteenth-century coat of arms. Skeptics predictably call any example of ogam or runic writing found on stones in America "plow marks," but a coat of arms is more difficult to ignore, especially since a similar carving found farther south in Massachusetts is very distinct. Opposite the coat of arms on the Vermont site was a partially obscured map. Although lichen had claimed part of the map, the Toronto-based researcher Joelle Laurel found it to be a fairly accurate depiction of the coastline from Nova Scotia to Mexico.

Lake Saint Sacrament

Farther west about forty miles is the large lake that divides modern New York State and Vermont. The southern reaches of Lake Champlain, named for the French explorer, are separated by a narrow strip of land from the northern tip of Lake George, named after the English conquest of lands that may have been explored first by French explorers. The original name of Lake George was Lake Saint Sacrament.

In this land where the Jesuits were hostilely received by the Iroquois tribe, the issue of just who explored the region and when is subject to debate. There is certainly an unrecorded history of the region.

What is known is that Jesuit priests in France were at war with the Sulpician order, and such hostility was carried to North America, where the two Catholic orders vied for control of Canada. Less well known is the secret society behind the Sulpicians, which we will meet later: the Compagnie du Saint-Sacrement, based in Saint-Sulpice in Paris, where a pro-Catholic yet openly tolerant group of priests strove to keep open Christianity's mind. It has been theorized that the company and the Priory of Sion are one and the same.

There is more reason than an emphasis on tolerance to connect Saint-Sulpice and the clan Sinclair. The Sulpician order, the Company of the Sacred Sacrament, and the Sinclair family all were on the surface ardent Catholics while sub rosa they shared at least the un-Catholic tolerance and possibly a full-blown appreciation of Gnostic thought.

Since the 1983 publication of *Holy Blood, Holy Grail* introduced the Priory of Sion, research has cast doubt on the long history of that group as presented to the authors by Gérard de Sède. A Priory of the Ordre de Sion was established in the mid-twelfth century at Orléans, and its original charter survives in the municipal archives. The Ordre de Sion and the Priory of Sion may not be one and the same. Some believe it was simply disinformation, and that the true secret organization was the Company of the Sacred Sacrament operating out of Saint-Sulpice. Modern Sulpicians use the initials *p.s.s.* after their name. The Priory of Sion was indicated by *p.s.* Both the Sulpicians and the Priory of Sion appear to share a devotion to a more mystic early form of Christianity. They conceal similar secrets, especially a strain of Gnostic thought that was common in the Church before Constantine. While this brand of Christianity did not indicate a specific dogma, it did allow the faithful an appreciation of the ability to explore issues of faith and science without the fear of inquisitorial persecution.

As Christ apparently concealed messages in parables, Sulpicians, Cistercians, Templars, and others concealed sacred messages and knowledge by other means. The baptistery buildings from Florence to Tomar and from the St. Clair Chapel in France to Orphir in the Sinclair-governed Orkneys concealed an astrological meaning that was not welcome in the Constantine Church but had played an important role in early Christianity. In Montreal stands the Sulpician tower, and in Newport the Templar-built tower. What connects the two is the Company of the Sacred Sacrament.

The intermarried clans of Sinclair and Drummond had connections to Saint-Sulpice, and in 1715 John Drummond, the first earl of Melfort and brother James, the fourth earl of Perth, were buried at Saint-Sulpice.

One is left to wonder whether it was the Sinclair expedition that gave the lake its name long before the English arrived.

Peterborough, Ontario, Boat Glyph

The Peterborough Provincial Park near Lake Ontario preserves numerous rock carvings that date from more than five hundred years ago to possibly over one thousand years. Most of these are readily ascribed to the neighboring Ojibwa tribe, part of the larger Algonquian language family, although just who carved the petroglyphs is uncertain. In Algonquian they are called *kino-man-age-wap-kong*, the "rocks that teach." Of the nearly one thousand petroglyphs, many appear to portray kinship relationships and family totemic symbols. One, however, stands out. It is a Norse-like boat with a serpent-head prow and a rudder. On the mast is a circle with six extending points.

Translating a visual image to stone does not, of course, allow for exact representation. Given no other evidence, the Peterborough glyph certainly seems to represent a European ship, but whether of Norse, Orkney, or French origin is unclear.

Vine Deloria Jr., a Native American spokesman, surprised many with his comments that Algonquians, specifically the Ojibwa, believe their original homeland was in the East, not the West. They entered the Americas through the St. Lawrence just as Europeans did much later. It is true that the Ojibwa and a few other Great Lakes tribes have a DNA strain that it seems is not shared with other American tribes or with Asians. The strain in fact demonstrates kinship with Europeans. Scientists, including paleoarchaeologists and geneticists, are debating just how that strain was brought to North America and whether recently or thousands of years ago. A recent arrival implies that a European population at the very least intermarried with the Algonquians.

Rather than allowing the artifacts at Lake Memphemagog and the Peterborough petroglyph to drag the Sinclair expedition across New England to the northern shores of Lake Ontario, however, it would certainly be neater to follow a straight line from Nova Scotia to Newport. Unfortunately, the route of the Sinclair-family expeditions is not so tidy. It is possible that the 1398 expedition took two courses, one along a St. Lawrence Seaway route that explored south to the Quebec-Vermont region, another that followed the coast. Many early maps depicted a fortified church at the mouth of the St. Lawrence River. Needless to say, there is no record of anyone building such a fortress. The second possibility is that there were several more expeditions.

Although it is obvious that the construction of the Oak Island complex happened later and required a great deal of time, intermediate voyages cannot be precluded.

The first Sinclair voyage most likely headed south, and nowhere is there more definitive evidence of its presence than in the small town of Westford, Massachusetts.

The Westford Ledge

In the small town of Westford, Massachusetts, lies a monument to the Sinclair expedition. On a granite perch is a life-size carving of a knight in effigy. The carving faces the sky and has been wholly exposed to the elements for six hundred years. Understandably, it shows a degree of wear. However, once chalk is poured into the indentations, punched holes, and incised lines, the work of the artist is revealed.

It is the full figure of a knight in chain mail holding a sword with a visible pommel, handle, and guard. As one picture speaks a thousand words, this carving speaks volumes. The helmet of the knight is the basinet style that was used in the late fourteenth century, placing the depicted knight in the time frame of the Sinclair expedition. At this time, it was common practice to leave a punch-hole monument (using the typical tools of an armorer) to a knight who fell in battle. Tellingly, in the Westford carving there is a break in the knight's sword, just below the guard, indicating that the owner was no longer alive.

The Sinclair expedition had either sailed upriver along the Merrimack to explore or made an overland journey. On the march inland they would have seen what is now called Prospect Hill. They may have climbed the 465-foot-high hill to get a better view of the area. It is possible that they also encountered members of a Native American tribe and fought a skirmish, which would account for the fallen knight depicted in stone. Fourteenth-century armor offered little protection from a strong bow and arrow.

The residents of Westford were aware of the carving in the 1880s but regarded it as Native in origin. When an amateur archaeologist named Frank Glynn rediscovered the monument in 1954, it was overgrown with vegetation. When he cleared it and applied chalk to gain a more accurate sense of the original image, a simple debate began over whether the man depicted was Native American or a European knight.

But Westford's knight had much more to reveal. The knight also holds a shield with a family crest. The crest itself holds a ship, a five-pointed star, and two buckles, or brooches. These brooches on a coat of arms were shared by few families, and beyond Glynn's capacity to research alone. By corresponding with T. C. Lethbridge, a museum curator in England, and engaging the help of a professional heraldist, he was able to determine that the crest belonged to a northern island family with a relationship to the Sinclairs. Sir Ian Moncreiffe, the heraldist, commented that there was "nothing remarkable" in a Sinclair expedition to Massachusetts, as his Norse-related family had been making westward excursions across the Atlantic for hundreds of years prior to Henry Sinclair's day. Lethbridge and Moncreiffe narrowed their search to the crest of the Scottish Gunn clan. This family was powerful in the north, and its lands included the isles and Caithness on Scotland's mainland. They were known as the "crowners of Caithness," meaning that anyone who ruled that region needed their consent. When Sinclair received Caithness through marriage, he would have met with the Gunn clan to reach a mutual agreement. Most likely a further marriage between clans sealed the deal. The Gunn clan became as important in the north to Sinclair as the Drummond clan was in Edinburgh.

It is believed that the James Gunn who died in Westford, Massachusetts, was a lieutenant of Henry Sinclair's. James was from Thurso, one of the northernmost towns in Scotland, facing the Pentland Firth and the Orkneys. Halfway between Inverness and Thurso is an ancient fishing village called Lybster and the Clan Gunn Museum, which commemorates the adventures of a widely traveled clan and the ancestor who lost his life in pre-Columbian America. The entire area is decidedly Norse and numerous place-names tell the history. The largest town north from Inverness is Wick, from the *vik-* prefix of Viking. Just north of that are two Sinclair castles and Sinclair Bay.

Both the Sinclairs and the Gunns were prominent enough that the death of one or the other entailed a monument almost as a matter of course. One Scottish researcher, Frank Tinsley, formerly an art muse-aum curator of arms, pointed out that effigies were very common on the slabs that covered burial vaults in chapels in Scotland. He noted that if the survivors of the skirmish had time enough to create the knight in stone, they also had time to give him a proper burial. Tinsley suggested he might be buried underneath the ledge. To date, no excavation has taken place.

When the Westford knight became a news item, a local farmer came forward and told of a boulder he had discovered in his field while plowing. It, too, depicted a galley-style ship (circa 1350–1400), as well as a number: 184. The number was only a clue. A local historian gave the typical response to the boulder, saying the marker was erected in 1840 to let the Native traders know when a ship was in Boston. The trading ships of the nineteenth century, however, were schooners, not galleys, and it is doubtful such SHIP IS IN signs were left along Native American trails. Alternatively, the number may have referred to a date in the perpetual calendar used by rune masters, indicating the year the stone was inscribed.

A final explanation is that the 184 could refer to units of measurement, such as the number of steps or miles between one thing and another. Unfortunately, there is no way of knowing where the rock was originally located. The boat stone is today in the lobby of the Fletcher Library in Westford.

In May 1966 a stone enclosure, measuring thirty-two feet by forty feet, was found, and investigators determined the original height of the enclosure to have been three feet. A few feet into the enclosure is a collapsed stone structure. The distance from the enclosure to the Westford knight may have been roughly 184 paces, indicating that the boat stone was a marker telling the distance between the effigy of the knight and his grave. It is impossible to know for sure, however, because the site of the stone enclosure has since been paved over and records from the 1966 discovery are little help in pinpointing the exact location.[9]

Fall River Knight

Farther south in Massachusetts is the modern city of Fall River. In 1831, at the corner of what is now Fifth and Hartley Streets, a male skeleton in full armor was dug up. Although others were revealed later, the first inspired a great deal of curiosity. The natural inclination, even a full century before Viking discoveries were made in Canada, was to believe that the knight was somehow a Viking. The poet Longfellow even wrote a poem connecting both the armored skeleton and the stone tower in Newport to the early Norse. The poem sees the author asking the skeleton to "Speak! Speak! Thou fearful guest," and the skeleton declaring, "I was a Viking old" who joined a corsair's crew headed across the ocean and built the "lofty tower." Longfellow said that he actually saw the skeleton on a trip he made from Newport.

His poem was a national and even international sensation and intensified the debate over a pre-Columbian Norse discovery. Even the Society of Northern Antiquaries of Copenhagen weighed in with a theory in support of a precolonial European presence. Others claim that Native Americans were no stranger to brass and copper and that shortly after Bartholomew Gosnold settled the area in 1602, the Natives were trading in copper. According to this view, the skeleton in armor could have survived hundreds of years underground. It would have less luck above ground, as it was destroyed in a fire a short time after being dug up. Because it was destroyed, there is no way to make a modern comparison to armor from any era. This has not stopped theorists from assigning dates to 1000 B.C. for Phoenicians, to 1000 A.D. for Vikings, to much more modern colonial times.

In 1921 five more skeletons in armor were discovered, in Charleston, Rhode Island. Curiously, Charleston and Fall River are almost precisely equidistant from the Newport Tower, one to the northeast, the other to the southwest. Three of the skeletons were missing skulls. One historian claimed that the Wampanoag tribe used armor and that copper as well as brass would be available to Native Americans once the English were in New England.[10] Others too have commented on the armor of the coastal New England tribes, including one piece found in the inner harbor of Pemaquid, Maine, comparing it to a breastplate found at Palenque, Mexico.[11]

Dighton Stone

From Fall River, it is no great distance to either Newport or the Taunton River, where lies one of the most controversial inscribed stones in America. A tiny museum now protects the seven-foot by eleven-foot rock. It is called the Dighton Stone.

Like the stone tower in Newport, the Dighton Stone was recorded very early in colonial times. Because it was discovered at such an early date in colonial history, most historians accept that it is authentic in some fashion. That is, however, where the agreement stops. Since 1677 scholars including Cotton Mather and Ezra Stiles have tried to decipher the stone's inscriptions and proffered widely divergent theories about its origin. Stiles claimed it was Phoenician. The Danish scholar Carl Rafn, two hundred years later, claimed Thorfinn Karlsefni was the artist. Edmund Delabarre of Brown University, declared in 1918 that it was Portuguese and claimed that it could be deciphered to read the date 1511. This somehow, he said, was the result of a Portuguese exploration by Miguel Corte Real in 1502.

There is little doubt that the Corte Real family was among the early visitors much farther up the Atlantic Coast. Gaspar Corte Real kidnapped fifty-seven Beothuk residents of Newfoundland to bring to his king in Lisbon in 1501. When he failed to return from a second voyage, his brother, Miguel, set out to look for him. Two ships departed Portugal; one returned. Like his brother, Miguel was never heard from again.

Delabarre is not the only one to claim a Portuguese explanation for the Dighton Stone. A large camp of local Portuguese historians and amateurs follow suit. There is little reason to doubt that the Portuguese reached New England at an early date, but again, nothing is certain.

Others have weighed in with explanations that range as far as Egypt and Japan. The most accepted explanation is Native American.

Sagres-Segregansett

In the early fifteenth century, some of Portugal's earliest explorers were trained in the navigation school in Sagres, on the coast of that country, founded by Prince Henry the Navigator. Within miles of the Dighton Stone is the village of Segregansett. The *–sett* suffix means "place" in the Wampanoag language, which has been used to bolster the theory that the Portuguese were the first to discover New England, as Segregansett could be construed as Sagres-place. The theory that early Portuguese explorers landed and interacted with the Wampanoag tribe depends on the Dighton Stone, as well as place-names and shared names between Portuguese and certain Native American peoples. Even if true, this connection may not do much to support those who believe that Corte Real discovered New England. As part of the House of Aviz, the Corte Real family was unlikely to have named a place in honor of their rival, Prince Henry of Sagres, the grand master of the Knights of Christ.

For that matter, Segregansett might even further the case for a

Norse or Orkney influence. The *–sett* suffix is similar to the *–ster* suffix in Old Norse, where it also means "place."

Whether Portuguese, Norse, or Native American, the name is unquestionably provocative. Ten years after the explorer Verrazano sailed the American coast, two Native Americans from the St. Lawrence River told Cartier of an elusive kingdom with a similar name: Saguenay. Cartier took two sons of the chief, Taignoagny and Damagaya, back to France, where they told all who would listen of a place where the people dressed in cloth garments like the white men, wore ropes of gold around their necks, and owned precious stones. The promise of gold waiting to be found in Canada, which would help France keep up with the Spanish, may have motivated the French king to fund subsequent voyages. Even as the stories of the two guests grew stranger, the French king stubbornly believed them.

The Narragansett Cannon

In 1921 a second breech-loading petriero was discovered off the North American coastline—this time in Narragansett Bay in Rhode Island. Again, the Zeno-Sinclair relationship suggests that it could have been aboard a Sinclair ship, or perhaps aboard a Hansa ship, as they too are known to have employed the cannon. The cannon's reputation for exploding caused it to be replaced at an early date, making it very unlikely that two were brought to America on post-Columbian visits.

King Magnus

Arlington Mallery was one of the first to suggest that Native American tribes had been influenced by pre-Columbian Europeans. When Cartier reached the Montreal area in 1535, he discovered Iroquois living in longhouses. One hundred years later, Champlain found the same longhouses hundreds of miles inland. Although not all Native Americans lived in tepees and wigwams—many erected at least one-room huts— the longhouses were notably atypical.

Native designs, too, suggest some Norse precedent. The Norse made steatite pots that were uncovered in Gardar in Greenland. These designs were often simple, and if they were not irrefutably European, the three small circles, or dots, on each pot would be called primitive. In Labrador, directly across the Davis Strait, Junius Bird uncovered the same three-dot steatite pots near Norse iron boat spikes. And Iroquoian potters crafted the same three-dot ceramic pot.[12] The three dots are supposed to represent the three most important gods. The Iroquois also used the chevron.

Both the Iroquois and the neighboring Huron tribe used a system of justice whereby the victim's family could demand an amount of payment based on the rank of the person killed. The Iceland Norse wergild system worked the same way, compensating the victim's family to a degree that was based on rank and standing.

Mallery was also among the first to compile a list of similar Old Norse and Iroquois words. The Norse trickster Loki is a devil type who is not found in non-Scandinavian cultures. As a trickster, he sometimes made deals with people and their gods; sometimes he broke deals and caused trouble. The North American trickster was similar—so similar that he was called Loki by the Huron and Oki by the Iroquois.[13]

The Iroquois were not in the Newport area or most of coastal New England. From Nova Scotia to Newport, the Algonquian-speaking tribes dominated. Consequently, they were the ones more likely to come in contact with Sinclair's expedition and early colony. Is it possible that the two peoples eventually became relatives? After all, Sinclair's men were just that, men. A lengthy visit might have seen Orkneymen marrying Algonquian women.

Verrazano's 1524 letter to the French king commented on the Wampanoag people "inclining to whiteness." Sieur de Roberval, the first governor general of New France, made a similar comment describing Iroquois he met in 1542. He said that "they are very white" and remarked that they could be mistaken for Frenchmen if dressed in the same clothes.[14] Roger Williams, of colonial Rhode Island, described the Wampanoag tribe as "tawnie . . . yet they are borne white." The Portuguese captain Estevez Gomez claimed to have taken white slaves in 1524 along either the coast of Nova Scotia or Maine.

The neighboring Narragansett tribe met with the early Pilgrim settlers at Plymouth. In their first spring, Governor Bradford recorded that a "certain Indian came among them, and spoke to them in broken English which they could well understand but were astonished by." This Indian was Samoset, and he brought a Wampanoag, Squanto, to visit as well. The Pilgrim fathers also commented on the Natives' advanced fishing skills. They knew when the shad were running and how to catch large quantities with nets. They also knew the benefits of using the crushed fish and bones as fertilizer. This productive use of by-products is something that modern fishermen still profit from today, selling the fertilizer.

The Algonquian myth system, too, has much in common with Norse mythology. The Algonquians' trickster god was Lox, similar to the Norse Loki and just as evil. Their view of the end of the world was decidedly Norse, with the good god, Glooscap, doing battle with the evil god, Malsumsis. This evil god was a wolf, similar to the Norse wolf Fenrir, who ended the world when he broke his chains. Orcadian sailors on Sinclair ships would undoubtedly have brought the Norse elements along with Christianity.

In 1884 Charles Leland, who spent a lifetime describing cultures from the Etruscans and Gypsies to the Algonquians, published *Algonquin Legends*. In it he claims there are six major similarities that connect the Norse culture with the Algonquians. At the same time, there was a twist. Glooscap was the good god but at the same time his name meant "liar." While this is not a name generally associated with the Christian God, surviving *m'teoulin* (the magicians and medicine men of the coastal tribes) explained that Glooscap had promised he would return. So far he hasn't.

In 1884 many of the m'teoulin were still alive, but little or no follow-up work was done on the Norse-Algonquian myth similarities. At the time there was no proof of the persistent myths of Norse exploration in North America, so Leland's observations went unnoticed.

When Frederick Pohl published *Prince Henry Sinclair* in 1967, he brought the Glooscap myth to the attention of a general audience. Pohl believed the 1398 voyage and exploration of Henry Sinclair exerted a great influence on the coastal Amerindian culture. Sinclair took on the role of the culture hero. Complete with tales of his travels on the backs of whales (an interpretation of the never-before-seen decked ships), sharp swords, and a large town of wigwams for his men, Glooscap took on a new meaning. The legend further tells how Henry, as Glooscap, taught the use of nets for fishing. Perhaps influenced by the fishermen's tale of just how appreciated this new knowledge was, Henry, with visions of establishing a colony himself, shared the knowledge with the local Micmacs.

And while other white men returned to Algonquian territory, Henry was not among them. Sinclair, in the role of Glooscap, would remain in legend like Britain's Arthur, the king whose return was long awaited.

The Algonquian Wampanoag people who met Verrazano had their own king, with a decidedly Norse name—King Magnus. It was through Henry Sinclair's first marriage, to the great-granddaughter of King Magnus of Sweden and Norway, that his landholdings increased. This might have made it an honorable name with which to dub a friendly Native chieftain. It also was simply a popular Norse name in the Orkneys and Caithness; it became "Angus" farther south in Scotland.

The Newport Tower

The final stop on Henry Sinclair's tour of the New World may have been the harbor of Newport. It is one of the most protected harbors of New England, and a favorite among yachtsmen for the safety it offers. The guardian of the remnant Templars would certainly have made a good choice in creating his Arcadia at this site. It offered protection from the sea, and it was out of the way of coasting ships. Discovery would, of course, have been unlikely, because transatlantic traffic was limited in 1398, but Henry, as a fourteenth-century military man, certainly would have insisted upon both access and security when planting his colony. When finished, the tower provided the ability to see eleven nautical miles to sea, and thus served as a beacon to the welcome or as a sentry to guard against the unwelcome.

It is said that churches are made of stone, houses of wood. Henry's men built the last Templar sanctuary of stone. It required at least a year to orient it to the solstices. Given that the expedition is recorded as landing in Nova Scotia in June 1398, the company may have wintered in Newport that same year. During winter they could get bearings, assuming Henry had at least one master mason among his men.

When the ground thawed in the spring, probably April, work would have started. The plan for the tower and even that for the placement of the light-admitting windows would have been complete by this time, possibly laid out by viewing the winter solstice. The Templar church of Ostrlars on Bornholm has similar slit windows that admit light upon the midsummer and midwinter solstices. Such architectural features could not be carried from one place to another by blueprint because the latitude of the location (and the consequent location of the windows) varied from structure to structure. Rather, the masons had to observe each site independently to develop their plans. The second step was in gathering the materials needed. Unlike the ancients, who often built with specific stones from far away, medieval builders worked with the materials at hand. New England is abundant in flagstones, so these were used at Newport. Cutting of timber might have also waited until spring.

Actual construction began with digging. A circle with a twenty-five-foot diameter was laid out. The tower has a foundation at least thirty inches deep to accommodate the footings of the columns. Stones were gathered and sized, timber harvested and made ready. Mortar was mixed and ready for building up from the ground.

Once the eight round columns were nearly complete, the floor of the first story was put into place, twelve and a half feet above the ground. Sockets and brackets were placed in the stone walls to hold the timber floor. Four very large pieces of timber were put in place to hold the floorboards. The thickness of the first-story floor is interesting, as it is more than three feet. In all of the Swedish Templar round churches we find this similar thickness, and it was used to fireproof the upper level. Clay was placed on top of the beams and then a level of mortar.

One clue to the age and origination of the tower is found in the measurements. In 1952 several architects measured distances and angles of the Newport Tower and decided it was not built by using the English foot. Instead, a Norse foot was used, measuring 12.35 inches.

More than eighty percent of Scandinavian baptisteries had an entrance on the southwest side, and so does Newport. Virtually nothing done in building such a structure is accidental. Even though the exact meaning of the entrance's placement, the floor's thickness, and the tiny slit windows may elude us, we can safely assume that someone had a reason for each feature.

The astronomer William Penhallow has determined that several astronomical alignments were built into the tower. The predetermined placement of the slit windows had to be done, then, to exact specifications. These include an alignment to the sun at the winter solstice, alignments to phenomena known as lunar majors and lunar minors, and even alignments to certain stars. The fireplace plays a role besides its practical use for cooking and warmth. On certain days it will be illu-minated through light entering the small windows. On one lunar extreme, the moon sets at the same spot on the horizon as the sun. Both will illuminate the fireplace when they set. When the full moon is observed at or near a lunar extreme, an eclipse is likely to occur three months later. Penhallow says this information was available in almanacs after 1600, which may imply that the tower was built prior to that time. He adds that because the alignments allow keeping the lunar months in phase with the solar year, the idea that the openings could have been random is "ludicrous."

To build above the first story, all of the work depended on workers below using a pulley system to raise the materials. Timbers and beams, brackets and sockets, stones and mortar were all brought up as con-struction of the second floor began. This time, the thickness of the floor was only sixteen inches. The use of recesses in the second-story walls may have had functional purposes as well, serving as tables and shelves for monks to take their meals. The thin slit windows, not unlike those found in a castle wall, might have served well if the occupants were under attack.

Finally, the roof was placed over the second story. In a majority of the round churches, the roof was the first to deteriorate for several rea-sons. Built of perishable materials, roofs are subject to frequent repair. Residents of croft houses in Caithness, Scotland, regularly clean or remove and replace thatching, which can absorb water, shelter insects, and suffer storm damage. Once the colony no longer existed, it was just a matter of time until the roof was gone. Another reason that so few roofs have remained intact could be that the roofs themselves were less important. It was the walls that either provided defense or made astro-nomical calculations. These were meant to last, and did, even longer than the floors.

Erecting the tower required that workers and soldiers be housed and fed through a cold winter and a hot summer. At minimum, this meant bunks for the men, a kitchen, and workshops. More likely, it also entailed private quarters for the leaders, a temporary chapel, and a recreation building. If we consider the later writings of Zeno, a ship was even needed to bring at least part of Sinclair's contingent home, requir-ing even more construction.

Critics of the tower's precolonial status wonder where the evidence of this small colony could have gone. The answer may lie in the abandoned fort of Ninigret, about forty miles away. Today the ruin is little more than three-foot-high mounds and rubble-work walls. An open breech cannon, a sword, and some skeletons have been found and historians argue over just who might have constructed the European-style structure. A theory of early, and probably lost, Dutch settlers was prominent until students of the Dutch West India Company refuted such a guess.

The open breech cannon was abandoned in 1540, a date that is too early for a Dutch presence. The five-sided fort, the cannon, and blue-and-white pottery more readily suggest sailors from Lisbon or from Portuguese islands of the Atlantic. It is just one more New England mystery whose evidence leaves historians without conclusions.

Possibly the most important question is What happened to the builders of the baptistery? Was Henry Sinclair or an heir supposed to send a relief expedition? Arcadia had been found and lost again.

6

Columbus and the
Knights of Christ

THE STORY OF COLUMBUS and his voyage has been oversimplified to the point of inaccuracy, and that has led to vilification.

In the shorthand version of the tale, the son of a Genoese weaver, poorly educated yet well read, decides the world is round and that, as a result, not only will one not fall off any earthly edges, but also one can reach the fabled lands of Cathay (China) by sailing the oceans. Queen Isabella hocks her jewels to raise money for three ships to cross the Atlantic. Despite a near mutiny by his boatloads of convicts, the hero presses on and finally reaches the New World. Slow to realize it is not India or China, he returns home and sells the king and queen on the potential of gold and possible converts to Christianity.

The second and more modern version of Columbus's tale starts with the same details, although we are now aware that the flat-world theory was fiction. Greeks and Romans writing one thousand years before understood the world is round. This version ends with Columbus selling the king on exploiting the gold, selling the people into slavery, and intentionally or not wiping out millions through greed and disease.

The truth is stranger than the fiction. Columbus actually was the son of a Genoese weaver and took to the sea at an early age. He traveled to Lisbon, where he married into a Knights Templar family and gained access to a trove of secret charts and maps. His wife's brother governed Porto Santo in Madeira, where the son of Elizabeth Sinclair and John Drummond had met and married into the family of Columbus's in-laws. Knowledge of four hundred years of Norse ventures in the West as well as the hundred-year-old saga of grandfather Henry Sinclair's voyage ended up in Columbus's hands.

It was there on Madeira that he made his decision to cross the Atlantic. Having gathered a wealth of input in a few short years after his marriage, from Madeira he also made voyages that served to increase his personal experience. The education gained on the tiny island chain was immeasurable. By 1479, Columbus was ready to make the voyage.

It is said that one of his pilots had also been to the Americas, just years before the 1492 voyage. In 1488 a ship belonging to Jean Cousin, of France, was hit by a storm in the Atlantic that blew it so far off course that it is believed to have reached either North or South America. Cousin's pilot was Martin Alonso Pinzon, of Palos, Spain, who would captain the *Pinta* for Columbus.

THE IBERIAN STAGE

Portugal's role in discovering the Americas has been relegated to second place; but Portugal actually did more to map the globe than neighboring Spain or, possibly, any other nation. The catalysts for the country's explosion of discovery were another prince, Henry the Navigator, and Portugal's king Dinis I, who saved the Templars from the pope. Portugal's role began as the Crusades ended. The Templars continued to play a key part.

Dinis I and the Knights of Christ
While much of the history of the Crusades centers on the goal of taking back the Holy City, as a whole the Crusades were just as much about territory as about religion. On the Iberian Peninsula, the territory

was the conquered homeland of what would later become Spain and Portugal. This reconquest of Iberia, called by historians the Reconquest or Reconquista, was important for two reasons. It was a military victory that kept Islam from dominating Western Europe. It also created new opportunity for the Templars. Just as the Western Atlantic had served as a barrier to many in medieval Europe, for the Templars it would serve as a gateway.

Alfonso Henriques (1139–1185) was the Conqueror King who turned back the tide of Islam. His country, Portugal, was a relatively small strip of land on the western edge of Iberia. While Islam was still the dominant force in Spain, the tiny kingdom of Portugal faced the enemy with its back to the Atlantic.

Alfonso sought help wherever it was available, including summoning the Knights Templar, who served as a fighting force in defense of his country, and the Cistercian order, whose members did not fight. Their role was as a religious force that would rededicate Portugal to Christianity and free it from Islamic influence. Merchants and traders of Genoa were also invited to join in the Portuguese efforts. Their knowledge of the sea made them pioneers in making voyages around the African coast as well as establishing avenues of trade with the continent's interior. Most would serve in a mercantile capacity, although some were initiated into the military orders.

Immediately after the Portuguese king recaptured Lisbon in 1147, Genoese merchants began arriving in the city and Alfonso expelled both the Moors and the Jews, who had coexisted peacefully with and thrived under the Moorish rule (thus were seen as being disloyal to Christians).* Quick to fill the void left by the Jews, Genoese bankers moved in and became the principal financiers of trade voyages and, later, of exploration.

When the Templars arrived in Portugal, they built a handful of castles and churches, possibly the most sacred structures being in Tomar.

---

*Lisbon's history is a kaleidoscope of changing rulers and inhabitants. The city was already ancient during the Roman Empire. One legend tells of Ulysses founding the city, and there is good reason to believe that the legendary Hercules was actually an Iberian prehistoric king. The Phoenicians, who had been there as early as 1200 B.C., called it Alis Ubbo (the Serene Harbor), a name the Romans altered to Olisipo. The Visigoths, who were instrumental in destroying the Roman Empire, called the city Olissibona. In their turn, the Moors called their captured seaport Ulixbona.

Upriver from Lisbon on a tributary of the Tagus, Tomar's region has an ancient mystical heritage that extends from the days of Hercules to modern time, when the Blessed Virgin Mary visited nearby Fatima. The town is dominated by the Templar church, which was first started in 1162, three years after the Order of the Knights Templar was chartered in Portugal. The Templars used Tomar as a base from 1159 to 1314, when the order was dissolved, but a nearby Templar church, Santa Maria do Olival, actually was the seat of the order in Portugal. Later, Santa Maria do Olival was considered the mother church of all churches in the colonies of Portugal, as it remained the seat of the succeeding order, the Knights of Christ.

Beginning in 1162, the stronghold of Tomar was constructed section by section, with the core portion following the model of the round church built by Constantine in Jerusalem, the Holy Sepulchre. Around the Templar church was built the Convent-Castle of the Knights of Christ, which over the years became an imposing complex of buildings. Judging by the order's predilection for building atop preexisting sacred sites, this too may already have been considered a holy place. It is probably no coincidence that not far from Tomar is Fatima, where the Blessed Virgin appeared in 1917. The entire town was dominated by the Templars. The central feature of the town itself is the Church of Saint John the Baptist; nearby is the octagonal chapel of Saint Gregory.

Shortly after Lisbon was freed from the Moors, the Cistercian abbey of Alcobaca was founded as a daughter house of Clairvaux in Burgundy. Saint Bernard had supported King Alfonso in drawn-out negotiations to gain from the pope recognition as a country. In return, the king gave Bernard the land he needed to establish his order within Portuguese borders. The monks brought the land under cultivation and introduced vineyards. They also established the first schools and played a role in establishing the first university at Coimbra.

The Templars built castles as well. The Torre de Belem, which still stands today, was built into the Tagus River and called the Castle of Saint Vincent. Its first commander was the Templar Gaspar de Paiva, and his mission was to defend the harbor at Restelo. Francisco de Arruda was the architect who designed the fort; his brother Diogo designed Tomar.

When the fourteenth century rolled round and the French king and his puppet pope sought to destroy the Templars, Portugal remained loyal to the order that had helped it do battle with Islam. The Templars were allowed to exist beyond 1307 in Portugal, simply by undergoing a name change to the Knights of Christ. The reconstituted order was founded for the purpose of strengthening the monarchy. As the age of exploration drew near, both the Templar knights and the Genoese seafarers still had a warm welcome in Portugal.

King Dinis I was Portugal's monarch when Philip IV and Pope Clement V declared war on the Templars. His country embraced this very early Renaissance man who brought about positive change in numerous ways. He established a university at Lisbon, in part because of his own love of literature, poetry, and writing. He was the prime mover for industry in his country, establishing commercial treaties with other nations. He promoted agriculture in Portugal as a way of resettling the country. For this he was affectionately dubbed "the Farmer."

At the same time, he did not like the autonomous control that the religious military orders enjoyed. The papal bull that disbanded the Knights Templar and gave away their assets played into Dinis's hands. After three years of limbo, during which he was the protector of the order, he became master of the Knights of Christ.

In exchange for direct control of the assets of the order, Templars in Portugal were free from the arrest and persecution others suffered in France. The new pope, John XXII, confirmed Dinis's new order and, interestingly enough, gave its religious rule to the Cistercian order, which had undergone no changes. The Knights Templar were alive and well in their new coastal home. Though the order itself unquestionably lost some autonomy, individual Templars, spared from arrest, torture, and death, were wholeheartedly grateful to the Portuguese king.

Historians have claimed that the province of Labrador was originally Lavrador, named for one of the sailors aboard Cartier's ship who might have been nicknamed *lavradore*, or "farmer." While the names of kings, queens, saints, and nobles grace the maps of the early navigators, few place-names were the result of an individual sailor. More likely, Labrador was named by a Portuguese Templar for King Dinis. Portuguese or Basque fishermen were certainly responsible for the word *baccaloas* (cod) being on maps drawn at the same time that Lavrador appears. Since the Phoenicians had settled along Portugal's Atlantic coast, the value of keeping secrets had been a tradition. Just how extensive the early voyages of Portugal were is something we may never resolve. The Templars kept secret their explorations as well, although for different reasons.

Thanks to the effort of the Farmer, the transition of both the country and the Templar order was rapid.

By the early fourteenth century, the Genoese were already trading in Morocco and exploring Africa, and a Genoese explorer had discovered the Fortunate Isles, now called the Canary Islands. Their renown may have served as a catalyst for King Dinis's invitation to a Genoese noble, Emmanuel Passagna, known as Manoel Pessanha in Portugal, to serve as the hereditary admiral for Portugal's navy. His title was lord high admiral of Lusitania. Passagna hired twenty Genoese as sea captains and pilots. He also invited several of Genoa's noble families to Portugal. As the navy expanded, with all the commanders coming from Genoa, so did the Genoese role in banking and trade. By the time Columbus washed up in Lisbon, the Genoese community had been established for more than 150 years.

In the fifteenth century, the most famous grand master of the reconstituted Templar order was Prince Henry the Navigator. He did much to increase the knowledge of the world, including sponsoring voyages around Africa and west into the Atlantic. When he started his navigation school at Sagres, he was in possession of many ancient maps, possibly recopied charts as old as the Phoenicians who had sailed around Africa. He was well read and his library contained works of Herodotus, Ptolemy, Strabo, and Pliny.[1] Henry recaptured the Muslim port of Ceuta and afterward settled down in his naval academy, never to sail again. His ships, however, began a series of explorations that would continue after his death.

The next grand master of the Knights of Christ was King Manuel I. He expanded Portuguese possessions in Africa and the East Indies, making the order the wealthiest in the Christian world.

Spain

The Reconquista in Spain is said to have begun nine years after the Muslim expansion ceased in the early eighth century. Islam had taken most of Spain in five years; it would take five hundred years to take it back. In the course of the wars, Christians fought Christians and Muslims fought Muslims. Between times, the long years of peace and the enlightened Islamic sciences brought Spain out of the Visigothic dark ages.

Universities opened in splendid Moorish cities, notably Córdoba, where Islamic and Hebrew scholars and philosophers brought back to Europe the higher education that had been missing since the classical days of Greece and Rome. A school of translators took works from Greece and translated them into Arabic, Hebrew, and finally Latin. Had it not been for the Muslim presence in medieval Europe, one can only wonder what secrets of the ancients would have been lost forever. Irrigation systems in place since the Romans were rebuilt; agriculture reached higher levels of production. Yet despite its high degree of tolerance, Islam was still an occupying force, and a factional one as well.

The Moorish caliphates also considered piracy just another occupation they could tolerate, and Muslim pirates nested on both sides of the Mediterranean Sea. The nadir for Christian Spain may have come when the Islamic vizier Almanzor sacked Leon in 996 and Saint James at Compostela the next year. This holy place ranked third in the world as a Christian pilgrimage destination after Jerusalem and Rome. The Cluniacs, who had a presence in Rome, responded by bringing in Norman adventurers, preceding the Cistercians and the Templar knights.

The Christian kings of Portugal and Spain invited the Templars to assist in turning back the Moors. When the Templars entered Spain, they began construction of castles and churches. In 1208, the Templars came to Segovia. Like Lisbon, the city was already ancient when the Romans arrived more than a thousand years before. Over Iberian foundations, the Romans constructed a circuit of walls to guard the city. The building started again in the eleventh and twelfth centuries, adding towers to protect the city. A Roman aqueduct dating to the first century A.D. still brings water from some ten miles away.

Outside the walls is the church of Vera Cruz (True Cross), a national monument. It began in 1208 as an early Templar church built on the model of the Church of the Holy Sepulchre. It still contains paintings from the thirteenth century. The area is rich in religious destinations, including the nearby convent of the Carmelite Friars, where the mystic Saint John was buried, and a pilgrimage church called the Virgin of Fuencisla.

In Calatayud, a little town near Zaragoza,* is the Templar Church of San Sepulcro. It was built in the twelfth century, somewhat earlier than the Segovia church. The smallness of the town does not reflect the significance it once had in guarding what was a major route from the south of France throughout the Pyrennees into Spain. Just outside of the town is the Cistercian-built Monesterio de Piedra, constructed at the same time as San Sepulcro. The area is a beautiful vacation spot with waterfalls, lakes, and caves.

When the Iberian crusades came to an end at the close of the thirteenth century, so did any tolerance. As in Portugal, Jewish residents were perceived as friendly to Islam and from city to city were expelled or massacred. Recurrent purges would last until the day Columbus sailed—when the expulsion was made official and nationwide. The Inquisition was set up by Isabella ostensibly to deal with the *conversos,* Jews who converted to Christianity to stay in Spain but who were not treating their new religion seriously. The Inquisition would later, of course, be turned against Christians, ostensibly for the same fault of failing to worship correctly. In reality, the Inquisition had always been about protecting the power of the Church.

Portugal turned its eye on the world; Spain's focus, however, was originally much more narrow.

The Templar Fleet

While Portugal was exploring for new lands and routes to the East, they were financing this exploration through trade. Both the Templars and the Genoese shared their expertise in trade with Portugal. To his credit,

---

*Zaragoza itself was once an important city of Spain. It began as an Iberian settlement called Salduba. When the Romans arrived, it was renamed Caesar Augusta, from which the present name was derived. The Visigoths arrived and controlled the city for nearly 250 years before being pushed out by the Moors. When the tide against the Islamic invasion turned, the kings of Aragon made it the principal residence.

Henry the Navigator, the son of King John of Portugal and Philippa of Lancaster,* took his role as grand master seriously. In the service of knowledge, he financed explorations around Africa and out into the Atlantic. To his discredit, much was financed by taking over the Arab lead in the African slave trade. Slavery had existed in Europe since Celtic and pre-Roman days, but the long-distance transportation of black slaves, which later expanded across the Atlantic, was Henry's innovation.

The Canary Islands were discovered (or rediscovered) by Europe early in the fourteenth century. In 1312 the Genoese explorer Lancelotto Malocelo attempted to colonize the easternmost island in the chain. He named the colony after himself, "Lanzarote," but his small expedition was not able to hold the island against the indigenous people called Guanches, who had been there for centuries and who had greater numbers if significantly less technology. To the Genoese, they were a persistent danger, like the "Skraelings" had been to the Vikings four centuries before. The Castilians would arrive in 1342 better prepared for war, wiping out the Guanches as a preview of the damage they would do to the "Indies." It was possibly the threat of losing the Atlantic isles to Spain that further motivated Portugal's race to discovery.

MADEIRA

Madeira was visible from the Canary Islands. In 1415, after Henry had established a foothold in Africa by taking the city of Ceuta, he retired to Sagres and established the school that became the new mecca for nautical knowledge. One of his captains was Bartolomeo Perestrello, an Italian whose family had come to Portugal a century earlier with the score of Genoese nobles invited by Lord Admiral Passagna. These Genoese nobles were admitted to the Knights of Christ order as knights. Perestrello, along with another knight, Tristao vaz Teixeira, was part of an expedition by João Goncalves Zarco to claim the Madeira chain in

---

*Portugal at the time was still in danger of being swallowed whole by Muslims in Africa or the warring kingdoms in Spain. Philippa of Lancaster was given to King John of Portugal to cement an alliance. She was the daughter of John of Gaunt, who was the brother of the Black Prince. The Portuguese king was reluctant to actually marry Philippa, but in 1387 the bargain was complete, as England threatened to cancel a loan. Portuguese and English merchant relations were not as cold.

1419. Henry rewarded the three knights with the titles of *capitanos,* or "hereditary governors," of Madeira. The Perestrello family would be responsible for Porto Santo in the Madeira chain.

It was no small honor, as a capitano could license all of the commercial activity on his island, including the baking of bread, the operating of mills, and the growing of agricultural products. Before the Americas were settled, Madeira's white gold was sugar, and slaves were imported to work on the plantations of the merchants who invested in sugar plantations. As important a commodity to Europe as tea would one day become—and as difficult to procure—sugar had been imported from India, where it was called *sakkara* in the Sanskrit language. The Arab merchants who transported it to Venice introduced it to Europe under the name *sukkar.* Venetian merchants acted as the middlemen, and their fleets carried the cash crop to the cities of Europe. The discovery of Madeira's ideal climate for sugar was no small benefit to the chain.

It was the Italian merchant families who first came to plant sugar. Commercial families who came from Genoa, and often made their headquarters in Seville, included Luis Doria, Antonio Spinola, Bautista and Urbano Lomellino, and Luis Centurione. The mills were built in the Sicilian fashion and the sugar was then exported to Flanders and England. Soon even Venice was buying sugar from Madeira.[2]

There was a grievous side to the business, the importation of black slaves to cut the cane. This gave rise to the plantation culture, which was exported to the New World.

The lands that Henry's exploring knights opened were quickly populated with slaves, owners, bankers, and traders. In the first half century of Madeira's new life as a Portuguese colony, eight hundred families moved there to start plantations, most paying fees to the three original capitanos.

One of the earliest colonists was a grandson of Henry Sinclair. Henry Sinclair's daughter Elizabeth had married John Drummond, uniting two of Scotland's most powerful families. English colonists were welcome in Madeira because the island chain enjoyed good relations with both mother Portugal and England. While Scotland and England were at odds, Portugal and Scotland had no ill feelings toward each other. In fact, they had much in common. Both had served as refuges for ex-Templars immediately following the order's dissolution, and both sent ex-Templars to the

Madeiras. Governing the early colonists were representatives of the Knights of Christ, who were joined by John Drummond, whose family was linked to the guardian of the Scottish Templars.

The first John Drummond on Madeira was the son of the master of Stobhall, John Drummond IV (1348–1428), who had married Elizabeth Sinclair. Significantly, John IV and Elizabeth Sinclair had signed a contract with Henry Sinclair on May 13, 1396, granting the couple Henry's claim to Norwegian property in case he did not return from his imminent expedition.[3] The couple were certainly aware of the Sinclair-Zeno voyage.

John IV and Elizabeth had vast estates in Scotland. They had a son Walter, and then a second son they named John (V). The elder John was also the nephew of Annabella Drummond, who married Robert III, king of Scotland. It is likely that John V's status as a second son would have left him without land, but it cannot be said for sure that this was the motivation that caused him to seek his fortune elsewhere. In any case, he left Scotland and went first to France, then arrived in Madeira the same year the Perestrello family settled on the island.

As one of the pioneering colonists, John Drummond prospered in his new home. He was dubbed John Escorcio, meaning "John the Scotsman," by the mostly Portuguese and Italian settlers. His first wife, Catarina vaz de Lordelo, had already been married to a relative of the Perestrello family. Later, John married Branca Afonso da Cunha and had at least six, possibly nine, children with her. Before long, this line of Drummonds had also married into the Perestrello family. Today the Drummond line, though split in two, still has two prominent lines tracing their ancestry back to the original John Drummond. One surname remains Drummond, the other, Escorcio, "the Scotsman."

Whether distance hindered the relations between the Scottish Drummonds and the Madeiran Drummonds for a time, we do not know. Because records are either nonexistent or were poorly kept, some interruption may have occurred. If so, it was brief. There is evidence of rekindled acquaintance in 1519 and much closer kinship in the early seventeenth century, when a Drummond was governor of Porto Santo.

From Madeira, not long after the voyage of Columbus to the Americas, many Portuguese moved on to Portugal's colony of Brazil, which was discovered by Pedro Alvares Cabral in 1500. Because the

French were also trading there, King John was in a hurry to establish his kingdom. He sold the three thousand miles of coastline to fourteen individuals who would act, like the Perestrellos in Madeira, as capitanos. Directly from the Drummond line in Madeira that began in the fifteenth century is Carlos Drummond de Andrate, one of Brazil's most outstanding twentieth-century poets.[4]

MADEIRA TO THE AZORES

In 1432 it was almost inevitable that the Azores would be rediscovered. The Phoenicians had been there in the sixth century B.C., and it is believed the Norse had reached the islands as well.[5] Although the islands were mostly forgotten for centuries, they did appear on an Italian map drawn in 1351. After Portugal's landing in 1431, Alfonso V gave them to his aunt, the duchess of Burgundy, and both Portuguese and Flemish settlers soon populated the islands.

Not all of the islands were immediately known, and the Portuguese explorer Diogo de Teive discovered Flores and Corvo in 1452. From Portugal to the Azores the distance was nine hundred miles, and from the westernmost island in the chain, Corvo, it was one thousand miles to Newfoundland. Diogo may have actually coasted Newfoundland. In 1447, the historian Antonio Galvao says a ship blown off course reached an island where the people were Christian and had a church.[6] Diogo may have been responsible for the Italian sword and Venetian earrings found among the Beothuk.

After the discovery of the Azorean chain, the Cape Verde Islands were next. They had been first spotted by a Venetian, Alvise Ca'da Mosto, sailing for Portugal in 1455. The were explored by Antonio Usodimare and a Genoese, Antonio di Noli, who served as governor until his death in 1496. From these islands, the Portuguese made successively longer expeditions down the coast of Africa until finally rounding the Cape of Good Hope and venturing into the Indian Ocean in 1488.

ENTER COLUMBUS

Even those who have tried to describe, rather than summarize, the role Columbus played in history have often oversimplified his life and the story of his explorations. The historian Samuel Morison, author of two books on the explorer, presents a good example. A young Genoese sailor is shipwrecked in Portugal. With his brother he opens a chart shop, where he regularly wines and dines a host of captains and pilots to increase his cartographic expertise. He soon becomes convinced that the world is round, and that Cathay lies a few weeks off the coast of Iberia. He travels and marries and is inspired by both to seek the assistance of the Portuguese king. Rejected, he moves to Spain, where he enlists Ferdinand and Isabella to sponsor his journey. Instead of Asia, he discovers America. While this story presents a broader picture than the one found in textbooks, the oversimplification at work even here has led many to believe that there were more dramatic and conspiratorial forces at work that led to the discovery of the New World.

It has often been claimed that Columbus was not Italian, but rather Castilian, Catalan, Corsican, Portuguese, Majorcan, or Jewish. The first claim may be taken as truth. Columbus was not Italian and did not write in Italian. He was Genoese. Centuries before Italy was unified as a country, it was inhabited by people who identified first with their extended family and second with the area in which they lived. Genoese did not always find kinship with Florentines or Venetians; in fact, they were often at odds. The Genoese dialect was quite removed from the Italian spoken in Rome. Columbus was educated first in and around Genoa. At an early age, he took to the sea.

On August 13, 1476, he was serving on one of five Flemish ships that were attacked by a small armada off the coast of Portugal. For this reason, some claim he was aboard a pirate ship, although the distinction between merchant and pirate was often blurry and could quickly change if the right opportunity arose. Legend has it that his ship was sunk and that he swam to Lagos. Having reached Portugal, he then made it to the Alfama district of Lisbon, where a brother who arrived earlier operated a chart shop.[7] The Alfama district had a notable Genoese community.

Thanks to the Knights of Christ, Portugal was the place to be to become knowledgeable in nautical skills. Columbus adapted quickly, and language never seemed to pose a barrier to the future explorer. Although he may have been able to write in his Genoese dialect, nothing he wrote prior to moving to Portugal has survived. The documents that we do have demonstrate a sort of pidgin that only a traveler would exhibit: part Portuguese, part Spanish, and grammar that was unconventional even in a time when syntax was not the exact science it later became. His Castilian dialect with Portuguese spelling does suggest he learned Portuguese first, then Spanish.[8]

This sequence makes sense. Even in Portugal, Spanish was the language of the educated class, and Latin better still. Columbus, as a seafarer and traveler, could probably get by in a handful of languages and dialects. He most likely spoke Genoa's dialect in Genoa and in the Genoese community of Lisbon, and Spanish aboard his voyages.

Facts and Theories

As complicated as Columbus's national affiliations may have been, his story presents much knottier problems. One of these may have been first brought to light with the 1940 publication of Salvador de Madariaga's *Christopher Columbus*. He insists the explorer was part of a converso family who were forced to convert or leave, and de Madariaga believes Columbus sought to create a homeland for the Jews in the New World. The evidence is flimsy at best and often insulting and stereotypical. The biographer claims that pidgin was commonplace among Jews, without pointing out that it is likely to be commonplace among any immigrant population in any era. Equally unfairly, Madariaga defines Columbus's interest in finding gold and precious stones in the New World as a Jewish trait. Using such flawed logic, nearly every explorer in North and South America and Asia must have been Jewish. Madariaga's last point is that Columbus left Spain on the same day that the Jews were expelled. Again, he misses a key point: Columbus and his crew came back.

As mentioned earlier, under Islamic rule the Jews had been provided protection in Iberia. Together with Muslim educators and cartographers, they had revived a knowledge of the world that had been either ignored or nearly suffocated by Christianity. The belief in a continent on the other side of the Atlantic was not regarded as heresy by the learned among Spain's Islamic and Jewish populations. Had Columbus made his case prior to Ferdinand's rule in Spain, he would not have been required to appear before the Inquisition, as it had just come into existence as an institution.

The end of the Reconquista was also the end of peace for the Jews in Spain and Portugal. Many went to Majorca, as the attitude toward

Jews was less intolerant there even though it was under the domination of King Ferdinand. In Majorca, mapmaking was an art and Jewish cartographers were masters of it. It is likely, therefore, that Columbus, as proprietor of a chart shop, had dealings with Jewish cartographers and traders.

There is, however, no evidence that he was actually Jewish. In fact, his very name works against this claim. Jewish parents in the fifteenth century often took biblical names for their children, but these were naturally Old Testament names. Christoforo, meaning "the Christ-bearer," would not be one of those. His brothers and sisters had typical Italian names, too—names of Christian saints. His mother's name, Susanna, although more typically Old Testament, implies little as its use was widespread in the period. Moreover, Columbus himself was devout and regularly attended church services, which is how he married into a family of Genoese expatriates who had immigrated to Portugal.

The flimsy evidence that Columbus was not Christian is based on the fact that many Jews were aboard ships on the same date that Columbus sailed for the New World. This is first coincidence and, second, the reason he left from Palos. Almost every port city in Spain had ships full of Jews ready to embark. Palos was one of the exceptions, and the Pinzon family of Palos owned both the *Pinta* and the *Niña*.

The less sensitive statements of Madariaga—concerning motivation for precious metals, Columbus's nose, and his ability to settle anywhere without allegiance[9]—could be made to fit quite a few Europeans of the fifteenth century. Genoese, in fact had settled in coastal cities in Spain, Portugal, England, and Africa. As merchants, they had the ability to assimilate, the desire to succeed, and an allegiance only to those with whom their business transactions took place.

Not all proponents of Columbus's Jewish heritage, however, can be so easily charged with maligning a people. Simon Wiesenthal, better known for his efforts in tracking Nazi war criminals, took time out to compile his own biography of Columbus and reiterated Madariaga's points concerning the prominent nose of the explorer and his "greed for gold," adding that many with the last name Colon are Jewish.[10] Again, the evidence applies equally well to other explorers. Columbus's Jewish heritage is simply a myth.

Yet Columbus did have a secret side. He developed his own unique signature that included an oversized *XPO* followed by the word *ferens* and a series of letters that are seemingly nonsensical. "Xpo ferens" referred to his spelling of his own name, "Christ-bearer." During Columbus's lifetime, the Saint Christopher myth was quite popular. Christopher is said to have been a Canaanite giant, a wild man who devoted his life to aiding pilgrims cross a river. One day he met up with a child who was such a burden that Christopher commented that he felt like he carried the whole world. The child was Christ, who replied to the giant that he had indeed just borne the weight of the world, as well as the one who had made it. This legend entitled Christopher to saint-hood until recently, when the Church reversed positions and said the story was simply that, a story. As the patron saint of travelers, Christopher still protects millions despite his reduced status.

The next letters, *S SAS,* are the initials of a motto in the admiral's mixed language: *Servus Sum Altissimi Salvatoris,* meaning "Servant, I am, to the Savior most high." This was followed by *XMY,* the initials of Christ, Mary, and Yago—Yago being San Iago or Santiago, whose name was rendered Saint James in English and who was the patron saint of Spain. The signature was not complete without still another coded reference, *SAM,* for Stella Ave Maris, the sailor's Star of the Sea and often a reference to the Blessed Virgin or the North Star. The entire signature could be an esoteric key to understanding the man.

The astronomer Adrian Gilbert points out the Saint Christopher tale actually describes the star Orion, which on May 9, the Eastern Church's feast day for Christopher, appears to carry the sun across that river in the sky, the Milky Way. Thus another myth reveals an accurate, complicated understanding of the scientific universe.[11]

It has been argued that the explorer's last name, Colombo in Genoese, was an invention. His son Ferdinand, who wrote the first biography of Columbus, declared that he chose his last name for its meaning, "dove," and because it was a symbol for Saint John the Baptist. The names of his parents, Domenico and Susanna (Fontanarossa) Colombo, however, have been documented, and even Ferdinand, later contradicting himself, says Christopher came from a line of seafarers, leaving his ancestry far from uncertain. Ferdinand's reference to Saint John the Baptist may bear some historical importance, hinting that Columbus was at least by marriage connected with the Templars' descendant order, the Knights of Christ. The Red Cross on his sails, a Templar symbol, may provide further confirmation.

As mythical as Columbus's Jewish heritage, although lacking any conspiratorial motive, is the story about Queen Isabella I pledging her jewels for Columbus's sake. The voyage of Columbus was financed by Luis de Santangel, the court treasurer, who entreated Francisco Pinello, a Genoese banker in Seville, to share the burden. The loan was made from the account of the police force that they comanaged. The expedition cost two million *maravedis,* and the Santa Hermandad, or Holy Brotherhood, a military police instituted to carry out Ferdinand's policies, put up 1.14 million. Columbus was required to contribute one quarter of the expedition, and for his 500,000 maravedis he went to the Florentine banker Juanoto Berardi.[12]

Iberia, particularly the coastal cities of Lisbon and Seville, were important trading centers between England and Ireland and the Mediterranean Sea. As the Islamic stronghold on sea trading was broken, the Italians quickly set up commercial outposts to take advantage. Some were very large houses and dealt in other commodities. Others, like Niccolo di Francesco Cambini's enterprise, specialized in a handful of select items, leather from Ireland, silk from Spain.[13] These smaller firms often represented the largest firms as well as trading for themselves. Juanoto Berardi operated throughout southern Europe as a representative for the Medici family. The voyage of Columbus and other ventures would eventually bankrupt him.

Portugal had a very close relationship with the Italian merchant cities. Both had seafaring and trading interests, and relations, especially with Genoa, were mutually beneficial. The import of Italian captains and commanders that had started with Emmanuel Passagna of Genoa ensured that Italians would play a long-term role in Portugal's commercial activities. Because of Passagna's influence, even the agents hired in Lisbon were mostly Genoese. They conducted trade with Flanders, Britain, and Africa. Portugal's navigators, too, benefited from knowledge from Italy. The Italian libraries held the classical writings on geography. Italian maps were the first to represent accurate distances. And Italian bankers made funds available for exploration.[14]

Columbus as a Genoese seafarer, therefore, was welcome in Portugal and especially, Lisbon, with its tight-knit community of Genoese. From

Lisbon, Columbus traveled in the employ of Genoese firms. In 1478 he made his first trip to Funchal, on Madeira, to pick up a cargo of sugar, but the Madeira merchants would not honor his letter of credit and he left empty-handed. The matter resulted in a legal case between the employers of Columbus and the Madeira merchants and Columbus visited Genoa the following year to testify. On August 21, 1479, he appeared in court and represented himself as a citizen of Genoa. He testified that he was in possession of one hundred florins, a considerable sum of money. Columbus stayed long enough to make up his will, employing the Bank of Saint George to act as executors. He then returned to Lisbon.[15]

Columbus and the Knights of Christ

One aspect of the life of Columbus that gets very little attention despite its significance is his marriage. Few biographies allow this important union more than a page, yet it was most likely the catalyst that propelled the explorer on the road west.

Columbus met his wife while attending Mass at the Monastery of All Saints. Part of the monastery was a convent to which the nobility sent their daughters for schooling and part was a chapel where Mass was said. It was not far from the mapmaking shop of the Columbus brothers.

Her name was doña Felipa Perestrello e Moniz. She was from noble breeding on both her father's and her mother's side. The mother's side was the Moniz family. She was a granddaughter of Gil Moniz, a knight rewarded with a governorship by Prince Henry the Navigator, his lifetime companion. The Moniz family was one of the wealthiest on Portugal's Algarve. Felipa's father's side was the Perestrello family of Genoa, who had settled in Portugal during the reign of John I and become the Perestrellos of Portugal. The children of the first Perestrello included Isabel and Branca, both of whom became romantically linked with the archbishop of Lisbon, don Pedro de Noronha, and bore his children, legitimized by decree. One of don Pedro's daughters married into the Braganza family. Three sons would rise in church and in politics.[16]

Felipa's father was Bartolomeo Perestrello, capitano of Madeira. She was possibly named for Philippa of Lancaster, the bride of the Portuguese king and the mother of Prince Henry the Navigator. Her sister, Briolanja, married into the wealthy Bardi family of Florence.

Columbus and his bride's family had a common origin in the Piacenza area outside Genoa. Biographers of Columbus often question how the mariner had married so well. He had connections to wealthy Italian families, although no wealth himself. But Felipa and family may have enjoyed the spirit of the future explorer and his connection to their home city of Genoa. For Columbus it may have been a marriage of love; it would certainly have been a pleasure to meet someone from the area where he had been born. One cannot help but wonder, however, if Felipa's family standing had anything to do with his affection. The marriage made Columbus a Portuguese citizen, and gave him the right to trade everywhere that Portugal could. The Perestrello family was also deeply connected to the surviving order of the Knights Templar, the Knights of Christ. To what degree this relationship broadened his horizons is a question worth considering.

For Columbus, everything was going well and would get even better. He moved with his new bride and her mother to Porto Santo, where Bartolomeo Perestrello had been governor until his death. Now Felipa's brother had taken over the office. According to Fernando, Columbus's son, Felipa's mother made Columbus a most precious gift: her late husband's maps, sea charts, and journals. Columbus was free to spend all the time he needed in the library of one of Portugal's first explorers. Columbus was now privy not only to the practical knowledge held by a captain of Henry the Navigator, but also to the navigational secrets of the Knights Templar and Knights of Christ.

Just how important this is cannot be overemphasized. The Templar knights, when not warring with Islam, were busy learning from Islam. Arab sailors, even from pre-Islamic times, were trading extensively in Africa and across the Indian Ocean. Adept at navigation and with a seafaring heritage born in prehistory, they had copied and recopied charts from Phoenician times. Before the Vikings reached Iceland, Arab traders were in China and as far as Korea, bringing home silk, camphor, musk, and spices.[17]

Like all seafarers, they guarded their knowledge, but not everything could be kept secret. From Morocco to Mozambique they used a lateen, a triangular, tall, high-peaked sail that provided balance and captured the winds. The Arab word *mīzān* means balance. The Italians called the sail *mezzana,* and the English corrupted the word further to *mizzen.*

Before the mizzen sail reached Europe, long voyages were at the mercy of the winds, and transoceanic sailors were subject to a problem recorded in Greek tales: being stuck for weeks because of inadequate wind. The mizzen sail, copied from the Arab ships during the Crusades, made sailors much less dependent on strong winds.

One of the earliest texts on long-distance travel by sea is the *Periplus of the Erythraean Sea*. It was written by a Greek sailor, who remains unnamed, and recorded at the time when the Christian Gospels were written. *Periplus* roughly translates to "sailing past," and the manuscript is a travelogue of the Red Sea and the Indian Ocean. It reports on cities and seaports, sailing conditions, products available, and the best time to sail. Such records were preserved by Islamic sea traders, as were secret maps.

Other volumes that Columbus read included the Roman and Greek texts of Pliny, Strabo, and Marinus. Marinus divided the globe into twenty-four hours of distance, and Columbus reckoned it was eight such "hours" from Cape Verde, which had been recently discovered, to Asia. Strabo believed Asia could be found by crossing the Atlantic; Aristotle and Seneca concurred. Gaius Julius Solinus, a third-century Roman, claimed the "Indies" were forty days sailing time from the Islands of the Gorgons (Cape Verde). Remarkably, Aristotle even claimed that a "Land of Cod" existed near a fertile island in the Atlantic.[18]

Columbus and the Sinclair–Drummond Connection

It was in Madeira that Columbus made his decision to cross the Atlantic. Prior to his marriage he had made several voyages, even one past Iceland in 1477. Just after his marriage he traveled to Africa. These voyages increased his knowledge firsthand. He also had the navigational records of the Knights of Christ and a wealth of connections through the Perestrello family.

As if that was not enough, he was also related to the family of John Drummond, because the son of John the Scotsman married into the extended Perestrello family. Although there are no records of the extent of their relationship, they most certainly met while on the island. Columbus lived briefly on Funchal, the main island, and then on Porto Santo, the Perestrello home island. His only son by Felipa, Diego, was born there. On the fairly remote and sparsely populated island outpost, both the birth and subsequent baptism would have drawn the family to celebrate, a welcome respite from overlooking agricultural enterprises. Christopher and Felipa would have certainly raised a glass to their child's health with Perestrellos and Drummonds.

Columbus had married into an extended family that brought together a great deal of knowledge of exploration and travel. Did John Drummond, the grandson of Henry Sinclair, and his wife share the knowledge of Henry's expeditions in the New World with Columbus? The Sinclair line had no doubt been aware of the Norse adventurers who reached islands to the west. The western lands discovered by the Norse did not hold the same promise of wealth that India and China did; however, there were other economic motivations, namely cod fishing.

By the time he set sail, Columbus had already made a journey to Bristol, England. Bristol, as mentioned, was a vital trading center where Spanish wine was traded for Icelandic cod. The Hanseatic League had attempted to cut off Bristol from trading with Iceland, so Bristol merchants and customs officials formed a partnership to seek other sources for cod, claiming all the while that they were searching for the elusive island of Hy-Brasil. Tellingly, when the Hanseatic League reversed its course and offered Bristol a share in the Iceland trade, the Bristol traders were no longer interested.

In his book *Cod,* Mark Kurlansky relates the story of the John Jay–Thomas Croft partnership and notes that the merchants were bringing their fish home dried. As that operation cannot be performed on a ship, they must have had a secret landing in the New World. Like the Basques, who may have been there earlier, fishermen keep secrets.[19] Columbus, on his voyage to Bristol, was not privy to such secrets, although he may have asked the right question. Just where were the rich fishing grounds to the west?

On his voyage beyond Iceland, Columbus was once again in the company of captains and pilots who had been in the waters of the North Atlantic for years. When Columbus and his brother operated their chart shop in Portugal, it had been his modus operandi to take visiting captains and pilots to dinner, where he would ply his guests with hospitality and hope to pry loose their navigational secrets. This inquisitive Columbus certainly returned from his visits north with some knowledge of the Norse who had landed on the North American continent long before he would reach the "Indies."

Let in on the secrets of the Portuguese Knights of Christ and their explorations, Columbus learned that Portugal's king, Alfonso V, had been corresponding with a Florentine cosmographer, Paolo dal Pozzo Toscanelli. A letter to the king dated June 25, 1474, proposed a shorter, direct route to Asia and so-called Cipangu, based on his study of Marco Polo's adventures. Toscanelli sent along with his letter a map of the Atlantic Ocean. Columbus was made aware of the letter in 1480, shortly after his marriage, and began a correspondence with Toscanelli of his own.

In 1482 he was part of the Diogo d'Azambuja expedition to Africa's Gold Coast, which was mounted by Portugal's king. After this voyage, Columbus calculated it was time to propose his journey to the lands across the Atlantic. It was 1484.

It is unknown just what evidence gave Columbus the greatest motivation to sail west, but the tale that he wanted to disprove the idea of a flat earth is just another myth. From access to his then modern charts and somewhat ancient books, to the library of the Perestrello family, to his own firsthand exploration and numerous interviews, Columbus was convinced that land lay beyond the setting sun and ready to make his own expedition. He was also well read in an age when the printing press had just been invented. Columbus was familiar with Seneca's *Medea,* in which is made the prophecy that one day the ocean would be crossed. He kept Pierre d'Ailly's *Imago Mundi* at his bedside, a text that referenced an estimated distance of the western ocean. He read Pope Pius II's *Historia Rerum Ubique Gestarum,* which also included references to just how far it was over the Atlantic to land. The conclusion that land could be reached across the Atlantic was obviously not new, although the acceptance of such claims was far from universal. What was new was that Columbus declared it was Asia, or "the Indies," that could be reached.

By the Light of Stella Maris

As a citizen of Portugal, Columbus applied first to the Portuguese crown. The Portuguese king John referred him to a maritime board, which rejected the idea. They claimed his notion of finding Cathay to the west was as mythical as Marco Polo's notion of an island called Cipangu, which of course later proved to be the real island of Japan.

Another possibility is that those privy to the information gathered by Portugal's explorers, adventurers, and even commercial fishermen understood that there were lands in the west, but they were not the fabled Asian lands sought by Columbus. Because from Corvo in the Azores they were only a thousand miles from Canada, and knew their fishermen were making the trip for cod to Canadian waters, they understood what to expect over the western horizon. Some in Portugal may have even had information as early as the eighth century.

When the Moors reached Iberia at that time, seven bishops were said to have left for western islands. In the far Atlantic they settled Antillia, calling it that after two Portuguese words, *anti* and *ilha*. It was the "opposite island." The Benhaim globe of 1492 carried the legend of one bishop of Porto in Portugal leading six others. Portugal was aware of this supposed colony and so was Columbus. His son Ferdinand recalled a 1430 Portuguese crew that landed on Antillia, attended church, and then headed home. In 1452, thirty years before Columbus applied for his expedition, the Portuguese king sent Diogo de Teive to search for "Anti-ilha." The voyage, like much of Portuguese exploration, may have been intentionally kept secret. Bartolome de Las Casas recorded the story in his *Historia de las Indias,* and because of the description it is possible that Teive reached the Grand Banks. It was he who on his way home rediscovered Corvo, the farthest in the Azore chain from Europe, the closest to Canada. It is possible that he too should be listed along with the numerous other "discoverers." After Teive's voyage, at least eight other Portuguese expeditions searched for Anti-ilha. It was recorded on numerous maps and even a point in the Treaty of Evora with Spain.[20]

By the time Columbus proposed his expedition, Portugal may have already understood that any western route would be interrupted by a vast continent. Unlike Columbus, they knew what was opposite Europe, and it was not Asia. This fact did not end their thirst for exploration, but the desire for Asian silk and spices was more vital.

There may be a third reason that Columbus's application was rejected. In 1485, as Portugal's maritime board was considering whether to approve the plan, Felipa died. Although Columbus may have considered Madeira home, her family wanted her to be laid to rest in the Carmen Monastery in Lisbon. He might have left his home forever at this point, although he was welcomed to Madeira years later en route to his third expedition to America.

Columbus had been allowed access to the Perestrello papers for five years, but he had known in advance that marriage into the family gave him no rights. Felipa's death may have meant a sort of divorce from her family as well, which would mean losing any influence he had held as a member of the Perestrello-Moniz family. Had Felipa survived, it is possible that with the support of the Perestrello family Columbus's plan would have been approved and the flag of Portugal would have been the first planted in the New World.

No longer a part of the Perestrello family, however, and turned down by Portugal's king, Columbus left the country. In 1485 he moved to Spain, while his brother Bartolomeo sought support for their mission in France and England. It took Columbus a year to get an appointment to meet Isabella I. She then had him make his case to her own maritime commission, which kept Columbus waiting for two years. He tried the king of Portugal again. The sailors in the employ of the Portuguese king, however, had just returned with news of passing the Cape of Good Hope, and Columbus returned to Spain. After a second refusal, it was Luis Santangel who moved the queen to change her mind.

With his backer's money, Columbus procured three ships, the *Niña,* the *Pinta,* and the *Santa María.** A four-hundred-page document titled the *Libro de Armadas* referred to the *Niña* as "also known as the Santa Clara."[21] Did Columbus still owe a debt of gratitude for knowledge he gained of the St. Clair expedition?

The three ships took on board a crew of locals. They are often described as convicts, and the story goes that Columbus could not find anyone else brave enough to sail west. These assertions are simply untrue.[23] Of Columbus's crew, all but four were Spanish mariners hired in Palos. The foreigners were Juan Arias of Portugal, Jacome el Rico of Genoa, Anton Calabres of Calabria, and Juan Vecano of Venice.

---

*The family of Columbus is rarely written about, outside of the attempts he and his son, Ferdinand, made to get a share of the gold and silver brought home. He did get a share, although less than the amount he had hoped for. It may have been enough to pass through successive generations however. One of his heirs, a five times great-granddaughter, Catarina Ventura de Portugal y Avala, married into the Scottish Stuart dynasty in 1716. Her husband, James Francis Stuart, was a grandson of James II.[22]

Did Columbus present his real intention to those he petitioned? If he had been hoping to discover a faster route to China and India, it would seem that he would have left laden with goods to trade. Into the land of rich silks and expensive spices, what gifts did the Genoese trader stock? His ships were filled with red caps, glass beads, and hawks bells. These trinkets impressed the semiclothed natives of the Caribbean islands, but it would seem that he was ill prepared to conduct serious trade. Gavin Menzies, a navigation expert and former Royal Navy submarine commander, writing on the worldwide explorations in 1421 by the Chinese, claimed that Columbus's calculations of latitude were inaccurate. If correct, he claims Columbus would have landed on Nova Scotia, indicating that he was actually heading elsewhere or that he was a very poor navigator.[24]

His voyage, of course, did not reach India or China; instead he discovered islands in the Caribbean. There he met up with native Arawak whose *canoa* could hold forty-five men. The word *canoe* in English came to mean a very small craft, but the canoa held almost twice the number of men aboard either the *Niña* or the *Pinta*.

The 1492 voyage of Columbus ended in March of 1493, when he was forced to land in Portugal. The king was gracious, but concerned that he had made such a great mistake. His courtiers urged him to assassinate Columbus.[25]

Nevertheless, he ultimately made three other voyages to the world he discovered, and suffered Spain's ingratitude to the point that he felt cheated. On returning home in chains on one voyage, he had time to write a very odd text called the *Book of Prophecies*. In it, he claimed he was the new Saint John the Baptist preparing the way for the Christ. As the Christ-bearer, he brought the *Niña* (the child) to the New World. The reason the *Niña* might have been known as the Santa Clara was that the Child was also the Sacred Light, in this case the sun. He also brought the *Santa María,* the Mother of the Child.

He declared that the Stella Maris stands in heaven between two guards, his namesake, Saint Christopher, and Saint James.[26] The Stella Maris, which may have shined for sailors long before Christianity, represents the Blessed Virgin: It is one of her many titles. The star is actually Spica, one of the brightest in the constellation Virgo. As we shall see in chapter 8, Virgo played a very critical role in Masonic planning of cities and is connected with the Egyptian goddess Isis.[27] Columbus, with his Knights Templar–Knights of Christ connection, may have been aware of the significance of such concepts of the stars and sacred geometry, but until the eighteenth century this was knowledge for the privileged few. Was Columbus part of the initiate? The Knights of Columbus founded four hundred years later called him "a mystic of the highest order."

He died in his home neither poor nor alone, but most likely suffering from Reiter's syndrome, which is caused by acute and chronic dysentery.

Evidence of Previous Discovery

For their part, the Spanish derided the explorer who brought their flag to the New World. The Portuguese were silent. Both debated their own role in the newly discovered lands.

When Columbus made his fourth trip to the New World, he encountered a galley larger than his own. It was similar to Mediterranean galleys, but the crew aboard, men and women, wore sleeveless cotton shirts with intricate designs. It is possible the crew were from the other Atlantic islands and could have been of Portuguese descent. Although it is possible that Portuguese ships followed quickly after the first voyage of Columbus, could Portuguese crews have arrived first? With numerous expeditions being made with the king's approval, and certainly others that were unknown except to fishermen, it is a distinct possibility.

From the Carolinas to western Virginia is a group of people who just do not fit neatly into any category of ethnicity or race. These people are darker skinned than Europeans in general, but they have European facial characteristics. Some of the earliest colonial Americans to come in contact with them reported that they were not black but were different from both Native Americans and Europeans. One English writer, James Needham, described them as "hairy," with whiskers and beards, wearing clothes, and living in log cabins. They claimed to be of Portuguese and sometimes of Moorish descent.

The most accepted theory is that they were Portuguese who reached America before Columbus. Some say they were Templars who, fearing the worst, headed west across the Atlantic in the early fourteenth century. They sported long beards, uncommon among Native Americans and very common among Templar knights. The discovery of the Hebrew Bar-Kokhba coins near a Melungeon settlement could be a hint that they had had at least Middle East contact. When they were discovered in Appalachian villages by English explorers, some were able to communicate in broken (Elizabethan) English.

Gene-frequency studies indicate that the Melungeons have much in common with Canary Islanders, Italians, and Portuguese. In addition, they suffered from a handful of diseases, including Machado-Joseph (Azorean) disease and familial Mediterranean fever, most common to those groups, thus confirming this unusual descent. Most had intermarried with Native Americans and black slaves to complicate the mix. If they are descended from fourteenth-century Templars, they could have crossed the Atlantic, then lost contact with any Europeans for as long as two hundred years. If they were fifteenth-century Portuguese, they could be a lost expedition sponsored by Prince Henry's Knights of Christ.

The historian Samuel Williams, writing on the early history of Tennessee, described a six-foot bell that one group of Melungeons owned. They rang the bell twice a day and then congregated. The Europeans had no idea what language they were speaking, but sensed a distinctly Christian air to their practices.

This is not the only incidence of odd groups of people turning up in colonial America. In 1650 merchant Edward Bland reached the area that was later divided into the Virginias and Carolinas.[28] He heard that there was a white tribe called the Mandoag that could be the result of another failed colony. Although he never found them, there were reports that they actually mined copper west of modern-day Chapel Hill, North Carolina. Their name may be Algonquian for "people who dig in the earth."[29] Perhaps they were descended from the 1587 Roanoke colony that waited for years for a relief ship or from an even earlier, unrecorded crossing. Paolo Marana, an Italian traveler in the Americas, heard of the Doeg tribe as being descendants of the Welsh.

It is possible that the Mandoag were in America even earlier, as the legend of Prince Madoc tells of a Welsh colony being established six hundred years before the Virginias. Settlers of both the Doeg and the Mandoag may have spoken Welsh or a Cornish dialect. Thomas Jefferson, Daniel Boone, and Francis Lewis, son of a signer of the Declaration of Independence, all described the Welsh-speaking Native Americans. In 1832 George Caitlin painted the pale-faced tribe with gray hair, beards, and blue eyes.

There is little reason to exclude the possible prior contacts: Pre-colonial American history no longer fits into a neat package. Vikings, Portuguese, Basques, and others certainly preceded Columbus. None of these considered North America a new world, but rather a secret one they were all too happy to keep secret. Columbus wanted publicity, and he achieved it. Because of his voyages, the New World was born in the European imagination—although it would not bear his name.

NEW WORLDS

The voyage of Columbus is not the story of the discovery of America as much as it is the story of uncovering lands to the west. For centuries they were known as rich fishing banks or, better for some, refuge from the wars and intolerance of Europe. Columbus tore off the veil of secrecy that had kept the West hidden. He had not, however, found the route to Cathay and the Indies he sought. Others found entirely different reasons to sail west across the Atlantic.

America

Amerigo Vespucci was born in March 1454, three years after Columbus. His family was both respected and influential in aristocratic Florence, one of Italy's most powerful cities. The Vespucci family was at the center of the Renaissance and played host and sometimes patron to such Renaissance pillars as Michelangelo, Botticelli, and Leonardo da Vinci. Amerigo's father commissioned Domenico Ghirlandaio to paint a family portrait that would hang on a wall in a Vespucci-built church. He received his education from an uncle, Giorgio Antonio, who tutored the children of the nobility of Florence at the convent of San Marco. One such noble was René II. Son of René the Good and Iolande de Bar, René was the future duke of Lorraine.

René II held several other titles as well. He was the count of Bar, of Guise, of Piedmont, and of Provence. He was the duke of Calabria and Anjou. He was the king of Aragon, Naples and Sicily, and Hungary. He held the title, albeit an empty one, of king of Jerusalem. He is also believed to have been a grand master in the Priory of Sion.[30] After his death, his daughter held that same title. Father and daughter, as well as René III, played a number of distinctly behind-the-scenes roles in

European history, including influencing the rise of Joan of Arc and building on the theme of an Arcadian paradise. His connection to Vespucci may have influenced getting Amerigo's name, rather than that of Columbus, on the map.

Vespucci studied literature in Latin and went on to the sciences of geometry, astronomy, and physics. It was a time when few enjoyed the luxury of reading the classics because they were too expensive. It is recorded, for example, that the bishop of Barcelona once paid a house and a piece of land for two volumes of Priscian.[31] As a Vespucci, Amerigo had access to books and maps that were available to only a handful. His uncle Giorgio was a collector of manuscripts and the owner of a well-stocked library, later presented to the Medici family. Vespucci also had access to Florence's most learned scholars, one of whom was Paolo Toscanelli, the director of Giorgio's library at San Marco. Toscanelli was Europe's greatest cosmographer and the map and chart collector whose correspondence with Columbus greatly influenced the explorer.

As a result of his father's death, Amerigo, still a young man, joined the business of the Medici family in the employ of Lorenzo and Giovanni. He was assigned to work in Paris under another uncle, Guido Vespucci, who served as Florence's ambassador. He renewed his acquaintance with René II, the duke of Lorraine, at this time.

In November 1491, Vespucci was sent to Seville for the Medicis. He was assigned to Medici banker Giannetto (Juanoto) Berardi, the merchant who financially backed Columbus. Vespucci struck out on his own as well, supplying ships, involving himself in both trade and exploration, and soon becoming one of Seville's largest outfitters of ships.[32] When Berardi's business was liquidated (in part because of his connection to Columbus), Vespucci handled the liquidation and saw to it that one of Columbus's debts disappeared. There was no lack of respect between the two.

Vespucci made his first voyage from Spain in 1499 and a second for the king of Portugal two years later. He found the Portuguese ships to be faster and stronger than the Spanish ships, and it is possible he found dealing with the Portuguese sailors easier than with the Spaniards. Relations between the Iberian states were apparently friendly at the time. Even after his voyage for Portugal, he was naturalized as a Spanish citizen by royal decree and made the pilot a major shortly afterward.

On his first voyage he gave Venezuela its name, after the Italian city of Venice. On his second, he headed straight for Brazil, and after exploring its long coast called it a new continent. In 1504–5, his letters recounting his explorations were in great demand. He not only described the new lands and immense rivers, but also went into great detail about the lustful women. The narratives were printed, copied and recopied, and circulated throughout Europe. Two important documents may have actually been forged. According to one account, Piero Soderini, a friend of Vespucci's, was annoyed that Vespucci wrote to the Medici family first, so he invented a letter from Vespucci to himself.[33] By most accounts, Vespucci made two voyages, although the Soderini letters tell of four.

A copy of the letter "sent" to Piero Soderini reached René II, the duke of Lorraine, who turned over the letter to his monks at the ancient monastery of Saint-Die in the Vosges. They possessed one of possibly two hundred of Europe's fine new inventions, the printing press. (It was just fifty years after the first press had printed the Gutenberg Bible.)

The monks put aside their work to produce a 103-page book of Vespucci's travels, along with a summary of principles of geography and cartography. Martin Waldseemüller is given the most credit for the work because he was a mapmaker and illustrator,[34] but the writing was in the hands of two poets, the German Mattias Ringmann and Jean Basin de Sandaucourt. They explained that the three known continents—Europa, Asia, and Africa—were named after women, so a female name should be given to the New World. It was not explained why this name would be America and not Columbia. It may be simply that Duke René was repaying a kindness. His tutor had been Georges Antoine Vespucci.

Arcadia

Another Italian served as the catalyst for a future transatlantic exploration, although he was not an explorer himself, but a poet. Jacopo Sannazaro was born in Naples in 1458. He studied classic literature and had the Aragonese princes as his patrons. When Frederick III of Naples, his primary patron, moved to Tours, so did Sannazaro, there writing under the name Sincerus. He was most influenced by Virgil, and authored poems and sonnets developed from his style. He was moved by the way Virgil blended the classic Roman era with pagan themes to create an idyllic world. Modern Europe manifested no such Golden Age. The Church violently suppressed anything that hinted at heresy, and Christian warred with Christian everywhere.

Sannazaro was regarded as a devout Catholic, but he openly criticized the pope and the Church's princes, and he blended the gods and goddesses of an ancient pagan past into his prose. In much of Europe this may still have been dangerous. But Florence was different. While artists risked prison elsewhere, here their freedom of expression was welcome. Liberty was the rule and every man had the right to become a guild member and a citizen. In comparison, Venice had a population three times the size but limited citizenship to two hundred families. In Florence's unshackled climate, literature could flourish.

Sannazaro's *Arcadia* was first published in 1502, and it received so much attention throughout Europe that not two years would go by in the entire sixteenth century without a new edition being printed. The book was so popular that the Tuscan dialect in which it was composed eventually eclipsed others to become the official language of a divided Italy.

Sannazaro captured the mood of his time, and although other mixtures of prose and verse were popular, he soared above the rest. In one sense, he recaptured elements of Grail literature and added the romance of the dawning humanist era. For three hundred years the style and themes of *Arcadia* would be built upon by other writers. Pastoral romances such as *Arcadia,* by Sidney; *Diana,* by Montemayor; and *La Bergerie,* by Belleau soon followed. Yet there was more to Sannazaro's work than a desire to return to paradise. Sannazaro incorporated into *Arcadia* a theme that was woven into the academies of Italy, that of the "underground stream" of knowledge—blending Pythagorean, Gnostic, Hermetic, and Kabbalistic teachings into the idea of a higher secret knowledge accessible only to the initiate. Sannazaro did not invent the pastoral style and themes; the body of writing that would follow, however, was labeled Arcadian.

In France, he came across a literary treasure trove, discovering lost and unknown works of Latin poets. As Sannazaro devoted himself to these texts, his *Arcadia* was pirated to Venice, where it was published without his knowledge. After the death of his patron, Sannazaro returned to Naples and published *Arcadia* again.

Giovanni da Verrazano was one who was deeply influenced by *Arcadia*. It is possible that within the text were messages that took on a different meaning to those who were able to understand them. Ten parts are tedious passages of sorcery, potions, and magic that have little merit compared to the dominant tale of lost love. The inclusion of an underground stream in the plot, however, may have conveyed that a secret knowledge was being transmitted. Sannazaro's description of the tomb of Massilia and the shepherds who lament her death became part of the Rennes-le-Château mystery four hundred years later. Sannazaro's often repeated line, "et in Arcadia ego" (and in Arcadia I am), was inscribed on the weathered tomb in a painting by Nicolas Poussin that one Father Saunière, the priest whose role was central to the Rennes-le-Château mystery, hurried to Paris to see. According to *Holy Blood, Holy Grail*,[35] the image of the underground stream "assumed obsessive proportions" to some powerful families including Medicis, Estes, Sforzas, and others from the north of Italy.

Apparently Verrazano was one of the initiates. Like Columbus, he may have been deserving of the title Mystic of the Highest Order. Verrazano brought Sannazaro's text to France and sold Francis I on the idea that there actually was an Arcadia. It had been settled and colonized by the Knights Templar and was in the New World. Like Arthur at rest in his mystical Avalon, so was France's greatest order. The tale had a powerful effect on the king.

7

The Secret Mission
of Verrazano

 THE MAN WHO CONVINCED the king of France to search for Arcadia was Giovanni da Verrazano. He was born into an Italian family at Val di Greve near Florence in 1485. The family's ancestral home, Castel Verrazano, is built on the foundation of a Roman structure that was in turn built on the foundation of an Etruscan structure, dating possibly to 500 B.C.

Verrazano played a mysterious role in the history of the exploration of the New World. His adventure in coasting the North American continent might have given France a claim to the new world, yet before he visited the French king, France had shown little interest in colonization, and did not do much afterward to press any such claim. As the seeker of a route to China, Verrazano avoided sailing into the Chesapeake Bay, the Delaware Bay, or up the Hudson. Where he claimed the Pacific could be reached over a narrow piece of land, he did not stop even to look. His voyage had an ulterior purpose.

VERRAZANO'S WORLD

Voyages with motives beyond those expressly named were not unusual. The mission of Sir Francis Drake was to circumnavigate the world but Queen Elizabeth really bestowed her blessing on his piratical attacks on the Spanish fleets. Merchants of Bristol sailed ostensibly to discover western lands but were prepared to pack in a haul of cod from a territory Hansa sought to monopolize. Such secrets were not kept well enough to avoid suspicion.

Verrazano, however, did keep his secret. His charts and his letter to the French monarch give only hints to why he sailed and what he uncovered.

He was the right man for the job. He was born into wealth and connections during the finest years of the Renaissance and in the city that fostered the birth of new ideas. But some of the new ideas and knowledge understood by the explorer and his family were not meant to be shared. Historians have very little to say about one of America's key explorers, testament to his having kept his secrets. To unravel the mystery of the man, one has to start in the city of his birth.

Gnostic Florence

Florence from the eleventh century on was a center of commerce for banking and for the wool and silk industry, employing about one third of the citizens in the cloth industry. For all the turmoil caused by Medici maneuvering, Florence was clearly a beneficiary. It had paved roads extending out of the city to a well-traveled trade route into France. Within Italy it was a crossroads city in the north, between Venice and Genoa and, more important, between Venice and France. Culturally, the city became the center of the Italian Renaissance. Dante was a Florentine, as were Donatello and Fra Angelico. Petrarch and Boccaccio were sons of Florentines. A legion of artists were incubated under the patronage of Florence's wealthy. Leonardo da Vinci, the exemplar of Florentine achievement, is linked permanently to the city's patron saint. His last painting was of Saint John the Baptist, as was his one work of sculpture.

Florence was also a religious crossroads. The Cathar movement was reaching throughout northern Italy, although its suppression there was nothing like the wholesale slaughter in the Languedoc, perhaps because the religion stayed underground to avoid controversy. As contraband, the new Gnostic teachings traveled with silk and wool on the road from Venice to Lyon.

It is most likely not coincidental that the patron saint of the city is Saint John the Baptist. Florence even minted coins with the saint and the emblem of the city, the lily. The florin replaced the silver penny of the Carolingians throughout Europe. The Medici family, who played a great role in the electing and disposing of popes, installed one of their own as Leo X. Leo carried with him the finger of Saint John as a talisman of his power.

As crusaders looted the works preserved in the East, a text called the *Corpus Hermeticum* was brought to Florence in 1453. It was believed that it had been written by Hermes Trismegistus, or even by Thoth, the Egyptian god of science and writing. In another city it might have been burned, but Cosimo Medici ordered that other translations be halted until the text could be deciphered. It proved to be nothing short of the secrets of Egyptian architecture and the geometry of the ancients, and it became one of the key texts in the Gnostic religion.

Florence already had been captivated by such ancient knowledge. In a fashion that later had Masonic overtones, the city had been laid out in four quarters. Each quarter had four wards, and they were named for mystical symbols, including keys, dragons, and unicorns. The center of the city was San Giovanni, Saint John.

It was understood by Florentines that the symbol of Saint John and the symbol of the goddess Venus was the same, the dove. Another of her symbols was the scallop shell, which was shared with the ancient goddess Brigit (and with Saint James in Compostela as well). Botticelli painted his famous Venus rising from the sea in a scallop shell using Simonetta Vespucci, the cousin of Amerigo, as his model. That image proclaimed that the ancient still had a place in the modern world.

The greatest secret of the Florentines, including the Verrazano family, was that whatever mystical leanings and beliefs were held within the city could be hidden in plain sight. The family crest of Verrazano is an example. It began as the same six-pointed star that could be found in the windows of churches in southern France and evolved into an eight-pointed star after his journey to the New Arcadia.[1]

The six-pointed star did not come to symbolize the Star of David until the seventeeth century. Long before that, it had a much different connotation. The triangle pointing up overlaid on a triangle pointing down represented what would become a Masonic creed: As Above, So Below. It is depicted on Masonic aprons as the square and the compass: the *A* without the bar over the *V.* Doubly useful, this symbol also stood for "Ave Maria," the words Gabriel used to announce to the Blessed Virgin she was with the Child of God. The number six itself had been a masculine symbol for the sun, as the number five and the pentagram had been female symbols for the moon. In Egypt six was the number of Ra, the deity of the Sun.

Five in becoming six creates time and space.[2] Our measurements used in dividing time have been based on six from the beginning of time. The ancient symbol for volume is the six-sided cube. Six was the event in which harmony exists as male and female principle come together.* It was an understanding present in early Christianity, but was later repressed in Roman Christianity as the female was pushed out of the equation.

The city of the lily and the dove was an Arcadia in itself until the backlash of the Church. The reincarnation of the vicious persecution of the Cathars that had begun in Lyon, Carcassonne, and a handful of other cities arose again when an Inquisitor was sent to Florence. Languedoc had been the heart of the Cathar religion, the land where the possible family of Jesus, led by Mary Magdalene, hid from persecution. It was also the land where Templar alliances had shifted from the pope to the religion, or antireligion, of Gnosis. Following the crusades against the Cathars in the thirteenth century, the people in southern France still held on to repressed beliefs. Ironically, Lyon became Verrazano's adopted city, as many Florentines fled the resurrected Inquisition in the late fifteenth century.

Verrazano himself may have been one of those who left the city before the onslaught of the mad monk Savonarola in 1494. Such hammers of God believed the arts and sciences and liberties of Florence

---

*For a full disussion of the symbolic nature of numbers and their meanings see West, *Serpent in the Sky.*

were a threat to the Church in Rome. Botticelli himself renounced his art in fear of the Catholic punishment for heresy. After a brief period of burning art and banning music, Florence reacted by burning Savonarola himself at the stake in the Piazza della Signoria. A stone slab still marks the spot.

Verrazano had been born into both wealth and connections. Castle Verrazano is still standing, and wine from Verrazano vineyards is still produced and sold. Although the family would never be mentioned in the same context as the Medici family, they had as peers some of Europe's greatest merchants and bankers.

City of the Sun God

After his flight from Florence, Verrazano may have been educated in Lyon, the southern French city that had been one of the holdouts against Christianity in Europe. It was a ceremonial center to the Black Virgin Cybele, an incarnation of Isis. Pre-Constantine, the goddess Cybele played an important role in Rome, also. Her prophecies were consulted regarding important matters of state, and bulls were slaughtered at the site of the Vatican until the end of the fourth century. She survived longer in Lyon. There it is recorded that the pagans viciously persecuted Christians as Rome had. When Christianity took over as the state religion, the temple to Cybele was built over by the sinister Basilica of Notre-Dame de Fourvière. Women now sacrifice to the new Blessed Virgin in the same fashion as they had to the Black Virgin and depart by walking backward.[3]

Founded by the Romans, Lyon was named for the sun god Lugh and called Lugdunum, literally, "city of Lugh." As Heliopolis, the Egyptian city, was the "city of the sun," Lyon too may have had great importance as a Celtic religious center. Lugh also represented the first fruits of harvest, a time when the sun begins its annual decline. His feast was August 1, but it was celebrated in the same fashion as Saint John the Baptist's on June 24. Saint John later replaced Lugh, just as Notre Dame, or Our Lady, replaced the Black Virgins Cybele, Isis, and—in Lyon—Rosmerta.

Lyon was a center of Templars, the tarot, occultism, and heresy long before the Florentines settled there. Indeed, Lyon and Florence had a great deal in common: They were both centers of Gnostic Cathar thought, they were both persecuted by the Church, and the tarot appeared in both cities after the demise of the Cathars and Templars. They shared one more significant characteristic: They were both centers of the textile trade. Most of the Florentines in Lyon were, like the Verrazano family, in the silk trade.

Lyon also had a large community of bankers. Most were Italians who traveled from one trade fair to another and sold letters of credit, stakes in trade, and shares of ships. Lyon was unique in being the only city where the Templar invention of branch deposit banking still existed. After the Templar demise, only a handful of cities offered such a service, and it soon ceased in most of these.

Verrazano may have belonged to an even more elite group than that of the Renaissance princes of northern Italy. He had been born too late to be a Knight Templar and too early to be in a Freemason guild. There was, however, a continuity between such organizations. Banking in the post-Templar years and in modern Switzerland is a tight-knit community where access is often limited to those who belong to certain lodges. The world of trade and banking often relies on trust. The expression "being on the level" is still more than a compliment. The phrase is a Masonic code meaning a person can be trusted. Verrazano's removal from one hotbed of heresy to another gave him even greater need to have and to use trusted connections. These granted him admission to the highest spheres of influence when he began to make his way into this world. After his education, he went to sea, most likely in the employ of the Guadagni family, equally prominent among Italian merchant and banking families. When the Guadagnis, to whom Verrazano was related by marriage, were expelled from Italy, they moved to France. Verrazano followed his now French in-laws and went to Dieppe in 1506 to earn his stripes as a seafarer. The city was a good choice.

The Port of Dieppe

The port city of Dieppe, in Normandy, had a longstanding tradition as a hub of commerce. By the time Verrazano arrived, it was showing great promise as a point of departure for explorers, thanks largely to two men, Jean d'Ango and the French king Francis I. Normandy itself had been the center of maritime France since the St. Clair ancestor Rollo arrived with his Norsemen. An Arab geographer, al-Idrisi, commented that as early as the twelfth century, it was the place from which expeditions started. The Arques River flows into the sea at Dieppe, and the inland forests of Arques provided the timber for ships. As early as 1362, a fleet of trading ships from the port of Dieppe sailed down the African coast to modern Sierra Leone and established a trading colony called Petit Dieppe. The Hundred Years' War, which greatly divided old loyalties and formed new ones, hurt Normandy, but by the early 1500s a revival was under way.

Nearby was the inland city of Rouen, where three great mercantile families held the power. One was the Dufour family, originally of Geneva and possessing strong connections to the home city of Verrazano's bankers and the center of the Italian silk trade, Lyon. The second was the Pelletier family of Provence, who were connected through business with the Rucellai family, again future backers of Verrazano. Verrazano was related to the Rucellais, who were banking partners with the Medici. Verrazano himself was close enough to his relatives to place Zanobio Rucellai in charge of his estate along with his brother, Girolamo.

The third was the family of Jean d'Ango. Born in 1481, d'Ango was perhaps Dieppe's most important citizen, serving the French as Henry the Navigator served Portugal. He built a manor called Varengeville, not far from the seaport, where he brought together navigators and scientists and King Francis I. Expanding the family business, d'Ango soon owned a fleet of ships ranging from large trading vessels to smaller coastal traders and several fishing boats. All flew his trading flag, a Turkish crescent, implying a trade with the Levant. For decades he could depend on the crown for political support; Francis often depended on d'Ango for financial resources. Together, they were soon sending explorers to America and to the Asian Pacific, often in secret.

In modern Dieppe, d'Ango may be more remembered than his king. L'Église Saint-Jacques is Dieppe's largest building and a monument to the merchant. Complete with twenty chapels, including the Templar-style octagonal chapel, flying buttresses, rose windows, and odd gargoyles, Saint-Jacques is the Normandy equivalent of Sinclair's Rosslyn. Inside is the oratory of d'Ango, with the family crest and a frieze depicting the "proof" that men of Dieppe discovered America.

Up to this point, France had been too busy to turn its full attention to the New World. King Louis XI had managed to increase the size of the country by annexing Burgundy and Picardy. Other areas such as Brittany, Anjou, and Provence were brought into France by marriage or bequest.

Francis I was at least as energetic. When he became king in 1515, he doubled the size of his kingdom by marrying his cousin. He then took on another role, importing the Renaissance from Italy. He welcomed the bankers, seafarers, artists, merchants, and explorers. He brought in Italian architects, advisers, and artists including Leonardo da Vinci, who served the king as an engineer, an architect, and a hydraulics expert.

While he played a fine Renaissance man, his feet were shod in the boots of yet another role, one that delayed France's start in the race to the New World. Francis had a compulsion to go to war. He himself led his army into battle, no doubt wearing the Italian armor he collected. An early victory may have caused the king to overestimate his army's strength, and a string of defeats followed that would extend through the rest of his reign. Most of his military campaigns were mounted against Holy Roman Emperor Charles V. His first lasted from 1521 to 1525, when he was defeated at Pavia in northern Italy and captured. What he lost on the field, however, was often recovered in negotiation, and Francis was never compelled to honor any agreements made under coercion.

Shortly after renouncing his claims to lands in Italy, he formed the Cognac League with Henry VIII, Pope Clement VII, Venice, and Florence and revived his rivalry with Charles V of Spain. The league was defeated in a war that lasted from 1527 to 1529, and the subsequent peace held for seven years, until Francis invaded Italy. This third war lasted from 1536 to 1538 and was again settled by treaty.

The peace lasted barely longer than had the war. After making a treaty with Süleyman I of the Turkish Empire, Francis attacked Charles again. When his Cognac League broke up because of religious squabbles and Henry VIII switched his allegiance to Charles V, Francis's fourth campaign was lost.

Nonetheless, being at war for nearly half of his thirty-two-year reign did not stop Francis from leading his country in a cultural renaissance and into transoceanic exploration.

With the support of the French king and the work of Jean d'Ango, Dieppe began to play a prominent role in the contest to discover new lands—not that it hadn't already done its part, at least according to legend. The Jean Cousin whose ship was supposedly blown to the New World four years before Columbus sailed was from Dieppe. Although numerous voyages of exploration and colonization were launched from Dieppe, more often it simply served as a very busy commercial port. It does, however, have many legends.

According to Desmarquets, an eighteenth-century historian, Cousin's ship was blown so far off course that it reached Brazil. As mentioned earlier, Columbus's future captain Martin Alonso Pinzon was on board. His actions on the voyage were so mutinous that Cousin filed a complaint against him once they reached safe harbor. To avoid the charges, Pinzon returned home to Spain. The Pinzon family, of Palos, was prominent as navigators and traders, and several Pinzons actually accompanied Columbus to the New World. One wonders whether Martin Alonso had been there before. The Cousin family was equally prominent in its home port.* Since the archives of the city were destroyed in 1694, there is no way to verify the tale of a Cousin-Pinzon discovery of pre-Columbian America.[4]

At the beginning of the sixteenth century, Dieppe launched numerous voyages, most to bring home fish. In 1504 a Norman ship first reached the Grand Banks of Newfoundland. In 1508 Aubert of Dieppe followed the route farther and explored up to the St. Lawrence Seaway. Aboard the d'Ango-owned *La Pensée* was Giovanni da Verrazano, meaning that he was already acquainted with crossing the Atlantic before he commanded his own voyage. In 1518 Baron de Lery of Dieppe landed on Sable Island, a floating island of mostly sand that would claim hundreds of ships in the centuries to come. He attempted to plant a colony; instead, he left behind only cattle, which survived and multiplied.[5] When John Cabot reached Newfoundland, he met men and fishing ships from Dieppe. Jean Parmentier of Dieppe was another early visitor to the New World, and in 1652 Jean Ribaut, also of Dieppe, mounted an expedition to start a Huguenot colony in Florida. In 1524, Verrazano embarked from Dieppe on his voyage to Newport.

Besides the d'Ango expedition to Newfoundland in 1508, Verrazano traveled east through the Mediterranean Sea to the Levant and Egypt. He had lived in Cairo for a while, which may have deepened his appre-

---

* Today Guillaume Cousin is quickly becoming a modern legend as a yacht racer.

ciation of Gnostic thought. His ability, as well as his banking connections, helped him acquire his letter of marque to prey on Spanish shipping. By 1510 King John III of Portugal was complaining that the French were capturing his trading ships. To the French, Verrazano was a hero; to the Spanish he was a pirate. In 1522 he took a ship valued in the millions of ducats that had been sent by Cortés to Spain for Charles V. Because of this one known act of piracy, he is sometimes confused with Jean Fleury, another captain in the employ of d'Ango and commander of a French Protestant fleet of corsairs who attacked an entire Spanish fleet in 1523 off the coast of Cape Saint Vincent in Portugal. Fleury took 52,000 ducats in gold, 140 kilograms of pearls, a cargo of sugar, and one of Cortés's ambassadors, who was ransomed two years later.[6] The Spanish were forced to defend their fleets more seriously and devised a system of annual and semiannual treasure fleets. The opportunity presented by such massive wealth was the catalyst for the golden era of piracy.

While France was fighting Charles V on land, Francis I and d'Ango wanted to catch up with their enemies at sea as well. The Parmentier brothers of Dieppe rounded the Cape of Good Hope and reached the islands of Sumatra and Java in 1529. The Portuguese had been there since 1512 and began fighting battles with the Spanish traders who arrived several years later. At stake was the lucrative trade for spices. Slower out of the starting port, Francis I now had his country's ships sailing as far and wide as Spain's and Portugal's.

As France began to catch up to other European nations in the burgeoning world trade, Verrazano came to the king with a new proposal. He was armed with Sannazaro's *Arcadia,* the lengthy poem that blended together the idyllic paradise of another age with modern ideas of arcane sciences. Within *Arcadia* was the theme of an underground stream of knowledge, which would be picked up by other artists and writers, including Sidney and Bacon.

It was a work that combines several writing styles, and it is written on several levels. As such, not everyone has the key to the mysteries concealed in the mixture of prose and verse. It is replete with goddesses and gods, references to astrology, and incantations to draw darkened stars from heaven, and often calls attention to the importance of astronomical events and their effects on earth.

Verrazano unlocked at least part of *Arcadia* for King Francis. There was an Arcadia, an idyllic world unspoiled by man and his institutions. It was not, however, in ancient Greece, but across the Atlantic. Just how much was revealed to the king is uncertain, but soon the Italian explorer was on his way west to the New World.

THE VOYAGE OF VERRAZANO

Verrazano sailed out of the port of Dieppe with four ships. The story of this early stage in the voyage is murky, and it is possible that two ships had been given a different mission, to attack Spanish shipping. Another ship was turned back by the weather. In any case, Verrazano crossed five hundred miles of the Atlantic to the Portuguese Madeiras on his own.

Verrazano was part merchant and part explorer. Although we know very little of his early life, we do know that he was in Portugal with Ferdinand Magellan when that soon-to-be-famous explorer decided to offer his services to the king of Spain. It is not clear why Verrazano decided not to join the ill-fated expedition of 1519. Magellan, however, was not the Florentine explorer's only Portuguese connection. He was mentioned in a letter from the governor of Portuguese Mozambique to the king of Portugal, so he must have had some degree of fame and traveled in elite circles.

There may be significance in the fact that Verrazano and his backers had a relationship with the Portuguese that enabled him to outfit his voyage from that island. There is also the possibility that he resupplied without any official knowledge. The relationship between Portugal's kings and Italian explorers tended to be on-again, off-again, the result of shifting alliances. Portugal had made discoveries by using a host of Genoese traders and adventurers, yet had turned away the most famous of the Genoese adventurers, Columbus, and also turned away Magellan.

On the other hand, a strong alliance could have existed that allowed Verrazano to be counted as a brother to members of Madeira's ruling class. It would not have been a shared sense of Italian nationality, as that concept did not yet exist; Genoese and Florentine individuals shared a language but not a national identity. If there was a bond, it may have been membership in the Knights of Christ. Moreover, the six-pointed star of the Verrazano crest may have signaled another esoteric connection, this one with Sinclair descendants on the island. Sinclairs have been involved with Catharism in France into the last century.

In any case, Verrazano's letter to the French king detailing the voyage says simply that he stopped at a deserted rock. If his visit could not have been official, we can only guess where he docked. The family of Columbus lived alternately on Porto Santo, the island it governed, and at Funchal, the main city of the larger Madeira isles. Porto Santo, then as now, is not deserted, but it is small, measuring four miles by seven miles, and is forty-one miles from Madeira.*

There are two groups of even smaller islands in the chain: the Desertas, whose name does not inspire hopes of resupply, and the Selvegans, also unpopulated. Both are legendary pirate hideouts, and expeditions to recover alleged booty of Captain Kidd and the treasure of Lima Cathedral took place every so often until the government declared the islands bird sanctuaries.

No serious expedition to find Verrazano's landing has taken place.

January 17

After making the trip to Portuguese-controlled Madeira, Verrazano set out again on January 17, 1524. The importance of particular dates is always debatable, yet an intriguing number of stories of exploration seem to highlight certain saints' feast days. Saint John the Baptist's feast day of June 24, for example, is somehow the day on which numerous explorers reach America. The practice of naming a place after the saint whose feast was the day of discovery accounts for the numerous Saint Johns on the Canadian seaboard and the Saint Johns in Florida.

January 17 is an equally significant date. The authors of *Holy Blood, Holy Grail* have made the case that this date in the mystery of

---

*Today Porto Santo, meaning "Sacred Harbor," is reached by a government-owned and -subsidized catamaran. Large enough to transport four hundred people, it is still an often difficult hour-and-a-half ride through choppy seas. Possibly to attract visitors, it was said that the sands of Porto Santo have curative properties and that a spring on the island, Fonte da Areia, can grant eternal youth. Today the tourism board has dubbed it Ilha Dourada, the Golden Isle. Besides the sandy beaches, the restored home of Columbus is its other attraction, down a narrow street from the town hall.

Rennes-le-Château is at least a tantalizing coincidence. In summary, the mystery is that an impoverished priest in a remote parish in the Languedoc suddenly became very wealthy soon after finding certain documents hidden in a church altar. He asked his bishop for guidance and was sent to Saint-Sulpice in Paris. There he bought copies of paintings by Poussin and Teniers, the *Shepherds of Arcadia,* which shows the quote from Sannazaro on a tombstone, and the *Temptation of Saint Anthony.* Whatever mystery was unraveled by clues in these documents and paintings is unknown, but the trip to Saint-Sulpice precipitated further digging in the countryside and church cemetery in his parish, and his instant wealth.

The tomb in Rennes-le-Château of the marquis d'Hautpoul de Blanchefort marking the death of his wife, Marie de Negre D'Ables, was dated January 17. Whatever secrets the tomb contained will remain secret, as Saunière defaced the inscriptions. That date in 1917 was also when Father Saunière had a heart attack, regarded as suspicious by the authors because, despite his robust health, his companion had ordered his coffin five days earlier. The authors pointed out it was the feast of Saint Sulpice and "Saunière himself had made something of a cult of Saint Sulpice."[7]

Part of Saunière's wealth went into civic improvements in the tiny village, including a strange church to Mary Magdalene and an oddly placed tower. Subsequent research by several writers, most prominently Henry Lincoln, revealed the whole area to be a reflection of astronomical significance. Churches and castles form a massive pentagram. Some are built on a line to meet the sunrise; others, dedicated to the Blessed Virgin and Mary Magdalene, are built to meet the sunrise on either July 22 or August 15. The latter, the Feast of the Assumption, is when the sun rises and sets near the star Regulus. The alignment of Virgo and Regulus is an auspicious occasion and featured prominently in later Masonic construction.

We can say with certainty only that there is a connection between the Church of Saint-Sulpice and Rennes-le-Château because of Father Saunière and the significance of astronomy in both places. Any more than that is speculation.

The original Saint Sulpice was a bishop in early France during the time of the Merovingian rule. He was born of wealthy parents but decided against marriage and from early youth worked to help the young and the poor. Sulpice became well known after restoring King Clotaire II back to health from his deathbed. He was named bishop of Bourges in 624 and waged a campaign for the rights of his people against another Merovingian king, Dagobert, and his minister, Lullo. It is claimed that by his piety and holiness, Sulpice inspired all the Jews of Bourges to convert to Christianity. He founded the now famous monastery at Bourges under the invocation of the Blessed Virgin. Resigning, eventually, from his active role, he lived out his life in piety and solitude, but he was not forgotten. At his death in 647, the crowds that gathered to show their love and respect were so massive that the clergy could not conduct the burial service. His feast day is remembered as January 17.

The rule of the Merovingians was not to last. King Dagobert II was murdered near Stenay in the Ardennes forest. Shortly afterward, his son Sigisbert IV arrived in Rennes-le-Château. The date was January 17, 681. He never actually had a chance to rule, as the Merovingians were soon forced out of power, but the Merovingian dynasty was preserved in the tiny French village by the survival of Sigisbert, who continued the family line.

That same date in the Catholic year is the Feast of Saint Anthony, who is regarded as the patron saint of lost treasures. As noted, the painting of the temptation of Saint Anthony played a role in the mystery of Rennes-le-Château. Saint Anthony died a hermit in 561 but inspired many. An order, the Hospitallers of Saint Anthony, never achieved the fame of the Knights of Saint John and of the Templars, but it is interesting to note that members wore a blue tau cross on a black robe.

January 17 is also given as the date that the family of Jesus left Egypt. The Gospel of Matthew is the only one that mentions the Magi—those astronomers from the East who understood that an important star, or possibly a planetary conjunction, indicated that the Savior King had been born. The year was very likely 7 B.C., a slight mistake in the Christian calendar. As King Herod received the Magi, we can assume that they were important men in their own lands. They were definitely intuitive, receiving in dream the knowledge that Herod planned to put the Christ Child to death. This they shared with the Holy Family, whose flight to Egypt ended when Herod died in 4 B.C. It is said that the day of their return, some three years after they had fled, was January 17.

Nicholas Flamel, alchemist and grand master of the secretive Priory of Sion, claimed to have made his first successful chemical transmutation around noon on January 17. And Henry Lincoln dated his introduction to *Holy Blood, Holy Grail* January 17 as well. The date provides links to the mysteries of the Templars and to Verrazano's quest, but no conclusions.

We will see later that the Society of Saint-Sulpice, founded in Paris, would play a powerful role in the French settlements in North America, specifically in Montreal, the city named for a Cathar-Catholic showdown and the home of a Templar castle. The society's organizer, Jean-Jacques Olier, did not want to establish a new order, which would have required the approval of the pope. Instead, in 1641 he created a "society." This society exists today and is much larger, with seminaries in several countries. Initiates must already be in the priesthood; therefore, they comprise an elitist group within the Church. In the United States, members use the initials S.S. after their name. In France they use p.s.s.[8]

Madeira to Arcadia

Verrazano's ship was called the *Dauphine,* for the French king, and was equipped with fifty men and provisions to last eight months. The only known crew member was his brother Girolamo, a mapmaker. Forty-nine days out of Madeira, around the second week of March, the *Dauphine* reached what is now North Carolina, and Verrazano headed north to avoid running into the Spanish. He did, however, have a chance to start placing names on his map of the voyage. The first land he saw he called Annunziata, for the Feast of the Annunciation of the Blessed Virgin. This was on the coast of North Carolina near the modern Cape Hatteras.

He noted that the strip of land along which he sailed was at most points only a mile wide. Had he been coasting opposite the Pamlico Sound, the other side of that isthmus can be twenty or thirty miles until continental North Carolina. He declared that it was the only thing separating his ship and the Pacific Ocean. He named the isthmus after himself, Verrazzania,[9] and the area itself Francesca.

If his mission was to find Cathay, it is surprising that he did not attempt passage through the numerous breaks in the shoals, or even a portage at some point. Instead, he hastened north without recording any attempt. Though the thin strips of land that serve as a barrier protecting the Intercoastal Waterway from the Atlantic may not have been as perforated in Verrazano's day as they are today, one would have to go far back in geological time to find a period when the Chesapeake Bay and the Delaware Bay were "closed." The narrow point of the entrance to the Chesapeake is twenty miles wide; the Delaware is much wider than that. Both must have presented an opportunity for a passage into the continent, especially if Verrazano really believed the Pacific was so close.

No such investigation took place. Instead, he headed north without stopping until he arrived in New York Bay. At the place where later it was named the Verrazano Narrows, he did a bit of investigating. Sailing north into the Upper Bay, he saw Manhattan and called it d'Angouléme. It is believed that he named it after the title of Francis I before he became king. Another explanation is that d'Angouléme is the actual home of a fourteenth-century Templar fortress near the port city of La Rochelle. As such, d'Angouléme may have stored the treasure of the Paris temple until it was placed aboard the ships of the fleet.

The small town of d'Angouléme has another connection with the secrets of underground France: Its symbol is a dragon writhing in flames. Montségur was the last stand of the Cathars and Paris the last stand of the French Templars; both saw their leaders and faithful go into the inquisitorial flames of church and state.

The Upper Bay itself he called Santa Margarita after the king's sister, the duchess d'Alençon. From the shores of the future New York City, he coasted the southern shore of Long Island. At its terminus, he headed north past Block Island to another island, which he named after Rhodes, the idyllic landscape in Sannazaro's *Arcadia*. It eventually became the name for the entire state of Rhode Island.

While Verrazano placed many names along the coastline, he applied the label Arcadia to the very large stretch extending from North Carolina to New York. The concept of Arcadia referred to an ideal landscape where a virtuous people could live in peace. Here Verrazano described the inhabitants as primitives who "goe altogether naked, except only certain skinnes of beastes."[10] On subsequent maps, based on Girolamo Verrazano's map, the Arcadia label was moved north to encompass New England as well.

There are a handful of facts that stand out among the records, letters, and charts of the Verrazano expedition. One is that at Narragansett Bay, he is recorded as having received help from the Natives, who guided him safely into the inner harbor. While it was custom in both Europe and Asia to engage a local pilot when navigating entrance into a foreign harbor, the availability of a Native American with the ability to communicate and experience piloting a large ship that required a much greater draft than a canoe is odd at best.

No less of a source than Samuel Morison, the maritime historian, affirms Verrazano's ship was "piloted by an Indian"[11] from Point Judith through the narrow divide between Beaver Tail Point on Conanicut and Breton Point on Aquidneck, past the small Dumplings, and into the inner harbor. This served as his anchorage. Although almost all of Verrazano's experiences with America's Native populations were awkward in terms of language and intentions, in Narragansett Bay he found an "Indian" who was trustworthy and somehow knowledgeable enough to pilot the ship.

Between Conanicut Island and Newport Harbor, Verrazano noted the defensive value of certain islands.* This was the only place where Verrazano records spending any time. For two weeks the *Dauphine* lay at anchor in the harbor of what is now Rhode Island while Verrazano interacted with the Wampanoag tribe and remarked on the tendency of some of the Native population to appear European. He made note of the bay, the mainland, the animals, and the trees, as well as the dress and customs of his hosts.

This was the domain of the Wampanoag, who were part of the Algonquian linguistic group and whose territory extended into Massachusetts. Verrazano made numerous notes on the charity and chastity of the people, which may come as a shock compared to other European explorers' descriptions, which so often highlighted hostility and licentiousness. There is evidence that the Wampanoag came in contact with Europeans before. Among the early possibilities, the suggestion that both Norse Vikings and Celtic sailors preceded them has merit. The Celtic/Norse word for boat was *bato;* the Algonquian word was *pados.*

---

*Verrazano named the islands, now called the Dumplings, Petra Viva, after the wife of one of his Italian backers, Antonio Gondi. Her maiden name was Marie-Catherine de Pierre-Vive.

The mission of Verrazano all along was to locate a Templar colony, founded under the leadership of the Sinclair family. In this mission he succeeded. Within the inner harbor of what is now Newport stood a Templar baptistery. Built out of the materials available, it nevertheless resembled European models and shared the measurements of those built by both Templars and Cistercians.

This Templar baptistery was so out of place in the New World that it could only have shocked a European discoverer. Yet Verrazano's reference to it shows no surprise, and the map of the voyage, drawn by Girolamo, refers to it simply as a "Norman Villa." Most likely, the secret nature of the mission explains his paucity of comments on the Templar baptistery. More enlightened than most other explorers, Verrazano would certainly have recognized the tower overlooking Newport Harbor as something more, and the very use of the term *villa* seems like an exercise in disinformation.

In his letter to Francis I, his surface mission—to coast North America and find an entrance to the Pacific or a northwest passage—also appears completely forgotten. He did tell the king that the people called the land Norumbega. That name stuck, although its location on maps wandered as far north as Nova Scotia.

Europe had a hunger for records of exploration and the newly drawn maps. Before the Verrazano brothers could print their own, the so-called Norman villa was mentioned on the 1526 map of Vesconte Majollo. Girolamo's map would actually be published second. The structure was also included on the Globe of Euphrosinus Ulpius in 1542.[12]

The map of Girolamo yields another clue, only slightly less important than the Norman villa, to the true purpose of Verrazano's cursory voyage. Verrazano and his brother named the port Refugio, "the Refuge." He does not enlighten us about just who he thought had been in need of refuge. One modern guidebook claims it was refuge to a sinking ship. However, Verrazano sailed in a one-ship expedition and his ship made it home. Encountering another European ship, even one that had sunk, would seem worthy of mention.

In his search for the Arcadia that served as a Templar refuge, Verrazano may have found everything but the people. They had been there, though, and the clues they left behind were Verrazano's evidence. The baptistery could only have been built by those trained in the sacred geometry and astronomy. It could not be the work of earlier Vikings or later colonists, it was far too complex for either. The Templar science that would be preserved within the craft lodges of Masonry and entrusted to the guardianship of the Sinclair family was something to which few were privy. This was the location of Sinclair's colony, the Arcadia refuge for those who were subject to the persecution of church and state in Europe. The sad truth was that it had not survived.

Other early maps corroborated Verrazano's practice and called the area Norumbega and Anorumbega. Both terms, the former meaning "Norse" and the latter "Norman," were Native American names for the village of the Northmen—the men who visited from the north. They would have included French Norman survivors of the Templar demise as well as Scottish ex-Templars and Orkney mariners.

The Gastaldi map labeled everything between d'Angouléme, which is a fair representation of the future New York City, and Cape Breton as Terra De Norumbega. Between the two is the Port du Refuge, a harbor with several islands. Accurate scale not being one of the great strengths of these maps, either Narragansett Bay or Newport Harbor could qualify. On a large scale, Narragansett Bay fits the map, as it has numerous islands and extends inland to the modern city of Providence. On a smaller scale, the harbor of Newport itself has a handful of islands as well.

Verrazano had completed his mission. He had crossed the ocean, searched for the lost colony, and found the evidence that he required. The stark message was that the colony had not survived. For Verrazano, the discovery ushered in disappointment. The Templar colony had been in the area, but whoever had once settled there was long gone. The Arcadia of Sannazaro was once there but was no longer. He bade adieu to King Magnus, the Orkney-sounding chief of the Wampanoags who had, surprising the Europeans, been a woman.

He then continued along the coast, rounding Cape Cod and heading north to Maine, where he ran into the Abnakis. He noted that their appearance was close to that of the Wampanoag, but in temperament they were hostile, a characteristic that might have been caused by early European sea captains' practice of taking slaves. Sailing away from Maine, he somehow missed the Bay of Fundy and Nova Scotia and instead sighted land at Cape Fogo in Newfoundland. Because he refrained from giving French names to Labrador, he may have carried aboard a Portuguese chart or possibly even a Portuguese mariner.

From Newfoundland he returned to the French port of Dieppe, where he landed on July 8 of the same year he had left. Ostensibly, his mission to find a sea route to Cathay was a failure. There is absolutely no evidence that he even tried. Was he instead attempting to fill in gaps of cartographic knowledge along the North American coastline? He did make a new map that added to what was known of the coastline, but it was of little value to his backers. They were silk merchants.

THE TRUE MISSION

The particulars of the Verrazano expedition tell a different story from his letter to the king. He sailed for the North American coast and seemingly only for the area around Newport. There he was guided to a safe harbor and, more dramatically, to a European building. Why did he spend time only in Newport?

As part of a secret society, Verrazano was privy to confidential knowledge that was not to be revealed in letters. Quite simply, he crossed the ocean in search of a colony planted the century before, and he knew exactly where to look for the American Arcadia. He found all the evidence he needed to understand that the Templars had been there; the baptistery left him in no doubt. Unfortunately, the Arcadian colony had not survived.

His voyage, though a personal disappointment, brought him a degree of fame. More significant, the crest of the Verrazano family was changed to an eight-pointed star after his mission to America, symbolizing in the Gnostic sense a quest completed and a rebirth, possibly a new mission.

Finding Arcadia, however, was not his destiny. Within a few years, his brother tells us, they made another voyage to the Americas. This time, most likely on the island of Guadeloupe, Giovanni waded ashore, leaving his men aboard the ship. Experience with both friendly and hostile Natives had not prepared him for the Caribs. He was quickly seized, killed, and torn apart. As his men looked on in horror, he was eaten by cannibals.[13]

8

In Arcadia

The Templar Colony in Montreal

 IN THE HEART OF PARIS is the Saint-Sulpice Church. When the sun rises on the morning of January 17, light hits a sundial that once marked the Paris meridian. Inside the church one can still see inlaid in the floor the brass strip called the Rose Line, which marks this once important zero-degree longitude. At noon the sun's rays reach an obelisk in the north transept. On important days, including both the solstices and the days of the equinox, sunlight through an upper window reflects off the brass strip and hits specific points on the obelisk. Combining visual techniques used from the windswept Orkney Islands to the dried sands of Egypt in ancient times, Saint-Sulpice was an important center.

In the mid-1600s, it was also home to a new secret society that had several things in common with the Knights Templar. This secretive group, even after being abolished officially, later founded a colony in the heart of French Canada. Although Canada did not survive as a French refuge, Montreal survived as a city, and Saint-Sulpice has survived and thrived in its Montreal base.

IN SEARCH OF AVALON AND ARCADIA

Verrazano had found unmistakable evidence of the Templar presence in America, but had located no colony. Nearly one hundred years later, France and England rekindled the efforts of both Verrazano and Henry Sinclair's Templars when a fervor for exploration and settlement was ignited, a fervor based on a mixture of arcane secrets and common greed.

France's colonial activity went beyond the burgeoning fur trade. In Saint-Sulpice in Paris a secretive Catholic society called the Compagnie du Saint-Sacrement would play a great role in bringing the message of Christianity to the New World. The message was broader than that of the exclusive Roman Catholic Church and the society included Jansenists and openly worked with the Huguenots. Cardinal Mazarin, the most powerful Roman Catholic in France, referred to the group as Le Cabal des Devots (the devout cabal), thus expressing his distrust.

The company served as the foundation of those who built the city of Montreal. They left few papers, although what is known is evidence that they had a very secretive way of operating, and both mystical and earthly intentions.

England had its own mystical motivations for exploration in the Americas. It was the alchemist and magician Dr. John Dee who prompted Queen Elizabeth I to back colonial efforts. He claimed America to be the refuge of King Arthur and thereby rightfully British. Yet the English had actually entered the race to North America quite early, following Spain's lead. They had even hired their own Genoese explorer, Giovanni Caboto. It is worth noting that Cabot, to use the Anglicized spelling, shared a home city with Columbus and Verrazano.

Born in Genoa, his family moved to Venice, where he lived until about 1490, at which time he, too, was in Spain, promoting his own venture to the East via the Atlantic. Neither Spain nor Portugal was buying, so he eventually landed in England. There he found sponsorship and a ship, the *Matthew*, for his expedition. The scanty records of his voyage keep us guessing even to the day he departed; we are told, however, that he landed on Saint John the Baptist's feast day in 1497. Most historians agree that his landing was either Newfoundland or Nova Scotia.[1]

Like France, England was not ready to commit to exploration and it wasn't until 1577, when Dee wrote his *Perfect Art of Navigation,* that

England took major steps. Around this time, a handful of England's men of learning were meeting at Dee's Mortlake residence, or the Syon house. Dee coined the word Britannia and put ideas of discovering Avalon in the queen's head at the same time that Sir Francis Bacon wrote of the New Atlantis. England's next ventures west would be cast in the rhetoric of myth.

Cartier

Verrazano's death ended Francis I's commitment to further exploration and the exploitation of his newly discovered lands in the New World. Moreover, his long war with Charles V had begun. The first decisive battle of that conflict may, however, reveal something telling about Verrazano's voyage. The man responsible for the capture of Francis I at the battle of Pavia was the Priory of Sion grand master, Charles de Montpensier. Now if Verrazano was, as he seems to have been, a member of the initiate, privy to what has been called the underground stream of knowledge, one would expect no rivalry between the man Verrazano sailed for (the French king) and an initiate of the innermost circles (Grand Master Montpensier). Montpensier's capture of Francis I suggests either that Verrazano used the French king as a pawn to achieve the undeclared goals of the underground stream or that Montpensier was not an actual member of the Priory of Sion. We are left to wonder whether Verrazano pursued his own agenda in one way or another in undertaking a search for Arcadia.

In any case, it was not until ten years after Verrazano's death that Francis I again focused west. He chose as his new discoverer Jacques Cartier. The king had been introduced to Cartier while on a pilgrimage to Mont-Saint-Michel. Believed to have been born in 1491 and described as a master mariner, there is little else known of the mariner from Saint-Malo.

Unusually, Cartier's voyage was directly backed by the king of France and paid for out of his treasury. More typically, the king would grant his blessing, establish his share of possible profits, then allow merchants to invest in such a voyage. Cartier sailed first to Newfoundland, making landfall in twenty days, possibly a record at that time. He was too early in the season and described the ice-clotted seas and a swimming bear as large as a cow and as white as a swan. He headed south and encountered another oddity, a large fishing boat that had sailed from La Rochelle.

After further exploration and a few days in fog, he finally sighted land—once again on June 24. He called the land Saint John's. Three days later he sailed to a handful of small islands that still bear the name he gave them, the Magdalen Islands. Naming these two places after the two most revered people in the Templar universe is interesting, as the Magdalen, popular during the Crusades, went out of favor after the Templar dissolution. The Magdalen Islands resemble the windswept isles of the Orkneys with high headlands and few trees, and have remained remote and sparsely populated.

After returning home in 1534, it was only a year before he returned to the Americas. This time he conducted a further reconnaissance, looking for the kingdom of Saguenay, that mythical land of the Algonquians that had been described to him much like the golden cities of Incan Peru were described to the Spanish. He sailed into the St. Lawrence River, named for the saint who saved the true Holy Grail. Along the way he called another small group of islands the Isles of Saint John. This name would be changed, no doubt because of the numerous capes, bays, cities, and islands named for that saint.

He anchored at the mouth of the Saguenay River at the trading post of Tadoussac. The name the Inuit people of the far north used to describe the rounded mountains nearby translates as "the Nipples." They brought their own trade goods down the fjordlike Saguenay to the St. Lawrence in the land of the Algonquian-speaking Hurons. This trading post, though off the visitor track, still explodes with activity in summer, for the junction of two rivers attracts five species of whales, as well as tourists who cannot miss seeing them whether from kayaks or on large whale-watching cruises.

Heading west into the St. Lawrence, Cartier probably reached the future city of Quebec before any other Europeans—except, of course, fishermen, whalers, and possibly other nonofficial voyagers. Past Quebec he stopped at the site of Montreal. The native name for this village was Hochelaga, and if the Ramusio map, based on Cartier's description, is accurate, it was a planned village that had numerous streets laid out in a grid pattern with a central plaza. Hochelaga later became part of the Cartier-named city of Montreal.

The word *hochelaga* may have been the French spelling of an Algonquian word for volcano. It is said that there is actually a dormant volcano in the city. It also resembles in its pronunciation the Norse Hecla, an active volcano in Iceland.

Cartier asked further about Saguenay only to be told that it was westerly. He was informed of Lake Superior and learned that tribes there brought copper ornaments to the Huron and other tribes for trade. He would never find the legendary kingdom, but this did not stop it from appearing on a French map, where its depiction includes a large group of Frenchmen, bearing their flag and encountering a white-bearded king on a throne. Cartier claimed there was a white race of people already in Canada, "as white as those of France."[2]

Both Cabot and Cartier played a role in the exploration process. Each would find land on June 24. Both of the early explorers had their own hopes and motivations for the New World. Sinclair had intended to build an Arcadia. Verrazano, in the hope that Sinclair was successful, wanted to find it. Cabot may have been like many other mariners, simply an adventurer; he left no journals. Cartier, born into a family of mariners, may have started as a commissioned captain but soon became enthralled by the potential the New World offered. Champlain was an enigma.

Champlain

The next step in the French attempt to colonize the New World was to send Samuel de Champlain. He was born in La Rochelle long after the Templars used the port to exit France and escape the king. It had remained an isolated port city and a Huguenot holdout against the Catholic Church. Champlain was Catholic, but would have accepted his Protestant neighbors. Little is known about his early life, but at some point he was taken under the wing of don Francisco Coloma, a member of the Knights of Malta. Prior to 1307, this order was a rival of the Knights Templar, but as many of the Templar properties were absorbed by the Knights of Malta, there is the possibility that so were certain individuals.[3] Coloma, named again for the dove, was in the Spanish navy when he met Champlain, and took him on voyages to the West Indies.

His first expedition to Canada was sponsored by another member of the Knights of Malta, Aymar de Clermont de Chaste, the vice admiral of France and the lieutenant general of New France. Isaac de Razilly, a sea captain and another in the Knights of Malta, organized a subsequent voyage with Champlain's assistance and brought over other knights. He proposed that a priory be set up in Nova Scotia and the Knights of Malta be made responsible for administering New France. Although it was not to be, Razilly died in the land he described as "an earthly paradise" and was buried not far from Oak Island in the Mahone Bay area.[4]

The Knights of Malta, the other order dedicated to Saint John, played prominent roles in the governance of Canada and in the American Revolution.

While Champlain was said to be an ardent Catholic, he teamed up with Sieur de Monts, a Huguenot. De Monts was perhaps the French version of his name, as he was described as "gentilhomme d'origine italienne." He may have been related again to the Knights of Malta because Pietro del Monte served as the Maltese grand master from 1568 to 1572.[5] De Monts had moved to France and purchased a castle from the Ardennes estate of Godfroi de Bouillon. To the French king, de Monts proposed creating a monopoly on the fur trade that would pay for colonizing the new lands. Along with two other ships, one commanded by de Monts and the other by Sieur de Pont-Gravé, Champlain sailed for Canada in 1603.

They first sighted land at Sable Island, and reached Nova Scotia at La Have Island, where they described a bay of many islands to the east. This was Mahone Bay, which harbors Oak Island. Champlain apparently missed Oak Island itself, as his record of the voyage mentions fir trees on the islands and oak trees on the mainland. At the same time, he may have spent three days in the bay.[6] His records are confusing and several errors exist on his map. He refers to this group of islands as the Martyrs, stating that some Frenchmen had been killed there.[7] The idea that Champlain was more knowledgeable about the Oak Island locale is an interesting possibility. Could he have heard of Templars killed in a battle with Micmacs a century before?

The record of the early part of their expedition has the three captains seizing ships that were in violation of the king's monopoly on trade in the region. Apparently, there were more ships in America than the expeditions of the various crowns could account for. Sir Humphrey

Gilbert had recorded thirty-six ships in Saint John's Harbor twenty years before, and by Champlain's day the Canadian fishing grounds were no secret. Basque whalers had discovered the entrance to the Saguenay River as a rich hunting ground. Fishermen from Saint-Malo, New Rochelle, and other Biscayan points needed no official blessing to harvest the Grand Banks. We know they were there only because Pont Gravé recorded confronting the whalers at Tadoussac, again declaring that they were infringing on the rights of the French king.[8]

While Champlain had no problems partnering with Huguenots, the religious wars in France were carried to the New World. When the admiral of France granted a trading license to William and Emery de Caen, the Huguenots they transported to Catholic Quebec outnumbered the entire population of the city. Huguenot singing so annoyed the Jesuits of Quebec that the Caen brothers lost their right to trade, and the Huguenots headed south. Ironically, the Arcadia of Sannazaro and the New Atlantis of Bacon were both supposed to be new lands where religious tolerance would be practiced.

The Jesuits were founded as a new militia of the pope in Rome. Often more learned than many other orders in both religion and the ways of the world, they were still rigid in their beliefs. The Sulpicians, just as learned, were tolerant of others, including the Protestants. Sadly, the infighting between the two orders hindered the growth of a unified New France and further jeopardized the dream of Arcadia, already threatened by Europe's greed and will to conquer.

THE NEW ARCADIANS

In France, the men who resurrected the dream belonged to the Compagnie du Très Saint-Sacrement de l'Autel. Like the original Knights Templar, they began as eight individuals and a grand master, between 1627 and 1630. On the surface, their goal was to alleviate the suffering of the poor. Most members were from the upper echelon of society, at a time when many showed little sympathy for the poor. The upper classes would be brought low for such an attitude 170 years later when the guillotine silenced the "Let them eat cake" attitude of French nobility. Yet although the order may have done its part toward helping the poor, it kept its affairs secret. The membership of the Compagnie itself was a secret; only members knew who the other members were. Letters that circulated within the society included no names, and nothing was ever signed.

Henri de Levis, the duc de Ventadour, was the founder, and his connections suggest long association with sacred secrets. An uncle was Henri de Montmorency and so Levis would simply buy his shares of New France. An Isabel Levis was the mother of Marie de St. Clair, who is said to have been the second grand master of the Priory of Sion. The Levis name was not rare in the Cathar-dominated south of France, and may reflect a Judaic origin. Henri claimed that his family was related to Mary, the Mother of Jesus.

Henri's eight knights included Henri de Pichery, an official of the king's household who acted as the French ambassador to Rome; the marquis d'Andelot; the archbishop of Arles; and Philipe d'Angoumois; a Capuchin priest.[9] Among additional early members were Father Suffern, confessor to the king, and Marie de Medici. Later members included Nicholas Pavillon, François de la Fayette, Charles Noailles, Vincent de Paul, and Nicholas Fouquet. Members met weekly as a pious confraternity, a charitable society, and a militant organization to defend the Church.

Nicholas Pavillon

Nicholas Pavillon was bishop of the out-of-the-way French village of Alet, whose church windows feature the six-pointed star. Nearby, Lyon was the adopted home of Verrazano's family, whose crest featured the same symbol. Pavillon had requested the position in Alet as bishop, which was actually a step beneath some of the other posts he was offered. He, like Father Saunière, began an extensive remodeling program in his village, reconstructing ancient sites including the cathedral, schools, roads, and canals. Unlike Saunière, his wealth was not a mystery: It was inherited.

Pavillon was a follower of Jansenism, an almost heretical form of Catholicism that was viewed by the mainstream as elitist and a threat. Jansenism has been described as being influenced by Catharism and as one of the holdouts of that simple and pure faith.[10] It was not, however, a Protestant movement or even an anti-Church movement. Rather, it came into conflict with the Church over the concept of predestination, an important belief shared in the teaching of Calvin. It was not a break-away sect like Calvinism, however, and attracted many of the clergy. This controversial side of Pavillon did not stop the city of Alet from naming an avenue after the rebellious bishop.

Vincent de Paul

Many have heard of the Saint Vincent de Paul Society, but few are aware of Saint Vincent's very unusual background. Born around 1580, he studied for the priesthood in the once Cathar city of Toulouse. He then borrowed a horse and sold it. He disappeared for two years, during which he was held as a slave in Tunis. His master was an alchemist and from this Islamic owner he learned the heretical science. He escaped the piratical Barbary Coast with his owner and made his way back to France. In 1608 he visited the papal vice legate in Avignon and then continued on to Rome. There he demonstrated his black arts for the pope.

It is said the pope had a mission for him that involved the king of France, although whatever this mission was may be less important than Saint Vincent's admission to elite society. In a short period, he raised money and started charitable groups to assist galley workers, prisoners, and the poor. During the period of the Thirty Years' War, when the Lorraine was besieged, many of the nobles who had given him money took refuge in Paris. Saint Vincent even started a relief program for such displaced nobles. His Sisters of Charity exists today and is responsible for the concept of "soup kitchens" as a place where the poor can find a warm meal.

Saint Vincent was also known to have an unusual devotion to the Black Virgin. He and Jean-Jacques Olier regularly prayed at the feet of the Black Virgin called Notre-Dame de Bonne Délivrance. Her shrine is a well-known pilgrimage site for Catholics in Paris near the Sorbonne. Saint Thomas Aquinas, Saint Dominic, and Saint Francis de Sales also prayed there. Saint Francis claimed to have found his vocation at the feet of the Black Virgin.

Saint Vincent also founded the Lazarist Fathers. In addition to the good works the order is known for, it also maintains a Black Virgin site in the Languedoc called the Notre-Dame de Marceille. Built over a pagan site in the eleventh century, it remains a pilgrimage site in the south of France today.[11] Lazarist fathers were called in to participate in

Father Saunière's ceremonies, marking various stages of completion of his Rennes-le-Château home.[12] On the land owned by the Church, and once owned by the Knights Templar, are underground vaults that have been connected to the Holy Grail legend.[13]

Today Vincent de Paul is remembered for the orders he established and their charitable works rather than for his forays into alchemy, his devotion to the Black Virgin, or his connection to Templar-Cathar secrets.

François de la Fayette and Charles Noailles

The families of the marquis de Lafayette and the Noailles had much in common, as they were two of France's royal and most wealthy lineages. They would be united in marriage by the young marquis himself, whose parents left him with a fortune but without a family. Jean-Paul-François de Noailles was the count d'Ayen, and his marriage to Henriette Daguesseau in the late eighteenth century was officiated by the king of France himself.

The Noailles name comes up again during the French Revolution, when even the enlightened nobles were the prey of the mob. The wife of the marquis de Lafayette, Adrienne Noailles, affirmed her loyalty to the Catholic Church despite it becoming a dangerous affiliation, and attended Mass at Saint-Sulpice in Paris. After three Noailles women had faced their destiny at the guillotine, the comte de Noailles attempted to start a colony very much like the Templar Arcadia in America. He chose a lonely outpost on the Susquehanna River, where a huge standing stone still marks a culture of America's ancient past. He called his colony Azilum (Asylum), as it was meant to be a refuge far from the mob rule in France. In the hopes of becoming a city, the colony was laid out in a grid pattern with wide streets. But the colony may have been too much of an Arcadia for nobles who had moved from palaces to log cabins. They had to hire farmers because they were not prepared for the work themselves. They did have time to erect the Troy Maze, a labyrinth in a flower and stone garden that has been maintained to the present.

After the French Revolution, Noailles property was gifted to start several abbeys and seminaries, including a secret society called the Ladies of the Sacred Heart and Perpetual Adoration. Part of their imposed rule was that at each hour a nun would be posted before the altar where the Blessed Sacrament was unveiled.[14] Such extra-liturgical cults may have existed from early Christianity, although no records were kept. The earliest that exist as recorded groups are at Chartres, Amiens, and Lyon, where parishes were divided into twelve groups, each group representing a month and members of each group assigned days and hours within their parish's month.

Jean-Jacques Olier

Just after the Company of the Sacred Sacrament began, a young Jean-Jacques Olier was ordained a priest. Born in Lyon, he studied as a Jesuit before going to the Sorbonne to learn Hebrew. With failing eyesight threatening his study, he made a pilgrimage to Loreto, Italy, where it was restored. He then spent time in the south of Italy, until his father's death brought him back to Paris. In Paris he fell under the influence of Saint Vincent de Paul, who was actively preaching the care of the poor. Olier also traveled in fashionable society, no doubt a result of his inheritance. In August 1641, he was in charge of Saint-Sulpice in Paris. There he established the Seminary of Saint-Sulpice.

The Church of Saint-Sulpice is referred to as the "New Temple of Solomon" by Gérard de Sède in his book *The Accursed Treasure of Rennes-le-Château.*[15] It has a colonnade-style facade and a large, cavernlike interior. It has two mismatched towers, one rounded, the other octagonal. Besides the Rose Line that marks the January 17 sunrise, there are several interesting features in and around the church. In the Place Saint-Sulpice is the Fontaine des Quatre Points Cardinaux, with four bishops on the four cardinal points of the compass. A play on words, the name has two meanings. One choice is the "fountain of the cardinal points." The other is the "four Cardinals who never were."[16]

The Company of the Sacred Sacrament actually did perform charitable work. It worked toward alleviating the burden of France's poor and correcting the conditions of its prisons. It urged the Church to correct the abuses within and, more significant, to curb the outrages of Catholic-against-Huguenot and Huguenot-against-Catholic skirmishes. While the goal of the society was to encourage conversion to, or back to, Catholicism, the members also encouraged a respectful dialogue. Such activities were not welcome within the Church. No official recognition ever came from Rome. Nonetheless, the society was said to have grown rapidly to more than fifty branches, although the Church was unaware of most of them. They have been referred to as "a politico-religious secret society that manipulated prominent leaders of the time."[17]

The group was feared by the French king and distrusted by Archbishop Gondi of Paris, who refused to bless the society. Worse still, they attracted the ire of the powerful cardinal Mazarin. While both Mazarin and the Gondi family had donated money to societies connected to Vincent de Paul, Mazarin did his utmost to have the group banned, and ultimately succeeded. His distrust may have been earned. According to Priory of Sion documents that may or may not be reliable, the Priory of Sion had worked to depose Mazarin. Since the Company of the Sacred Sacrament was also opposed to Mazarin, it is speculated by some that the two organizations were one and the same. It has also been said that the company was a front for the Priory of Sion. The existence of the company has never been in doubt. Both historic and modern references mention the group despite its secrecy. The priory, however, has been called a modern-day invention, and lacking a variety of credible, contemporary references to the organization, historians are forced to build their arguments on modern and thin foundations.[18] There is no proof of the possible connection between the two organizations. What clues there are seem to weigh in favor of the Priory of Sion being a modern front for the company.

In any case, the company may have worked to depose King Louis XIII as a way to get rid of Mazarin—who used Louis to accumulate power. It had been assumed that because the king and his wife, Anne of Austria, failed to produce an heir, both the king and Mazarin would soon be gone. Quite suddenly, Anne did have a child and rumor spread that the child was fathered by Cardinal Richelieu. A handful of families, possibly connected to the company, attempted to keep the child off the throne. Soon thereafter, the company found itself dissolved.

Templar-like, they did not disappear, but rather changed their name. It would not be the first or last such change. Calling themselves the Society of Notre-Dame of Montreal, they remained in Paris, where membership remained mostly the same and their headquarters remained in Saint-Sulpice.

The new members were most likely recruited by the old members. We cannot be certain, as few papers ever survived in an organization whose policy was not to keep records. We do know that the Society of Notre-Dame listed as its founder the mysterious Jean-Jacques Olier, a member of the Company of the Sacred Sacrament from the time he was ordained. Its leader was Paul de Chomeday de Maisonneuve, who was from the city of Troyes, important as a Templar center and the home of the handful of ancient families that had been instrumental in Templar and Cistercian history. Funds for both societies were raised privately and often come from Guise-Lorraine families.

Paul de Chomeday de Maisonneuve eventually left for Montreal from the Templar, later Huguenot, stronghold of La Rochelle.

AS ABOVE, SO BELOW

In the thirteenth and fourteenth centuries, the Templars revived the art of sacred architecture. Saint John the Baptist and Mary Magdalene personified the sun and the moon in the then modern Christian concept. Cathedrals and churches employed this geometry to announce the most relevant days of solar and lunar activity. Thus the structures were at once a place to conduct ceremonies of the Church and, at the same time, a way to preserve a science known only to the initiated.

This wave of building was halted with the repression of the order, but it was never forgotten.

The settling of Atlantic Canada and specifically Montreal saw a revival of the thirteenth- and fourteenth-century reverence for Mary Magdalene and Saint John the Baptist in the form of churches that bear their names. Even Notre-Dame is subject to question. It means, of course, "Our Lady," but in the south of France the lady in question could be one of two Marys, either Mary, Mother of Christ, or Mary Magdalene. It was after all, the Magdalen that came to the south of France.

The thesis of *Holy Blood, Holy Grail* is that this Mary brought the Sacred Grail—that is, the sacred blood (or bloodline)—to France. That bloodline may have flowed through the very tangible body of a child. The Templars often referred to each other as the "son of a widow." Was the widowed Mary Magdalene the "mother" of the Templars? Bernard, whose instigation in developing the order cannot be overestimated, had an unusual zeal for the Magdalen. As a boy, he received three drops of milk from the breast of the Black Virgin of Chatillon, which is the inspiration that brought him to be ordained.[19]

Ean Begg, author of *The Cult of the Black Virgin,* found that more than fifty of the Magdalen sites in France were places where a "black" Madonna was depicted. There have been numerous attempts to explain her color. The Church asserts that the wood of certain statues has been charred or aged, although this explanation does not hold up. The painting *Black Virgin of Padua* by Donatello, for example, was clearly intended to be black.

A second explanation is that the Mother and Child image of Mary and Jesus was modeled after the image of Isis and Horus. The question of whether the similarities were deliberate or simply coincidental is not relevant, as the goddess Isis was just one of several Gallo-Roman and Celtic goddesses worshipped in Europe who are depicted as black. The party of the three Marys, Mary Magdalene, Mary Jacobe (possibly the mother of James), and Mary Salome (possibly related to Jesus) who escaped the post-Crucifixion Jerusalem landed on the Isle of Ratis near Marseille. This story recalls the three goddesses Artemis, Isis, and Cybele who had been worshipped long before, and whose statues graced an acropolis. As the three Marys might have been a modernization to the three goddesses, then the servant Sara too takes on a different meaning. As the three Marys brought their black Egyptian servant girl, she may have served as an avatar for the black goddess Isis.[20]

Another explanation is that the virginal mother of Jesus represents one aspect of the goddess. Another aspect, the sexual side, or dark side, is represented by the Magdalen, the companion of Jesus.

The Church lost its simplicity after being altered for the worse by Constantine. Although Jesus never spoke against marriage and treated women as equals and companions, the Roman Church quickly became embedded with the teachings of men who neutered themselves in fear of temptation. Jesus declared that the law was made for man and not man for the law; however, the Church did not hesitate to create new laws. Transgressions of such arbitrary laws became punishable by torture and death. The mixed brew of popes who ran the Vatican as decadent kings and unholy clerics who saw only the evil side of such activities as earthly love, sex, and marriage created an institution that promptly lost its way.

The Church had no room for joy or for the troubadours of the twelfth century who glorified courtly love and chivalry. They had no room for medicine, as all sickness was the result of sin. They had no room for science and declared Galileo a heretic for claiming the sun moved around the earth.

Saint Bernard may have understood differently.

Bernard had an unusual zeal for the science of building and the connection of God to proportion. This zeal is evident in the remains of Cistercian and Templar construction. After the Templar repression, the lodge system of Craft Masonry would also place great emphasis on the sacred geometry. In Masonry, the *G* symbol is said to be a mystery, but there is reason to believe it represents both God and geometry. The fact that one symbol represents both alludes to Bernard's comment on God and proportion. If Masonry is any indication, we can infer that there are layers to such secrets. A myth is not a simple tale; it is a tale told simply.

The artisan would take great pains to fit the hidden into the obvious. Magdala in English means the "tower of the dove." Mary Magdalene then is Mary of the Tower. When Father Saunière constructed his tower at Rennes-le-Château, he situated it where it would line up as part of a geometric shape. The redundantly named Tour Magdala (Tower of the Tower of the Dove) "had been placed to conform with the alignments" that tied together certain critical points in the Rennes-le-Château landscape.[21] To get it to conform, it was perched over a sheer drop on the west of the hilltop village. Henry Lincoln's *Holy Place* demonstrated that the area surrounding that mysterious French village contains a sacred key—a configuration of landscape features that form both a six-pointed star and a five-pointed star. The two stars have centers that are connected to each other by a straight line. The center of the pentacle is at Levaldieu, literally, the "valley of God."

This union of two geometric shapes represents the union of the sun symbol and the moon symbol. While some medieval castles and churches can be used to determine key events in the solar and lunar calendars, the origin of their astronomical magic lies below them: in the much older temples and holy places upon which they were built. Here, in the megalithic structures of ancient Europe, the secrets of the sun and the moon, and of the union of sun god and mother earth, were made manifest.

Because of the pioneering efforts of a handful of modern

astronomers and mathematicians, we now know that the monuments from the Orkneys, New Grange in Ireland, Stonehenge in England, and Carnac on the coast of France were built in an attempt to understand the moon and sun. Until recently, this was not understood, at least by the uninitiated. In 1740 William Stukeley published his thesis claiming that the Druids were responsible for Stonehenge. He was wrong, as the Druids came much later, but his book led to the understanding that the monument was keyed to the midsummer sunrise. In 1846 Rev. Edward Duke discovered the midwinter alignment as well. Sir Norman Lockyer would later calculate Stonehenge's eight-month calendar, which counted in terms of forty-five days from midwinter to midsummer. Gerald Hawkins found ten sun alignments and fourteen lunar alignments in Stonehenge.

Until the twentieth century, such research was limited to Stonehenge, yet larger, older, and possibly more complex calculators exist in numerous places. During the last century, in addition to the contribution of Professor Alexander Thom, who determined a megalithic standard of measurement, we have come to understand that the ancients were aware of Pythagorean geometry—notably, well before Pythagorus was born.

Megalithic building, and the scientific insight required by it, faded after 1700 B.C. in Europe, Africa, and Asia. There is evidence, however, that down the centuries such knowledge was always maintained by someone.

In the south of France, the marriage of the sun and moon is left in stone by ancients very much aware of such sacred geometry. Furthermore, the pattern of the five-pointed star created by the placement of such monuments is aligned with the Paris meridian, having a key intersection of the lines of the star on the meridian. The first Paris meridian was drawn in 1669 by Giovanni Domenico Cassini. He had been invited to Paris by the Sun King, Louis XIV, from the University of Bologna. The budget to study geometry and astronomy may not have known a limit, and the Paris Observatory was built as just part of an elaborate mission that would not be complete even through four generations of Cassinis. Founded in 1671, the Paris Observatory had four facades, each facing a cardinal point of the compass.

The line created by Cassini ran from Paris to the Cathar Carcassonne and along the way made some important intersections.

Henry Lincoln's *Holy Place* discusses the invention of the Paris line and its passage through the area of the Valley of God. He points out that the line is less than one quarter of a mile from the Pouisson tomb.

Patrick Byrne's *Templar Gold* picks up the story by explaining the role of Saint-Sulpice. First, while the 108-foot-high Church of Saint-Sulpice was said to be built from 1646 until 1780, Byrne found evidence of an older Saint-Sulpice on a 1630 map.[22] Before the Paris meridian was adjusted in 1744, the brass strip known as the Rose Line was inserted in the floor to mark its passage through the church. As we have seen, the Rose Line was used to ensure the noon service in an era when clocks were not yet commonplace.* Obviously, someone in the late seventeenth or early eighteenth century could still work wonders with the wisdom of the ancients.

Montreal

From the time that Cartier planted the flag on the spot he called Montreal until the end of the sixteenth century, little was done to create a city. Fur traders hunting and trading for beaver pelts made up the largest group who frequented Montreal and the future city of Quebec. Other, more established posts had more traffic. Explorers searched for gold and a passage to the Pacific Ocean and to Cathay. A new development in Europe was the catalyst to populate the city Cartier named.

The same year that he planted the flag, religious war began plaguing Europe again. The new enemy of the Catholic Church was not Islamic or Jewish, but rather fellow Christians who had questioned the practices of the Church. In 1535 an edict banned Protestant worship and the French Huguenots found themselves the target. It was a civil war often turning family members and neighbors into enemies. As Catholics battled Huguenots, they also found themselves at odds with fellow Catholics.

---

*A very interesting coincidence also connects the church named for Saint Sulpice and the Rose Line: There is a Saint Roseline whose feast occurs on January 17. It appears that Roseline was a real person, unlike some "saints" who are obvious borrowings from pagan cultures. She lived in the thirteenth century, and oddly enough, her father was an alchemist. Alchemy encompasses more than one science, and Roseline's father was transmuting salty seawater to a sweeter liquid. In later times, he might have been simply a chemist. Roseline's brother was named Helios for the sun god. This Helios, too, was an actual person who fought in the Crusades.

The Jesuits, as discussed, had been organized as a new military priesthood. Their mission was not to serve as soldiers, but instead to serve Rome with as much authority as could be mustered. The Church in Rome found little margin for accepting criticism. The Jesuits would root out any ideas that did not conform with Rome's doctrine.

Taking transport on one of Champlain's ships to the newly discovered lands were four Recollet fathers. Their goal was to baptize the inhabitants of the new continent. Ten years later, in 1625, they invited the Jesuits. The Jesuits came in force and set up trading posts in Canada and the area that would become New York State.

At the same time, Jean-Jacques Olier established his Society of St. Sulpice. His Sulpicians were not an order as much as they were a seminary for training priests from other orders in how better to serve God and God's people. They placed great emphasis on helping the poor and the sick and in bringing converts to Catholicism. Tolerant, they had little in common with the Jesuit order, and Sulpicians and Jesuits proved to be rivals in the New World. Both served God, but they had dividing differences.

Operating from Paris, Saint-Sulpice was then in the seventeenth century and even much later in the twentieth century a clearinghouse for esoteric ideas within the Catholic Church. It was the center of several secret societies that could quickly change names while operating at the same place with the same members. Openly tolerant, it attracted the suspicion and occasionally the wrath of the Church in Rome.

From Sulpice sprang the Society of Notre-Dame of Montreal, whose members became the seigneurs of that city island. This meant they acted as a sort of corporate board in governing the city. They were almost all members of the Company of the Sacred Sacrament.

In February 1642, a ceremony was held in Notre-Dame. Paul de Chomeday, Sieur de Maisonneuve, and Jean-Jacques Olier were present, along with all of the founders of the Society of Notre-Dame, including seventeen who were in the Company of the Sacred Sacrament. They were consecrating their new church. Although they named their settlement Ville Marie, or the House of Mary, it was the beginning of Montreal as a city. They would espouse ideals of the "primitive" church of Jesus—that is, the pre-Constantine Church. Women could play roles as significant as men, and a true sense of communal poverty and charity would ensure the betterment of individuals as well as the group.

There is no doubt that the group was first Catholic and second loyal to a French monarchy if not certain monarchs. It just may have been Gnostic enough to tread on dangerous ground. That an enmity existed between the group and the Jesuit order was very clear in the early formation of Canada as both orders fought for control. The Sulpician order represented the humanistic church; the Jesuits, like the Dominicans, who were such an important part of the Inquisition, represented the law and, on a regular basis, the dark side of the Church's power.

The sixteenth century began a critical time for the Church in Rome. Its authority was threatened by both humanism and the rebellious Protestant movement. Sulpicians and others would lean toward tolerance as a means to preserve the Church; the Jesuits, however, were born to combat such tolerance. A section of the Exercises of the Jesuit Code of Obedience declares, "We must hold fast to the following principle: What seems to me white, I will believe black if the hierarchical Church so defines."[23] Templar-like in its militant course of achieving a goal, this order, which was originally limited to sixty plus a grand master called the superior general, had no question about its mission.

Such unyielding principles and a reputation for secrecy led the Jesuits themselves to being suspected of conspiracy, banned more than once by the pope, and ejected from several countries. In fledgling Canada, the Jesuits and the Sulpicians often worked toward opposite goals.

The Sulpicians, with the Company of the Sacred Sacrament, founded Montreal. As the Cistercian Order of Saint Bernard had used the Knights Templar as a military vanguard, the Sulpicians hoped that they would rule Canada with the help of the Knights of Saint John. Now known as the Sovereign Knights of Malta, the Knights of Saint John have remained powerful and influential even in modern times. General Georges P. Vanier, who died in 1967, was the governor general of Canada. The most well-known Canadian Knight, he is being considered for beatification, the first step toward sainthood.[24]

The Sulpician order wanted Montreal to be the new Arcadia, where diversity, science, and open-mindedness would be tolerated. This Arcadia, like the New Atlantis of Bacon, would specifically allow the expansion of scientific thought. Their city of Montreal shared its name with a Templar castle in the Languedoc, the area of the Cathar "heresy" in France.

Although the order has been suspected of being less Catholic than it proclaims, its actions have always served to sustain the Church's potential for goodness rather than to thwart it. They acted within the Church to contain a warlike attitude toward the Protestant movement. They acted within the Church to promulgate a less didactic role than Rome. They accepted variations of philosophy within the context of their Christianity. And they apparently accepted science not as the work of the devil or a challenge to faith, but as a way of finding God in the world.

The tolerant attitudes of the Sulpicians promised a new role of both state and church in the Americas. Had they the chance, they may have built an idyllic Arcadia where men and women were equal, where questions of faith and science were not resolved by violence, and where peace was more attractive than the endless wars that wracked the Old World.

One of those wars resulted in the British becoming the owners of Canada in 1763. This effectively ended the Arcadian experiment even though some of the original attitudes remained. Evidence that such toleration survived is found in Canada's acceptance of diverse culture, a lack of involvement in foreign wars, a wide safety net for the poor, and medical coverage for all.

The monument to the Sulpician achievement is the last baptistery. Far from the Newport structure left behind by Sinclair's Templars, this building can be found at the Seminary of Saint-Sulpice in Montreal. There it survives and so do its secrets. Upon entering, a visitor is greeted by a statue of Our Lady. Hanging from her neck is the six-pointed star.

America's Secret Vault

Montreal was not the only colony planted and influenced by a secret society. While the Sulpicians and the Company of the Sacred Sacrament were at work in Montreal, another society was at work in the colony that would become Virginia.

England during Elizabeth's reign (1558–1603) was a hotbed of mysticism. Her coronation date was decided on by the magician and astrologer John Dee. He was a scientist on the caliber of Copernicus, but his magic mirrors, crystal balls, tricks of levitation, and experiments with alchemy were and are held against him. Dee's influence on England is incalculable: He convinced Elizabeth of England's rightful ownership of the seas, planned a royal navy, and coined the term Britannia. He also influenced her to believe she was a linear descendant of King Arthur, which endowed her with such rights. In return she granted him a patent on all lands north of the five-degree line. Despite such influence, he is regarded by the Royal Society as a crazed alchemist although Isaac Newton, who also studied the transmutation of metals, is honored.[25]

Dee's circles of intimates included Sir Francis Bacon, Walter Raleigh, Sir Francis Drake, Edmund Spenser, and Robert Devereaux, the earl of Essex, whose power and learning combined with a touch of adventurism would have a great effect on early colonial history. As much power as these men had in the court of Elizabeth, they knew they were satellites revolving around her power. A misstep could lead to losing a lucrative position, confinement in the Tower of London, and the ultimate threat of execution.

Bacon was an avid writer whose works often could not see the light of day. *The New Atlantis* would not be published until one year after his death but it was known within his circle. It begins with a crew of shipwrecked sailors blown off course arriving in a new land. The New World (described as being in the South Pacific) is called Bensalem, or the Seed of Peace. The New World is led by a wise man named Solomon and a council of philosopher-scientists. While this ruling council was not unlike Bacon and his circle of friends, the idyllic Arcadia he described had a peaceful existence and tolerated scientists and writers, two occupations that could be dangerous in England.*

After the death of Elizabeth, Bacon was free of her capricious nature, which had always been a threat. With James I he organized the colonization of the Americas that had been proposed while the Virgin Queen was alive. The symbol of the new colony was the goddess of wis-

---

*Writing was so dangerous, in fact, that Bacon published some of his greatest literature under the name of William Shakespeare. While this may be a shock to some, since the 1770s, the list of those who have written about Shakespeare's inability as a barely literate butcher's apprentice to write the texts attributed to him is long. It has included Mark Twain, Nathaniel Hawthorne, Oliver Wendell Holmes, Ralph Waldo Emerson, Benjamin Disraeli, and Walt Whitman. It has been pointed out that Shakespeare did not own a book, or even a manuscript. His parents were both illiterate. There is little evidence that he could write. His only signature was an X. At his burial there was no service that attracted anyone either in London or Stratford-on-Avon. England's greatest playwright apparently was forgotten in his own lifetime. In his will he gave away such

dom, Athena, who appeared in the texts of works attributed to both Bacon and Shakespeare. As wisdom was power, her depiction includes her spear and shield. Author Henrietta Bernstein points out in her *Ark of the Covenant, Holy Grail* that Bacon and his select group were those who shook a lance at ignorance, which is why they chose the goddess called the Spear Shaker as their symbol.

Into the new colony of Athena, Bacon's supporters and family members carried documents and sacred artifacts, which they preserved in a church tower in Jamestown but later moved. By 1676, they were in a ten-foot-square vault twenty feet under the original brick church in Bruton Parish. The church was in Virginia's first settlement, the Middletown Plantation, which later became Williamsburg. The esoteric researcher Marie Bauer Hall made this discovery in 1938 through anagrams, cryptograms, codes from books, Masonic texts, and symbols found in the graveyard. There was more than one obstacle in her excavating the Bruton vault, which Masonic records called the Bacon vault. First, the original church had been moved. And Masons, including a descendant of Sir Walter Raleigh, resisted, letting Hall know they wanted the vault untouched. Third, the Rockefeller family had bought up most of the area to restore colonial Williamsburg.[27] Hall's research led her to believe that the vault has been moved again, although others have provided this author with information that the secrets of the Bruton vault remain in place.[28]

Manly Hall, author of *The Secret Destiny of America,* claims that a Brotherhood of the Quest exists both to keep alive the ideals of a free society and to protect the documents, preserved in the Bruton vault, that helped inspire the new nation.[29]

---

mundane items as a bed but there is no mention of a single book. There exist no uncompleted texts or works.

Bacon had studied law and botany, was experienced in government, had traveled and read history, and obviously spent a great deal of time writing. In all he was everything Shakespeare was not. Like his *New Atlantis,* which may have had subsequent chapters that have never been revealed, there is a body of work that remains, some believe, literally underground.

Bacon is also credited with editing what became the King James version of the Bible. In Psalm 46, the forty-sixth word down from the first verse is "SHAKE," while the forty-sixth word from the end is "SPEAR."[26] Many believe that the man who contributed so much may have felt that, at least postmortem, he deserved recognition.

Hidden in Plain Sight

In recent years it has come to light that the layout of the city of Washington, D.C., was executed to Masonic specifications. Baigent and Leigh's *The Temple and the Lodge* includes a map indicating two octagonal patterns, one centered on the White House, the other on the Capitol.[30] Tupper Saussy discovered pentagrams over Washington that form the icon of the Knights Templar called Baphomet. Saussy, a descendant of Huguenots, believes that the Templar intentions were evil. The word Baphomet, though, when put through a decoding scheme called the Atbash Cipher, spells Sophia (Wisdom). Within the same downward-pointing pentagram is the head of Aeneas on the Congressional Medal of Honor.[31] David Ovason found numerous zodiacs incorporated in the buildings and statues of the capital city.[32] He notes that there are even more of these in Washington than in Florence. Most significant, he notes the importance that the constellation Virgo played in both the founding of the city and in the positioning of the White House. This cannot be coincidence and the planner had to have a "considerable knowledge of astrology . . . [and] a vested interest in emphasizing the role of the sign Virgo."[33] The entire city was oriented to the sun, with the Capitol building as a symbol of the half arc of the heavens, the point where the equinoctial and solstitial points meet.[34] "As above," the constellation of Virgo is encased in a celestial triangle marked by the stars Arcturus, Spica, and Regulus. The city of Washington, "so below," has a triangle of the White House (Arcturus), Regulus (the Capitol), and Spica (the Washington Monument). The position of Regulus, which featured so prominently in the construction of the pyramid of Cheops, is featured again in the construction of the Capitol.

When Virgo is ascendant, a period exists when the path of the moon intersects the path of the sun. What astrologers call the Dragon's Head marks that point. The cornerstone of the White House was laid in 1792 when the Dragon's Head was in Virgo. The next year the cornerstone of the Capitol was laid when the Dragon's Head was again in Virgo. More than fifty years later, the Washington Monument foundation stone was laid when the Dragon's Head again was in Virgo.[35] Clearly, the tradition of placing an emphasis on the Virgin as a positive portent was still alive, even if by then Masonry had given itself a black eye by its haughtiness.

Even Detroit, a remote frontier town when Washington was built, would reflect a hidden knowledge of Masonic geometry. Named for the Templar fortress of Destroit, it would be a planned city laid out to reflect a map of the heavens.

From the most remote times and places to modern times and densely populated places, the knowledge of a relative handful of initiates is there for all to see. Jesus' command, "He that hath ears to hear, let him hear," is a message to us all, or at least all of us who wish to understand. It may also serve to remind us, and all future generations, of the wisdom of the past.

On a cynical note, such devices could be said to be a show of power. However, the Pyramids of Egypt and the Capitol in Washington already reflect power without the additional understanding that they are lined up to reflect Orion and Virgo. A Druid might once have used his ability to predict (or to be seen to create) an eclipse to make the uninitiated cower, but a *Farmer's Almanac* utilizes the same knowledge today without need to show power. Likewise, the pyramids of Egypt and the Washington Monument can be seen to be a simple display of knowledge and scientific ability.

Such architectural wonders are evidence that there are those with higher ideals. The coded knowledge hidden for all to see in structures built over the span of thousands of years may be meant to remind us that humankind has a greater potential than it has achieved. Genesis says the stars were put in the sky as signs, and below it may be that we have created a way to read them. We can only hope the aim of such wisdom is in promoting an Arcadia where the law is made for men and women instead of the opposite. Modern times make it easier to be skeptical.

To quote the anthropologist Keith Laidler, "All great religious leaders are doomed, upon their death, to have their high ideals usurped and corrupted by men and women who only vaguely understand the teachings that their revered leader tried to promote."[36] And so too are the well-intentioned founders of nations.

Epilogue
Under the Rose

THERE IS A SECRET HISTORY of the colonization of the Americas. From Canada to California, there are secrets that find no place in the history books, and many subjects have been purged from historical discussion in the hopes that they will be forgotten.

In the province of Quebec, a land that still resists assimilation into a non-French Canada, the motto on the seal of the province is *Je me souviens,* meaning "I remember." While the man who designed the seal, Eugène-Étienne Tache, offered no explanation for the ambiguous statement, in 1978 the motto was the subject of much discussion, and his great-granddaughter brought its meaning to light. Helene Paquet, in a letter to the *Montreal Star,* said it was from an anonymous poem. While many do not remember the reference, the full line of that poem is "Je me souviens, que née sous les lis je crois sous le rous." (I remember, born under the lily, I live under the Rose.)[1]

Paquet's explanation may have put the debate to rest. The lily may represent France and the rose England. Quebec certainly started as a colony of the French and ended up a colony of England. For French Quebecois, the motto may represent a bit of the rebellious spirit that still remembers the history and desires a French-speaking, separate province within Canada.

But the lily in the poem may not be the Bourbon triple fleur-de-lis it is

248

believed to signify. The earliest use of the lily was in Sumero-Babylonian times, when it represented the mother goddess. The pre-Christian goddess of the Celts was Eostre, symbolized by the lilies that are now part of the Christianized Easter celebration. Christian art often married pagan and Christian symbols more meaningfully than the Church could have intended. Renaissance art depicting the Annunciation, for example, shows the angel Gabriel announcing to Mary her conception. Gabriel holds out a lily while the dove hovers overhead.

Such symbols were not lost on residents of Florence, where the lily and the dove of Saint John the Baptist convey that Florence, too, remembers. They would not have been lost in Lyon, the second city of the Gnostic faith where the Verrazanos and others took up residence when the Inquisition threatened Florence's tolerant society. There, the lily was the symbol of the balance in life that religion had distorted. A symbol known and used from Babylon and Palestine to France and Ireland, it represented the sanctity of the female part of life's equation. It was not the property of Zion, although the Priory of Sion used it for its insignia.

Like the Star of David that was used in the original coat of arms of Verrazano, the meaning of any symbol extends far beyond the confines of any state or even any religion.[2] This same star is secretly concealed in the depiction of the compass and the level, used as a Masonic symbol for the architectural principle "As above, so below." This should not be taken as an implication that such a symbol is limited to a sacred geometry. Like the lily, the triangle over the triangle is also a symbol of the unity of the male and female principles, of light and darkness, of balance and harmony. It is not unlike the Eastern symbol for the relationship between yin and yang.

In this sense, all are born under the lily—born male and female and able to share in the fruit of knowledge untainted by dogma or decree. And in a sense, all live under the rose. Not the rose of the House of Tudor or of York, or of any one nation, but the symbol of a Creator whose love is for all. While the Romans claim the rose to represent the mysteries of the goddess Venus, the Christian Church would claim the same rose as the sign of the Blessed Virgin, but no religion has a monopoly on the symbols of harmony.

And in a third sense, all who share in a culture that admits everyone to the pursuit of happiness in this life and the paradise of an afterlife live under the rose, in the secretive sense of *sub rosa*. Those who understand that as above the Creator does not deny access to the afterlife along imaginary borders and rigid philosophical principles understand, too, that so below we must be tolerant. Such a philosophy, of course, may not find acceptance within religions whose shamans and bishops find it necessary to exclude, deprive, and kill in the name of God.

The first chapter of Mark's Gospel in the New Testament begins with the dove that ascends over the head of Jesus at the moment of his baptism. This dove is the Holy Spirit, the female principle of wisdom. It recalls the first chapter of Genesis when the Spirit, again wisdom, moves over the waters and God begins creation. The message is the same. Space and time are created only within the harmony of male and female.

The message of Jesus was understood by some. It was not of an earthly kingdom, but of an earth that was part of God's kingdom. It was of the balance and harmony that allowed for birth and rebirth of man and nature. Long before Jesus, this message was understood by the Neolithic builders of the Orkney Isles who created temples to celebrate the marriage of the earth mother and sun at the winter solstice for the purpose of continuing life. But as the truly wise are doomed to have their high ideals corrupted by those who only vaguely understand their teachings, Jesus' message was distorted and contaminated. Religion has failed. Its true message of balance, harmony, and understanding has largely been lost, though not to all.

This may have been the dream of Henry Sinclair, of Jean-Jacques Olier, of Sir Francis Bacon, and of Giovanni Verrazano: to restore the Grail. In creating a refuge, a New Jerusalem under any name, they sought to restore the Eden, the idyllic world. As St. Lawrence carried the Holy Grail to safety, the river named for him carried still one more order, of knights and priests, of men and women, who would try again. They were the guardians of the sacred gnosis, tolerant of neighbors and friends, dreaming once again of creating a land of Arcadia.

Notes

Introduction: From La Rochelle to Newport
1. Samuel Eliot Morison, *Great Explorers*, 155.
2. Holand, *Explorations in America*, 246.
3. Ibid., 226–29.

Chapter 1: Sun Gods and Sea Kings
1. Hedges, *Tomb of the Eagles*, 11.
2. Ibid., 93.
3. Poertner, *Vikings*, 125.
4. Palsson and Edwards, trans., *Orkneyinga Saga*, 15.
5. Ibid.
6. Graham-Campbell, *Viking World*, 110–11.
7. Gordon, *Before Columbus*, 29.
8. Mallery and Harrison, *Rediscovery of Lost America*, 17.
9. Mowat, *Farfarers: Before the Norse*, 188; "Crime Rate for Selected Large Cities 1997." *Time Almanac 2001*, 363.
10. Mowat, *Farfarers: Before the Norse*, 243.
11. Ibid., 193.
12. Anderson, *Norse Discovery of America*, 281.
13. Lansverk, *Runic Records*, 70–71.
14. Pohl, *Viking Settlements of North America*, 12.
15. Ibid., 87.
16. Ibid., 134–35.
17. Holand, *Explorations in America*, 81.
18. Bradley, *Grail Knights in America*, 225.
19. Baigent, Leigh, and Lincoln, *Holy Blood, Holy Grail*, 112.

251

20. Holand, *Explorations in America*, 91.
21. Pohl, *Viking Settlements of North America*, 145.
22. Mowat, *Farfarers: Before the Norse*, 204.
23. Ibid., 291.
24. Holand, *Explorations in America*, 125–26.
25. Kurlansky, *Cod*, 17.
26. Mowat, *Farfarers, Before the Norse*, 319–20.
27. Brent, *Viking Saga*, 213.
28. Pohl, *Viking Settlements of North America*, 95.
29. Swaney, *Iceland, Greenland and the Faeroe Islands*, 369.
30. Brent, *Viking Saga*, 213.
31. Thompson, *American Discovery*, 277.
32. Lemonick and Dorfman, "Amazing Vikings," 3–5.
33. Picknett and Prince, *Turin Shroud*, 53.
34. Lemonick and Dorfman, "Amazing Vikings," 3–5.

Chapter 2: The Sun, the Moon, and the Knights Templar

1. Gilbert, *Signs in the Sky*, 195.
2. Ibid., 77.
3. Penhallow, William S., "Astronomical Alignments in the Newport Tower," *NEARA*, March 21, 2004.
4. Runciman, *History of the Crusades*, vol. 2, 63.
5. Runciman, *History of the Crusades*, vol. 1, 138.
6. Read, *Templars*, 91.
7. Ibid.
8. Runciman, *History of the Crusades*, vol. 2, 181.
9. Ibid., 95.
10. Begg, *Cult of the Black Virgin*, 103.
11. Runciman, *History of the Crusades*, vol. 2, 253.
12. Addison, *History of the Knights Templar*, 38.
13. Deuel, *Testaments of Time*, 5.
14. Gilbert, *Magi*, 247.
15. Miles, *Christmas Customs and Traditions*, 221.
16. Knight and Lomas, *Hiram Key*, 74–76.
17. McClusky, *Astronomies and Cultures*, 26.
18. Ibid.
19. Goodrich, *King Arthur*, 280–89.
20. Facaros and Pauls, *Italy*, 564.
21. Young, *Sacred Sites of the Knights Templar*, 49–50.
22. Picknett, *Mary Magdalene*, 104.
23. Bernier, *Templar Legacy in Montreal*, 52.
24. Hancock, *Sign and the Seal*, 102.

25. Frankl, *Gothic Architecture*, 218.
26. Haagensen and Lincoln, *Templars' Secret Island*, 19.
27. Carlson, "Loose Threads in a Tapestry of Stone," *NEARA Journal* 35, no. 1 (summer 2001), 25.
28. Ibid.
29. Haagensen and Lincoln, *Templars' Secret Island*, 31.
30. Holand, *Explorations in America*, 144.

Chapter 3: The Knights Templar: Death and Rebirth

1. Addison, *History of the Knights Templar*, 128.
2. Markale, *Montségur*, 55.
3. Ibid., 164.
4. Ibid., 203.
5. Oldenbourg, *Massacre at Montségur*, 94.
6. Markale, *Montségur*, 217.
7. Ibid., 49.
8. Wasserman, *Templars and the Assassins*, 194–96.
9. Baigent and Leigh, *Temple and the Lodge*, 73.
10. Runciman, *History of the Crusades*, vol. 3, 442.
11. Starbird, *Tarot Trumps and the Holy Grail*, 21–25.

Chapter 4: From Scotland to the New World

1. Morrison, *History of the Sinclair Family*, 20–21.
2. Baigent and Leigh, *Temple and the Lodge*, 64.
3. Robinson, *Born in Blood*, 27.
4. Sinclair, *Sword and the Grail*, 13.
5. Previte-Orton, *Shorter Cambridge History: Twelfth Century to the Renaissance*, 914.
6. Pohl, *Prince Henry Sinclair*, 68
7. Ibid., 90.
8. Thompson, *Friar's Map of Ancient America*, 2.
9. Ibid., 98.
10. Johnson, *Phantom Islands*, 116.
11. Davis, *Mother Tongue*, 42–44.
12. Mallery and Harrison, *Rediscovery of Lost America*, 151.
13. Pohl, *Prince Henry Sinclair*, 132.
14. Mowat, *Farfarers: Before the Norse*, 293.

Chapter 5: The Templar Trail in America

1. Holzer, *Long Before Columbus*, 29.
2. Imbrogno and Horrigan, *Celtic Mysteries in New England*, 38.

3. Crooker, *Tracking Treasure*, 47–51.
4. Ritchie, *Viking Scotland*, 67.
5. Sinclair, *Secret Scroll*, 133.
6. Samuel Eliot Morison, *Great Explorers*, 62.
7. LeDuc, "Did the Templars Seek Refuge?" 26–27.
8. Conversation with Michael Bradley, April 2000.
9. *Glynn Papers Bulletin*
10. Childress, *Lost Cities*, 441.
11. Stapler, "Ancient Pemaquid,"
   http://www.neara.org/ROS/pemaquid.htm.
12. Mallery and Harrison, *Rediscovery of Lost America*, 178.
13. Ibid., 187.
14. Ibid., 170.

Chapter 6: Columbus and the Knights of Christ

1. Sanceau, *Henry the Navigator*, 26.
2. Thomas, *Slave Trade*, 70–71.
3. Gardner, *Bloodline of the Holy Grail*, 399.
4. Bruce, *Mark of the Scots*, 204.
5. Baumgarten, *Baedecker's Portugal*, 68.
6. Sanceau, *Henry the Navigator*, 286.
7. Wilford, *Mysterious History of Columbus*, 65.
8. Samuel Eliot Morison, *Great Explorers*, 359.
9. De Madariaga, *Christopher Columbus*, 90–91, 114.
10. Wiesenthal, *Sails of Hope*, 100, 134.
11. Gilbert, *Signs in the Sky*, 265–66.
12. Wilford, *Mysterious History of Columbus*, 94–95.
13. Thomas, *Slave Trade*, 84.
14. Crone, *Discovery of America*, 30–31.
15. Morison, *Christopher Columbus, Mariner*, 13.
16. De Madariaga, *Christopher Columbus*, 84.
17. Hourani, *Arab Seafaring*, 70–74.
18. Keen, trans., *Life of Admiral Christopher Columbus*, 27.
19. Kurlansky, *Cod*, 27.
20. Johnson, *Phantom Islands*, 95.
21. Wilford, *Mysterious History of Columbus*, 111.
22. Sale, *Conquest of Paradise*, 328.
23. Granzotto, *Christopher Columbus*, 141.
24. Menzies, *1421: The Year the Chinese Discovered America*, 258.
25. Samuel Eliot Morison, *Great Explorers*, 425.
26. Wilford, *Mysterious History of Columbus*, 215.
27. Ovason, *Secret Architecture*, 87.

28. Miller, *Roanoke,* 237.
29. Ibid., 256.
30. Baigent, Leigh, and Lincoln, *Holy Blood, Holy Grail,* 136.
31. Haskins, *Renaissance of the Twelfth Century,* 72.
32. Wilford, *Mysterious History of Columbus,* 200.
33. Pohl, *Americus Vespucci,* 151.
34. Wilford, *Mysterious History of Columbus,* 206.
35. Baigent, Leigh, and Lincoln, *Holy Blood, Holy Grail,* 140.

Chapter 7: The Secret Mission of Verrazano
 1. Baigent, Leigh, and Lincoln, *Holy Blood, Holy Grail,* 396.
 2. West, *Serpent in the Sky,* 46–48.
 3. Begg, *Cult of the Black Virgin,* 59.
 4. Parkman, *Pioneers of France in the New World,* 145.
 5. Ibid., 149.
 6. Lane, *Pillaging the Empire,* 18.
 7. Baigent, Leigh, and Lincoln, *Holy Blood, Holy Grail,* 37.
 8. Society of St. Sulpice, "Who We Are," http://sulpicians.org/whoweare /pop_why_stsulpice.html (accessed December 16, 2003).
 9. Samuel Eliot Morison, *Great Explorers,* 144.
10. Ibid., 218.
11. Ibid., 155.
12. Holand, *Explorations in America,* 256.
13. Samuel Eliot Morison, *Great Explorers,* 167.

Chapter 8: In Arcadia
 1. Firstbrook, *Voyage of the* Matthew, 123–25.
 2. Anderson, *Norse Discovery of America,* 142.
 3. Bradley, *Holy Grail Across the Atlantic,* 251.
 4. Seward, *Monks of War,* 238.
 5. Bradley, *Holy Grail Across the Atlantic,* 253.
 6. Ibid., 227.
 7. Ibid., 231.
 8. Parkman, *Pioneers of France in the New World,* 243.
 9. Costain, *The White and the Gold,* 99.
10. Facaros and Pauls, *South of France,* 54.
11. Begg, *Cult of the Black Virgin,* 112.
12. Picknett and Prince, *Templar Revelation,* 196.
13. Ibid., 199.
14. Marois, *Life of the Marquis de la Fayette,* 440.

15. De Sède, *Accursed Treasure*, 22.
16. Radula-Scott, ed., *Paris*, 191.
17. Picknett and Prince, *Templar Revelation*, 196.
18. Picknett and Prince, *Turin Shroud*, 71.
19. Begg, *Cult of the Black Virgin*, 23.
20. Ibid., 15.
21. Lincoln, *Holy Place*, 105.
22. Byrne, *Templar Gold*, 319.
23. Saussy, *Rulers of Evil*, 48.
24. Seward, *Monks of War*, 329–30.
25. White, *Isaac Newton*, 172.
26. Bernier, *Templar Legacy in Montreal*, 176.
27. Ibid., 188.
28. Conversation with Fletcher Richman, September 3, 2003.
29. Hall, *Secret Destiny of America*, 110.
30. Baigent and Leigh, *Temple and the Lodge*, 258.
31. Saussy, *Rulers of Evil*, 226–29.
32. Ovason, *Secret Architecture*, 3.
33. Ibid., 65.
34. Ibid., 83.
35. Ibid., 254–56.
36. Laidler, *Head of God*, 62.

Epilogue: Under the Rose

1. Bernier, *The Templars' Legacy in Montreal*, 13.
2. Baigent, Leigh, and Lincoln, *Holy Blood, Holy Grail*, 396.

Bibliography

Addison, Charles G. *The History of the Knights Templar.* Kempton, Ill.: Adventures Unlimited Press, 1997. First published 1842 in London.

Anderson, Rasmus, ed. *The Norse Discovery of America.* London: Norruena Society, 1906.

Baigent, Michael, and Richard Leigh. *The Temple and the Lodge.* New York: Arcade Publishing, 1989.

Baigent, Michael, Richard Leigh, and Henry Lincoln. *Holy Blood, Holy Grail.* New York: Dell, 1983.

Baumgarten, Monika. *Baedecker's Portugal.* Norwich: Jerrold & Sons, 1992.

Begg, Ean. *The Cult of the Black Virgin.* London: Penguin, 1996.

Bernier, Francine. *The Templars' Legacy in Montreal: The New Jerusalem.* Enkhuizen, The Netherlands: Frontier Publishing, 2001.

Bernstein, Henrietta. *Ark of the Covenant, Holy Grail.* Marina del Rey, Calif.: DeVorss Publications, 1998.

Bradley, Michael. *Grail Knights in America.* Toronto: Hounslow Press, 1998.

———. *Holy Grail Across the Atlantic.* Toronto: Hounslow Press, 1988.

Brent, Peter. *The Viking Saga.* New York: G. P. Putnam, 1975.

Bruce, Duncan A. *The Mark of the Scots.* Secaucus, N.J.: Citadel Press, 1996.

Byrne, Patrick. *Templar Gold.* Nevada City, Calif.: Symposium, 2001.

Carlson, Suzanne. "Loose Threads in a Tapestry of Stone: The Architecture of the Newport Tower." *NEARA Journal* 35, no. 1 (Summer 2001).

Childress, David. *Lost Cities of North and Central America.* Kempton, Ill.: Adventures Unlimited Press, 1992.

Costain, Thomas B. *The White and the Gold.* New York: Doubleday, 1954.

"Crime Rate for Selected Large Cities 1997." *The Time Almanac with Information Please 2001.* Boston: Time Magazine, 2001.

Crone, G. R. *The Discovery of America.* New York: Weybright and Talley, 1969.

Crooker, William. *Tracking Treasure: In Search of East Coast Bounty.* Halifax, Nova Scotia: Nimbus, 1998.

Cunliffe, Barry. *The Extraordinary Voyage of Pytheas the Greek.* New York: Penguin, 2002.

Da Silva, Manuel Luciano. "Ninigret: A Portuguese Fort," www.apol.net/dightonrock/pilgrim_chapter_10.htm (accessed April 19, 2002).

Davis, Joel. *Mother Tongue: How Humans Create Language.* New York: Carol Publishing, 1994.

De Sède, Gérard. *The Accursed Treasure.* Surrey, England: DEK, 1967.

Deuel, Leo. *The Testaments of Time.* New York: Alfred Knopf, 1966.

Facaros, Dana, and Michael Pauls. *Italy.* London: Cadogan, 1994.

———. *South of France.* Guilford, Conn.: Globe Pequot Press, 1992.

Firstbrook, Peter. *The Voyage of the* Matthew. San Francisco: KQED Books and Tapes, 1997.

Frankl, Paul. *Gothic Architecture.* Baltimore: Penguin, 1962.

Gardner, Laurence. *Bloodline of the Holy Grail.* New York: Barnes & Noble, 1996.

Gilbert, Adrian. *Magi: The Quest for the Sacred Tradition.* London: Bloomsbury, 1996.

———. *Signs in the Sky.* London: Corgi Books, 2000.

Glynn Papers Bulletin, no. 26, 1967.

Goodrich, Norma Lorre. *King Arthur.* New York: Harper and Row, 1989.

Gordon, Cyrus L. *Before Columbus.* New York: Crown Publishers, 1971.

Graham-Campbell, James. *The Viking World.* New York: Ticknor & Fields, 1980.

Granzotto, Gianni. *Christopher Columbus: The Dream and the Obsession.* Translated by Stephen Sartarelli. New York: Doubleday, 1985.

Haagensen, Erling, and Henry Lincoln. *The Templars' Secret Island.* Gloucestershire, England: Windrush Press, 2000.

Hall, Manly P. *The Secret Destiny of America.* Los Angeles: Philosophical Research Society, 1944.

Hancock, Graham. *The Sign and the Seal.* New York: Crown Publishers, 1992.

Haskins, Charles Homer. *The Renaissance of the Twelfth Century.* New York: Meridian Books, 1957.

Hedges, John W. *Tomb of the Eagles.* New York: New Amsterdam Books, 1984.

Holand, Hjalmar Rued. *Explorations in America Before Columbus.* New York: Twayne Publishers, 1958.

Holzer, Hans. *Long Before Columbus: How the Ancients Discovered America.* Santa Fe: Bear & Company, 1992.

Hourani, George F. *Arab Seafaring.* Princeton: Princeton University Press, 1995.

Huyghe, Patrick. *Columbus Was Last.* New York: Hyperion, 1992.

Imbrogno, Philip, and Marianne Horrigan. *Celtic Mysteries in New England.* Saint Paul, Minn.: Llewellyn, 2000.

Ingstad, Helge. "Vinland Ruins Prove Vikings Found the New World." *National Geographic* 126, no. 5 (November 1964): 708–35.

Johnson, Donald S. *Phantom Islands of the Atlantic.* New York: Walker and Company, 1994.

Keen, Benjamin, trans. *The Life of Admiral Christopher Columbus by His Son Ferdinand.* New Brunswick, N.J.: Rutgers University Press, 1959.

Knight, Christopher, and Robert Lomas. *The Hiram Key.* Boston: Element, 1997.

Kurlansky, Mark. *Cod.* New York: Penguin, 1997.

Laidler, Keith. *The Head of God.* London: Orion, 1998.

Lane, Kris E. *Pillaging the Empire: Piracy in the Americas 1500–1700.* Armonk, N.Y.: M. E. Sharpe, 1998.

Lansverk, O. G. *Runic Records of the Norsemen in America.* Rishford, Minn.: Erik Fris, 1974.

LeDuc, Gerard. "Did the Templars Seek Refuge in French Canada?" *Ancient American* 7, no. 44 (March/April 2002): 26–27.

Leland, Charles G. *Algonquin Legends.* New York: Dover, 1992. First published in 1884.

Lemonick, Michael, and Andrea Dorfman, "The Amazing Vikings." *Time Magazine* 155, no. 19 (May 8, 2000): 3–5.

Lincoln, Henry. *The Holy Place.* London: Corgi, 1991.

Madariaga, Salvador de. *Christopher Columbus.* New York: MacMillan Company, 1940.

Mallery, Arlington, and Mary Roberts Harrison. *The Rediscovery of Lost America.* New York: E. P. Dutton, 1951.

Markale, Jean. *Montségur and the Mystery of the Cathars.* Trans. by Jon Graham. Rochester, Vt.: Inner Traditions, 2003.

Maurois, André. *Adrienne: The Life of the Marquise de la Fayette.* New York: McGraw Hill, 1961.

McClusky, Stephen C. *Astronomies and Cultures in Early Medieval Europe.* New York: Cambridge University Press, 1998.

Menzies, Gavin. *1421: The Year the Chinese Discovered America.* New York: William Morrow, 2002.

Miles, Clement. *Christmas Customs and Traditions*. New York: Dover Publications, 1976. First published in 1912.

Miller, Lee. *Roanoke*. New York: Arcade Publishing, 2000.

Morison, Samuel. *Christopher Columbus, Mariner*. Boston: Little, Brown, 1942.

Morison, Samuel Eliot. *The Great Explorers: The European Discovery of America*. New York: Oxford University Press, 1978.

Morrison, Leonard. *The History of the Sinclair Family in Europe and America*. Boston: Damrell & Upham, 1896.

Mowat, Farley. *The Farfarers: Before the Norse*. South Royalton, Vt.: Steerforth Press, 2000.

Oldenbourg, Zoe. *Massacre at Montségur*. London: Weidenfield and Nicholson, 1961.

Ovason, David. *The Secret Architecture of Our Nation's Capital: The Masons and the Building of Washington, DC*. New York: HarperCollins, 2000.

Palsson, Hermann, and Paul Edwards, trans. *Orkneyinga Saga*. London: Penguin, 1981.

Parkman, Francis. *Pioneers of France in the New World*. New York: Library of America, 1983. First published in 1885.

Penhallow, William S. "Astronomical Alignments in the Newport Tower." *NEARA*, March 21, 2004.

Penrith, James, and Deborah Penrith. *Orkney and Shetland*. Oxford: Vacation Work, 2002.

Picknett, Lynn. *Mary Magdalene*. London: Robinson, 2003.

Picknett, Lynn, and Clive Prince. *The Templar Revelation*. New York: Touchstone, 1997.

———. *Turin Shroud*. New York: HarperCollins, 1994.

Poertner, Rudolf. *The Vikings: The Rise and Fall of the Norse Sea Kings*. Trans. by Sophie Wilkins. New York: Saint Martin's Press, 1971.

Pohl, Frederick J. *Americus Vespucci, Pilot Major*. New York: Octagon Books, 1966.

———. *Prince Henry Sinclair*. Halifax, Nova Scotia: Nimbus Publishing, 1967.

———. *The Viking Settlements of North America*. New York: Clarkson Potter, 1972.

Previte-Orton, C. W. *The Shorter Cambridge History: The Twelfth Century to the Renaissance*. Cambridge: Cambridge University Press, 1952.

Radula-Scott, Caroline, ed. *Paris*. London: Insight Guide, 2002.

Read, Piers Paul. *The Templars*. New York: Saint Martin's Press, 1999.

Ritchie, Anna. *Viking Scotland*. London: B. T. Batsford Ltd, 1993.

Rixson, Denis. *The West Highland Galley*. Edinburgh: Birlinn, 1997.

Robinson, John J. *Born in Blood*. New York: M. Evans and Company, 1989.

Runciman, Steven. *A History of the Crusades.* First pbk. ed. Vols. 1–3. Cambridge: Cambridge University Press, 1987.

Sale, Kirkpatrick. *The Conquest of Paradise.* New York: Penguin, 1991.

Sanceau, Elaine. *Henry the Navigator: The Story of a Great Prince and His Times.* New York: W. W. Norton, 1947.

Saussy, F. Tupper. *Rulers of Evil.* New York: HarperCollins, 1999.

Schledermann, Peter. "Eskimo and Viking Finds in the High Arctic." *National Geographic* 159, no. 5 (May 1981): 575–601.

Seward, Desmond. *The Monks of War.* New York: Penguin, 1972.

Sinclair, Andrew. *The Secret Scroll.* London: Sinclair-Stevenson, 2001.

———. *The Sword and the Grail.* New York: Crown Publishers, 1992.

Society of St. Sulpice. "Who We Are." *Sulpicians.* http://sulpicians.org/whoweare /pop_why_stsulpice.html.

Stapler, Mead W. "Ancient Pemaquid and the Skeleton in Armor." *NEARA Journal* 32, no. 1 (Summer 1998). http://www.neara.org/ROS/pemaquid.htm.

Starbird, Margaret. *The Tarot Trumps and the Holy Grail.* Boulder, Colo.: WovenWord Press, 2000.

Swaney, Deanna. *Iceland, Greenland and the Faeroe Islands.* Hawthorn, Australia: Lonely Planet Publications, 1994.

Thomas, Hugh. *The Slave Trade.* New York: Simon & Schuster, 1997.

Thompson, Gunnar. *American Discovery.* Seattle, Wash.: Argonauts/Mist Isles Press, 1994.

———. *The Friar's Map of Ancient America.* Seattle, Wash.: Laura Lee Productions, 1996.

Walker, Barbara G. *The Women's Encyclopedia of Myths and Secrets.* San Francisco: Harper & Row, 1983.

Wasserman, James. *The Templars and the Assassins.* Rochester, Vt.: Inner Traditions, 2001.

West, John Anthony. *Serpent in the Sky.* Wheaton, Ill.: Theosophical Publishing House, 1983.

White, Michael. *Isaac Newton: The Last Sorcerer.* Reading, Mass.: Addison-Wesley, 1997.

Wiesenthal, Simon. *Sails of Hope.* Trans. by Richard and Clara Winston. New York: Macmillan, 1973.

Wilford, John Noble. *The Mysterious History of Columbus.* New York: Alfred A. Knopf, 1991.

Young, John K. *Sacred Sites of the Knights Templar.* Gloucester, Mass.: Fair Winds Press, 2003.

Index

Books of Related Interest

THE LOST TREASURE OF THE KNIGHTS TEMPLAR
Solving the Oak Island Mystery
by Steven Sora

SECRET SOCIETIES OF AMERICA'S ELITE
From the Knights Templar to Skull and Bones
by Steven Sora

THE KNIGHTS TEMPLAR IN THE NEW WORLD
How Henry Sinclair Brought the Grail to Acadia
by William F. Mann

AMERICA'S SECRET DESTINY
Spiritual Vision and the Founding of a Nation
by Robert Hieronimus, Ph.D.

THE TEMPLARS AND THE ASSASSINS
The Militia of Heaven
by James Wasserman

ART AND SYMBOLS OF THE OCCULT
Images of Power and Wisdom
by James Wasserman

THE TEMPLARS
Knights of God
by Edward Burman

THE LOST TREASURE OF KING JUBA
The Evidence of Africans in America before Columbus
by Frank Joseph

Inner Traditions • Bear & Company
P.O. Box 388
Rochester, VT 05767
1-800-246-8648
www.InnerTraditions.com

Or contact your local bookseller